Intervention and Underdevelopment

Jon V. Kofas

Intervention and Underdevelopment

Greece During the Cold War

The Pennsylvania State University Press
University Park and London

Library of Congress Cataloging-in-Publication Data

Kofas, Jon V.
  Intervention and underdevelopment : Greece during the cold war / Jon V. Kofas.
   p.   cm.
  Bibliography: p.
  Includes index.
  ISBN 0-271-00661-7
  1. Greece—Economic conditions—1918–1974. 2. Greece—Dependency on other countries. 3. Greece—Relations—Great Britain. 4. Great Britain—Relations—Greece. 5. Greece—Relations—United States. 6. United States—Relations—Greece. I. Title.
HC295.K565 1989
330.9495′07—dc19   88–26572
                                                                  CIP

Copyright © 1989 The Pennsylvania State University
All rights reserved
Printed in the United States of America

Contents

Foreword by Professor L. S. Stavrianos		vii
Preface		xi
Introduction		1
I	Economic Dislocation and the Demise of British Influence in Greece	5
	The Financial Dependence of Greece on Great Britain: An Overview	5
	War Devastation	8
	UNRRA and the British in Greece	13
	The Failure of Reform Under Varvaressos	18
	The Anglo-American Struggle for Hegemony in Greece	31
	White Terror and Profiteering	37
	The London Agreement	43
II	The Origins of Greek Dependence on the United States	51
	The Twilight of British Influence in Greece and the Venizelos Mission	51
	The Soviet-American Confrontation and the Outbreak of the Greek Civil War	61

	Policy Antecedents to the Truman Doctrine	66
	The Communist Threat	74
	The Truman Doctrine	79
III	The AMAG and United States Ascendancy in Greece, 1947	89
	Conditions for United States Aid to Greece	89
	Protracted Economic Dislocation, Refugees, and Guerrillas	92
	AMAG's Preeminence and the Failure of Foreign Aid	98
IV	Greece Under the Marshall Plan	107
	The Marshall Plan, Greek Finances, and the Defense Budget	107
	The Four-Year Plan in Greece	117
	The Failure of ERP in Greece	120
	From Foreign Aid to Private Investment	132
V	The American Mission and the Greek Labor Movement	137
	United States Infiltration of the Greek Labor Movement	137
	United States Intervention in Greek Labor Affairs	144
	Labor Unrest and United States Ascendancy in the GSEE	149
	Organized Labor Under the ICFTU	158
	The Economic Status of Organized Labor During the Early Cold War	163
Epilogue		169
Notes		181
Bibliography		201
Index		211

Foreword

Pity the unfortunate Greeks. Their country is so beautiful but also so strategically situated at the junction of three continents. This location has made Greece a pawn on the global chessboard throughout its history. In 1841 the British Minister to Athens, Sir Edmund Lyons, declared: "A truly independent Greece is an absurdity. Greece can either be English or Russian, and since she must not be Russian, it is necessary that she be English." A century later, in 1944, Greece received the same cavalier treatment when Churchill and Stalin divided the Balkan Peninsula between themselves, with Greece relegated to the British sphere. President Truman sounded more altruistic when in March 1947 he proclaimed his famous "doctrine," in which he stated that his proposed aid program was designed to help "Greece survive as a free nation." But a few years later General James Van Fleet penetrated the rhetorical veil when he declared that Greece was important to the United States because "it offers [an] important base for collection of strategic intelligence" and also "a secondary front to Soviet diversion in [the] event of war." The general therefore concluded that *"The United States is here to stay"* (ch. 4, p. 117).

Van Fleet's optimism has proved well-founded thus far. Major American bases are still located on Crete and the Greek mainland. On the other hand, the status of the bases has become so uncertain that

Secretary of State George Schultz sought assurances concerning their future when he visited Athens in March 1986. Three days before Schultz's arrival, a bronze statue of President Truman in the center of the capital was dynamited. The Athens City Council then voted against restoring the statue to its pedestal. Few who were involved during the heady days of the Truman Doctrine proclamation could have foreseen such an ambiguous outcome.

This boomerang syndrome in American foreign policy is manifest today in many regions besides Greece. Hence the significance of this ground-breaking study by Jon Kofas. It is obviously important for Greek history since it provides an insightful analysis of the American aid program that determined the political and economic configuration of postwar Greece. Kofas's analysis, however, is equally significant for United States history because it was on Greek soil that American counterinsurgency, pacification, and containment tactics were evolved, tested, and later applied elsewhere in the Third World. In some countries, such as Guatemala, the tactics proved as successful as in Greece. In Vietnam, however, the end result was defeat, withdrawal, and agonizing reappraisal which is still in process, as evident in the current Reagan Doctrine and the organizing of Special Operation Forces for quick action anywhere in the Third World.

Those who seek meaningful reappraisal rather than beguiling rationalization might well begin with this study solidly grounded on all available sources. It presents a revisionist perspective regarding both the economic and the political development of Greece under American tutelage. The declared objective of the economic aid was to avoid restructuring the Greek economy and to preserve Greece as an exporter of raw materials and an importer of manufactured goods. Kofas asserts that an alternative industrialization program similar to that of the northern Balkan countries was feasible, and that failure to undertake such a program is responsible for the dependence and vulnerability of today's Greek economy.

Likewise in the political realm, Kofas rejects the Washington dogma (the counterpart of Lyon's theory in the mid-nineteenth century) that Greece has to be in either the Soviet or the American camp, and therefore must be in the latter. Kofas proposes as a "plausible alternative" a social-democratic regime that, in addition to socioeconomic reforms at home, could have pursued abroad a pro-Greek rather than a pro-Soviet or pro-American course.

The victory of the American-supported forces in Greece obscured this alternative vision for decades. Yet it was persistently propounded, in the face of discouraging odds, by a variety of centrist and leftist leaders. With the coming to office of Andreas Papandreou, this vision has become official policy in Athens. Furthermore, assorted versions of this alternative strategy are cropping up globally, which is the underlying reason why the Third World today is out of control. And also why superpower doctrines and projects not recognizing this indisputable and irreversible fact are experiencing difficulties as embarrassing as they are predictable. Hence the broad significance of this thoughtful and thought-provoking study.

L. S. Stavrianos

Preface

This book focuses on the effects of British and American intervention in Greece during the Cold War. Written from a revisionist perspective, the work attempts to do two things. First, it seeks to trace a different model of development for Greece within the Western framework. There is serious debate whether there was an alternative for Greece other than becoming pro-United States or pro-Soviet. Prominent historians of modern Greece, such as William H. McNeill, argue forcefully that there was not. This study proposes the contrary thesis as it argues that there was a plausible alternative, though it was not accepted by either the Foreign Office, the State Department, or the Greek elites. That alternative was the formation of a social-democratic regime that would have pursued fundamental socioeconomic reforms to make the country more competitive in the international arena. American policymakers decided to restore Greece's prewar economy rather than restructuring it to meet the postwar challenges. Consequently, Greece's economy was outwardly prosperous but dependent, vulnerable, and incapable of meeting the people's long-term needs.

The book does not argue, by any means, that Greece could or should have remained neutral between the two superpowers, for it was not in its best interests to pursue such a course. On the contrary, it points out that it was to the country's benefit to have better relations with both its communist and noncommunist neighbors, for only through regional economic integration could Greece realize its development potential.

The second part of the work analyzes the consequences of the policies that were actually followed by the British Foreign Office and the United States State Department. This section is historically valid, and one can accept the second part of the analysis without necessarily embracing the first.

This study has been made possible by the kind and generous assistance of worthy colleagues. I would like to thank Professor Alexander DeGrand, chairman of the Department of History at North Carolina State University, who read the entire manuscript and made many useful comments on content and style. Professor Lewis Erenberg of Loyola University made perceptive observations regarding American foreign policy during the Cold War, which were very helpful in shaping the final draft. I am also greatly indebted to Professor Theofanis Stavrou, director of the Modern Greek Studies Program at the University of Minnesota, who read the manuscript and encouraged me to publish it. I owe profound gratitude to Professor William McNeill of the University of Chicago, who was very kind to comment on America's role in Greece during the 1940s and to offer many insights into the subject matter. Finally, I am especially indebted to Professor L. S. Stavrianos for his most generous contribution to this book, and for the kind support he has given me.

Introduction

The most significant period in the history of contemporary Greece was the tumultuous decade of the 1940s, when the country was engulfed by war and revolution and its future course was decided largely by foreign intervention. During the war the Greek Communist party, KKE, led a popular resistance movement that was composed of heterogeneous elements committed to defeating the Axis powers in the country and establishing a popular democratic regime after liberation. The KKE operated on the principle of the "Popular Front Policy," which was promulgated by Georgi Dimitrov, secretary general of the Third International, in 1935. The Greek Communist party was under Stalinist leadership, but it was uncertain that it had either the capability or the resolve to seize power by force, for it was unprepared for a proletarian revolution similar to that of China under Mao Tse-tung.

Greece was in dire need of systemic socioeconomic changes after the war, and only a regime with a broad popular base, one that would have included or at least tolerated the KKE, could have undertaken the monumental task of reconstruction and development. The centrist and rightist political parties opposed the idea of a coalition government in which the KKE would have had some political influence. It must be noted that the centrist parties had a long tradition of refusing to collaborate with the KKE, dating back to 1936, when General John

2   Introduction

Metaxas imposed a four-and-a-half-year dictatorship on the country. The democratic parties, which Metaxas had suppressed during the late 1930s, reemerged in the postwar years determined to reclaim their rightful places in the political arena and resume the struggle for control of the state. World War II and the resistance movement, however, had changed sociopolitical conditions drastically, shifting the pendulum of popular support toward the center-left and leftist factions, which opted for structural change rather than a return to the status quo ante—restoration of the monarchy and installation of a conservative regime.

Great Britain, which had played an important role in Greece's internal affairs since the War of Independence in 1821, was an influential force in the resistance movement. The British were obviously concerned about the ubiquitous influence of the KKE in the resistance and acted to counterbalance its role. Great Britain assisted the anticommunist forces in the civil war of December 1944—the Athens Revolt—and successfully defeated the National Liberation Front, EAM, the political arm of the communist-guerrilla resistance movement. After the Athens Revolt was crushed by the British invasion of Greece, the government in London assisted in the formation of "Service Governments" in Athens. These transitory governments were designed to quell the communist threat while giving the royalist forces time to consolidate and prepare for restoring King George II. The Service Governments, however, engaged in terrorist acts against the leftists, with the encouragement of the British authorities in Greece, and were partly responsible for provoking the civil war of 1946–49. While the Greek Communist party's egregious policies were also to blame for that fateful conflict, there is no doubt that most of the republican and monarchist parties did not have a propensity toward compromise and deliberately sought confrontation. Finally, the Cold War policies of Great Britain and the United States exacerbated the tensions in the Greek political arena and contributed to the polarization of the country during the three decades after liberation.

The United States replaced Great Britain in Greece after 1947, when it had become apparent that the British empire was crumbling and could no longer afford large-scale economic and military assistance to the Greek regime. The Truman administration internationalized the Greek civil war by linking it to a bipolar foreign policy and the Soviet-American confrontation. The government in Washington poured massive military and considerable economic aid into Greece between 1945 and 1951 as part of an effort to efface the communist threat and secure the country as a staunch ally of the West. American intervention in Greece during the late 1940s had far-reaching consequences not only for the future of the Greek people but also for United States relations with the Near East and the Third World. The government in Washington opted for military solutions rather than political compromise in securing areas of vital strategic and/or economic importance to North American interests. Such solutions did not serve the best interests of the Third World, which has been the arena of the East-West power struggle since 1945, and it is questionable whether they have been in the best long-term interests of the United States.

The legacy of Anglo-American intervention in Greece during the 1940s was underdevelopment under a right-wing regime during the 1950s, dependent development since 1960, and the preeminence of foreign advisers in the country's internal affairs. The reformist forces—communist, socialists, and some centrists—which were committed to Greece's modernization/structural development were thoroughly suppressed from the end of the civil war in 1949 to the end of the military junta in 1974. There is no doubt, therefore, that the country's contemporary history has been determined largely by exogenous factors. This is not to say that internal sociopolitical forces did not play a role in shaping Greece's economic and political orientation. But the conservatives were co-opted by foreign elements, while the centrists and leftists were too weak to effect change in a preindustrial society that lacked a dynamic bourgeoisie.

In this study, an attempt is made to analyze the obstacles to Greece's structural development and the mechanisms the British and United States governments used during the Cold War to keep Greece linked to the Western sphere of influence. The antecedents to the Truman Doctrine are covered extensively and particular focus is placed on the ramifications of American military and economic aid to Greece by the Truman administration. Greece was reduced to a military satellite and an economic dependency of the United States and became part of the Near Eastern strategic network—part of the Northern Tier, which included Turkey and Iran as a buffer zone against the Soviet bloc. There was a metamorphosis in Greece after the promulgation of the Truman Doctrine in 1947 because the country was permeated thoroughly by American advisers who exerted inordinate influence on the future course of the nation.

As will be seen in the following chapters, the transition of Greek political, military, and economic dependence from Great Britain to the United States was necessitated by the new global balance of power and by Greece's geopolitical importance to the West. The catalyst of the transition of Greece's dependence from England to North America was foreign aid, which entailed the acceptance by the recipient of constrictive conditions imposed by the donor. Such conditions were tantamount to United States control of Greece's destiny, especially during the Truman administration. Moreover, the process of political reform, which was an imperative of socioeconomic reform, was halted as a result of the same conditions.

I

Economic Dislocation and the Demise of British Influence in Greece

The Financial Dependence of Greece on Great Britain: An Overview

Greece became an aid recipient and a client country of the United States after 1947, but the roots of its dependence on the West predate the nation's founding. The provisional government during the War of Independence (1821–27) commenced a foreign borrowing trend that was responsible for Greece's financial dependence on the Great Powers—Great Britain, France, and Russia—throughout the nineteenth and twentieth centuries. The Greek state borrowed 2.2 billion gold francs from the Great Powers, primarily from England, between 1821 and 1932. The service paid on the debt until the outbreak of World War II amounted to 2,383 million gold francs. When foreign borrowing ceased in March 1932 due to international financial retrenchment caused by the Great Depression, Greece still owed approximately 2,000 million gold francs to foreign financiers; in other words, almost the entire original amount of the principal borrowed between 1821 and 1932.[1]

The proceeds from the foreign loans were absorbed primarily by the military sector, leaving a small percentage for economic development. In fact, only 6 percent of the foreign loans were allocated for productive works between 1821 and 1893. From 1924 to 1932 Greece borrowed heavily amid a period of political instability and economic dislocation after 1929. The interwar loans were used largely for the civilian economy, but not for structural economic development; that is, there was no effort to build the secondary sector of production. Foreign loans, therefore, were not an economic stimulus, but simply constituted a drain on the economy as they deprived Greece of domestic savings.

Financial dependence entailed economic, political, and military dependence of the borrower on the lender. Greece was a dependency of Great Britain throughout the nineteenth century and until the promulgation of the Truman Doctrine. In the course of the nineteenth and twentieth centuries, the Greek government devoted as much as 40 percent of its national revenues to service the public debt, of which three-fourths went to foreign, primarily British, financiers. "The claim of the foreign debt on the national income," wrote L. S. Stavrianos, "was 9.25 percent for Greece, as against 2.98 percent for Bulgaria, 2.32 percent for Rumania and 1.68 for Yugoslavia."[2] Greece remained unable to develop its own resources by industrializing partly because a substantial portion of its capital formation was drained by European financiers.

The burden of the foreign debt was particularly heavy during the 1930s, when the country experienced major economic problems that were aggravated by the pervasive political instability. The public-debt service absorbed 3,587 million drachmas in fiscal 1931–32 out of a budget of 9,904 millions. The democratic governments of the early 1930s allocated a small fraction of the budget for public-works programs and substantial amounts for debt service and the defense sector. Such flagrant policies simply perpetuated the underdevelopment process and precluded any progress toward modernization.

Although Greece's capital resources were drained principally through the foreign debt, foreign investors had permeated the private sector as well. Foreign investors sunk 850 million gold francs in Greece between 1832 and 1938, of which 310 million accounted for the interwar (1922–38) investment. Of the 850 million gold francs, 610 millions accounted for direct investment and the remaining for portfolio investments. Most of the direct investment was in businesses as well as in the form of loans. The annual installment payments on the foreign investments and the public foreign debt had amounted to 130 million gold francs by 1938, when General Metaxas was in power. The massive capital outflow was the catalyst in Greece's retention in the periphery of the world economy.[3]

Ever since the War of Independence, England played a preponderant role in Greece's internal and foreign affairs. Greece was not allowed to pursue a multidimensional foreign policy based on its national interests because it was subservient to the British government and financiers. One historian described the degree of British penetration of the Greek economy as follows:

> Half of the Greek public debt of 89,000,000 [pounds sterling] was held by private British investors [in 1935]. The Whitehall Securities Ltd. was the largest single straight investor with 5,000,000 [pounds sterling] invested in public utilities such as lighting, tram and bus services in Athens and 5,000,000 in loans to mortgage banks. The Habro Bank had over 1,000,000 [pounds sterling] in chemical and other industries which operated through the Hellenic and General Trust. Habro also owned the Ionian Bank in Greece. General British capital was sunk into general private enterprises to the tune of 15,000,000 [pounds sterling].[4]

Greece's location as the gateway to the Near East made it strategically invaluable to the British empire. Moreover, British economic interests in Greece compelled the government in London to protect and expand them. British intervention in the southeastern Balkan peninsula was inevitable, therefore, during times of crises, such as the Crimean War (1853–56) or the Athens Revolt of 1944. Besides military intervention, England also used missions that investigated Greece's finances and influenced domestic policy. Finally, there was diplomatic intervention by the Foreign Office designed to secure Greek foreign-policy support for the empire's Near Eastern interests.

The British empire disintegrated after World War II and the United States inherited England's legacy in Greece. The massive destruction in Greece after the war, occupation, and the Athens Revolt required external financing for reconstruction. The government in London was not in a position to provide it and relinquished its responsibilities to the United States. The government in Washington could not allow Greece to fall under the domination or even partial influence of the communists, and the likelihood of Greece becoming another Yugoslavia—nonaligned—was not within the realm of possibility in the 1940s. Consequently, American intervention on a very wide scale, which affected every societal sector, became inevitable during the early Cold War when the defunct British empire proclaimed its inability to continue carrying Greece as a dependency.

War Devastation

Every sector in Greece, with the exception of a small clique of war profiteers and Nazi collaborators, was left utterly devastated by the Italo-German occupation. Approximately 550,000 people, or one-eighth of the population, perished during the war, which ended in Greece in the autumn of 1944. Many people died because of widespread famine and disease, primarily malaria. Several tens of thousands fell in battle and some died in concentration camps, while still others were executed by the occupying forces.

The material privation to Greece was astronomical compared with that of other European countries. The delegation that represented Greece at the Paris Conference on Reparations—19 November to 21 December 1945—claimed that total material losses amounted to $7,181 million, or 2.18 percent of Europe's losses due to the war. According to the Greek Ministry of Public Works, the damages to the public sector alone amounted to 44,721 million prewar drachmas. The total cost of the war damages to Greece has been estimated at one trillion drachmas or one billion gold pounds. Although the above figures are no doubt inflated, the losses to the country were extensive. It must be noted that the country's economy and finances were strained under the Metaxas regime, and there was an inevitable decline following the invasion by Italy in October 1940 and the occupation by Germany and her allies after the spring of 1941.[5]

The national income in 1945 was a mere 41 percent of the prewar level, industrial production stood at 36 percent, agricultural production was 54 percent, and wages were just 40 percent of the prewar level; all measured against 1939 constant drachmas. Thirty-four percent of the entire national income was destroyed during the war, with the building sector leading the list in property losses. Estimates concerning the number of housing units that were either totally or partially destroyed vary depending on the source. It has been estimated that 120,000 to 400,000 homes were obliterated during the war and that 1,000,000 to 1,500,000 people were left homeless, representing one-fourth to one-fifth of the entire population.

The rural sector, which was the backbone of the Greek monocultural economy, suffered enormously and was the slowest to recover. About 60 percent of the Greek population earned its livelihood from agriculture, yet only 20 percent of the land was tillable. This meant an average of 1.31 acres of arrable land per person as compared with the world average of 1.90 acres per individual. Such statistics are indicative of the chronically poverty-stricken peasantry in Greece and of its predicament during the 1940s. The number of villages destroyed during the war has been estimated at 1,400 to 1,700. Forestry and agricultural production suffered cataclysmic losses as 25 percent of the forests were burned in a country with few such precious resources. Between 1941 and 1944 there was a 40 percent decline in cereal production as compared with the 1938 output. That figure must be viewed against the background of a nation that has always been a large wheat importer. There was a 66 percent reduction in the output of grapes and raisins, 89 percent in tobacco, and 75 percent in cotton—the four products constituting the bulk of Greece's prewar export commodities. Animal husbandry was also affected as there was an 80 percent loss of small animals, 65 percent of cattle, sheep, and goats, and 50 percent of the horses, which were the principal means of transportation for rural Greece. Finally, 80 percent of the 1,300 tractors were destroyed, leaving the country with practically no agricultural machinery after liberation. The overall decline in agricultural production for the period under consideration was 40 percent, while the population remained relatively steady.[6]

Since the urban sector was a target of frequent bombings, it too suffered considerable deprivation. Transportation and communications networks were either totally demolished or damaged irreparably. About 90 percent of the large bridges and 50 percent of the smaller ones were blown up. Tunnels and mountain passes as well as canals were bombarded. Fifty-six percent of the roads and most harbors, railway tracks, and airports were destroyed. The telephone network was dismantled and 70 percent of the telegraph equipment was confiscated by the Germans, who took it out of the country. The Nazis seized 75 percent of the automobiles and left behind the inoperable ones. Upon liberation Greece had a mere 14 percent of its prewar automobiles.

The shipping industry, which along with banking represented the most dynamic sectors of the economy, sustained substantial losses. Unlike the other segments of the economy, however, shipping recovered very rapidly in the late 1940s. The Greek merchant fleet consisted of 583 vessels, amounting to 1,878,403 tons in 1939. Only 154 ships, totaling to 531,403 tons, remained in 1945. The loss to the shipping industry was no less than 72 percent of prewar capacity. About 99 percent of all coastal craft (caiques), on which 60 percent of the aggregate internal transportation depended, were decimated during the war. The coastal craft were virtually the sole means of transportation and of livelihood for many islanders. But since most harbors and canals were also destroyed, there was little use even for the operable vessels. The wealthy shipowners, whose property was insured primarily by British companies, actually benefited in the long run as a result of the war and its aftermath. The shipping industry became even more lucrative in the postwar period than ever before due, in large part, to the Greek government's efforts and the United States government's desire to revitalize Greece's economy by aiding the most dynamic sector.

The occupation authorities in Greece dismantled entire industrial plants and moved them to Germany. Moreover, they destroyed many factories, so that after liberation industrial production was drastically below prewar levels. As a result of the condition of the factories and the overall chaotic economic and political condition of Greece in 1945, urban unemployment was as high as 50 percent. The absence of a strong and stable regime, combined with the lack of productive investment by the private sector, was largely responsible for the country's incessant economic problems in the aftermath of the Athens Revolt. It must be stressed that the value of the currency declined very rapidly due to gold speculation by the wealthy and exorbitant defense expenditures by the British-appointed Service Governments. Workers and peasants spent up to 75 percent of their income for food alone, while the wealthy few, primarily in Athens, reaped the benefits of postwar economic dislocation. That situation persisted throughout the 1940s and was not redressed until the early 1950s, when political stability was restored, though at a high price—the loss of political freedom for a large number of people.[7]

The official historian of the United Nations Relief and Rehabilitation Administration, UNRRA, concluded that the German occupation of Greece was chiefly responsible for ruining the country's finances. George Woodbridge has written: "By April 1944 note circulation was 1,400 greater than before the war; by October 1944 more than 2 million times. Prices increased even more. In this respect, Greece suffered more than any other European nation."[8] But the German occupation and the ensuing civil war in December 1944 were not the only factors responsible for the calamities that befell Greece after liberation. The indigenous oligarchy, the Greek government, and the British and United States authorities played a significant role in Greece's postwar economic, military, political, and social developments. The aforementioned forces were largely responsible not only for failing to offer constructive solutions for the country's problems but also for exacerbating existing sociopolitical tensions and economic dislocation.

One of the major causes of Greece's postwar financial crisis was hyperinflation, which most countries experienced because of the war economy and the difficult transition to a peace economy. Inflation reached record levels in the autumn of 1944 and the monetary system was in total disarray. The government issued a new paper in currency in November 1944 whose exchange rate was fixed against the American dollar at 150 drachmas and against the British pound sterling at 600 drachmas. The old currency was eliminated as it was made redeemable at 50 billion old drachmas to one new. The nominal exchange value of the currency circulation was reduced from 80,000,000, which was the estimated currency in circulation in 1939, to just 1,000,000 in November 1944. The price of the unstable gold sovereign was fixed at 2,850 drachmas.[9]

The new drachma lost its value almost as soon as it was issued, and the nation's finances remained in perpetual chaos until the early 1950s. One of the reasons for the depreciation of the currency, according to Lincoln MacVeagh, United States Ambassador to Greece, was that people, especially the wealthy, did not support the government's monetary policy. Many merchants, financiers, and industrialists preferred to make short-term investments in gold and foreign currencies, which yielded large profits, rather than commit long-term investments in the productive sector. Investment in gold was a common practice before the war, but it reached inordinate proportions during and after World War II. The Germans poured 2,000,000 gold sovereigns into Greece in order to stabilize the country's war economy under the quisling governments and finance their operations. The British, who were involved in the resistance, poured an amount estimated to be equal to that of the Germans, thereby setting the stage for widespread gold speculation after liberation.[10]

Most of the gold was concentrated in the hands of the few wealthy Athenian families who constituted the indigenous oligarchy. The entire population, however, was infected by the psychology of economic dislocation and skepticism regarding Greece's political future. Ambassador MacVeagh analyzed the causes of the ominous monetary crisis facing Greece as follows:

12   Intervention and Underdevelopment

> Practically no-one deposits it [the drachma] in the bank or otherwise retains possession or title to this currency any longer than absolutely necessary. It has no value abroad and even in the case of domestic transactions its use is limited principally to day-to-day purchases of necessities. A sale involving the equivalent of $25 or more is almost invariably calculated in gold.[11]

One of the factors conducive to the devaluation process was the printing of new notes to finance the war against the leftist guerrillas during the Athens Revolt. The number of notes increased from 126 million in November 1944 to 25,762 million in May 1945. The official value of the currency dropped from 150 drachmas to the dollar in November 1944 to 500 drachmas in May 1945, while the price of the pound sterling increased from 600 drachmas to 2,000 during the same period. The black-market rate was much higher, reflecting the actual value of the drachma. It must be stressed that currency devaluation was a useful device for governments throughout the world to meet their needs and balance their budgets since there was little or no reservoir of national credit, and it has been a practice of Third World governments since the war. Moreover, currency devaluation was not endemic to Greece but was a global phenomenon that resulted in large part from the strong dollar. The devaluation process per se need not have dire consequences, however, if there is economic growth and fair income distribution. But that was not the case either in Greece or in other Third World countries during the 1940s and 1950s. Finally, in Greece currency devaluation was symptomatic of a larger process of economic dislocation and political instability. There were gross inequalities of income distribution as society was polarized between the few wealthy families and the millions of poor.[12]

The unofficial value of the gold sovereign soared from 2,100 new drachmas in November 1944 to 25,000 drachmas in May 1945. During the same period the cost of living increased two-and-a-half times. The manipulation of the gold sovereign by speculators caused substantial hardship for the volatile national economy. The price of the sovereign in New York remained steady at about $8.40 throughout the 1940s. Therefore, there can be no question as to the gross manipulation of the gold market in Greece. There were other mitigating factors that contributed to monetary instability, such as the excessive costs of the Athens Revolt, the anemic industrial and agricultural production, and the wasteful spending by the government for defense, especially after the signing of the Varkiza Agreement. That agreement officially ended the civil war on 12 February 1945, but the pro-British Service Governments in Athens continued to spend excessively for defense. Finally, Greece was an underdeveloped country and suffered considerably more as a result of the war than the developed Western European nations that had an industrial base upon which to rebuild.

The reconstruction requirements of Greece, according to a contemporary estimate, totaled $3,172 million—funds which the Greek government hoped to obtain from reparations and foreign assistance. Great Britain, Greece's principal source for capital since 1821, did not have the resources to underwrite Greek reconstruction. Certainly no other Western European country could have financed Greece's economic resurgence, and the Soviet Union, which was willing to have economic relations with Greece, was anathema to the ruling class in Athens and to the British and the Americans who stood behind the Greek government. The United States, therefore, which emerged as the strongest economic and military power on earth after the war, was the only possible country upon which the Greek politicians and business community could depend. Greece was destined to become a dependency of the United States given the absence of a dynamic revolutionary movement similar to that of China during the same period and the determination of the Truman administration to include Greece as part of the American strategic network in Europe.[13]

UNRRA and the British in Greece

The United Nations established UNRRA in 1943 as a humanitarian agency to provide relief supplies and essential services to war victims in areas under the jurisdiction of the UN. Forty-four nations signed the UNRRA Agreement on 9 November 1943; each signatory nation had one vote and pledged to contribute 1 percent of its revenues to UNRRA's treasury. Since America's contribution was about 73 percent of the total, the organization was subject to Washington's preeminent influence, if not actual control. UNRRA spent $3.5 billion for relief and rehabilitation in devastated areas. Since it was not above politics, it became subject to the nascent Cold War and served those countries that were friendly to the West. In the case of Greece, UNRRA played a very significant role, for it paved the way for the Truman Doctrine as well as for subsequent United States aid to Greece.

Greece applied for UNRRA assistance in July 1944. The government-in-exile, established in Cairo under the auspices of the

British, asked for a minimum of $550 million after enumerating areas in dire need of relief and reconstruction. Herbert H. Lehman, UNRRA director-general, informed A. Sbarounis, the Greek alternate representative at the UNRRA Council, on 4 September 1944 that Greece had qualified for relief assistance. On 23 October 1944, ten days before the last Germans evacuated Athens, UNRRA representatives arrived in Greece to study conditions for relief-aid allocation.

Before UNRRA assumed its functions in Greece, another foreign agency, the British Military Liaison, ML, had been in charge of relief operations. The ML's source of financing was Anglo-American, and the agency had delivered 387,000 tons of supplies to Greece before relinquishing its obligations to UNRRA. The British-backed government-in-exile, headed by the centrist George Papandreou, supported the ML's operations. The Papandreou Government, however, under the advice of the British, used relief supplies as a political weapon against the leftist guerrillas. Supplies were not delivered in the areas which the National Liberation Army, ELAS, controlled. ELAS was the resistance army of the communists and the socialists. The ML program benefited a minority of the population because four-fifths of Greece was under ELAS's control. Consequently, the ML played an important role in the defeat of the revolutionary movement in 1944.[14]

The replacement of the ML with UNRRA was only a first step in Britain's replacement in Greece by the United States. Winston Churchill, prime minister of Great Britain, made serious efforts to retain Greece within the British sphere of influence, but the government in London was facing a multitude of problems at home as well as in India and Africa with the rise of the decolonization movements. Churchill attempted to preserve the long-standing pattern of British influence in Greece by supporting the pro-British politicians in Athens, advocating the restoration of King George II, and refusing to allow the fruition of an independent coalition regime to form after the war. In all likelihood the formation of a broad center-leftist coalition government would have resulted in a faster and better reconstruction process, a more democratic society, the avoidance of a bloody civil war in the late 1940s, and the absence of the preponderate American influence in Greece.[15]

William H. McNeill, the eminent historian who studied Greece's postwar problems since the 1940s extensively, has written that England wanted to exert influence in the formation of a postwar Greek regime for economic and strategic considerations.

> Their [Britain's] first and principal concern was that the government of Greece should always be friendly towards them; and the men who shaped British policy for Greece were convinced that an EAM (National Liberation Front) government would not be friendly. Exactly what "friendly" meant was not clear. Probably the reestablishment of economic concessions to British-owned public utility and other companies; but in the last analysis, and far more important, it meant a government that would side with Great Britain in case of another war.[16]

Of course, the question that arises is whether the alternative to a pro-British regime in Athens was an EAM-controlled government. That was certainly not the case after the Varkiza Agreement, and it is questionable whether it was even a plausible alternative before the Athens Revolt. The real objective of the British regarding the type of government in postwar Greece was to avoid the possibility of a reformist—social-democratic—regime that would have limited the role of foreign capital, perhaps nationalized certain foreign firms such as utilities, and pursued a multidimensional foreign policy.

A large part of the Greek foreign debt was owed to British bankers and financiers. According to one source, British bondholders and bankers possessed $400 million worth of Greek bonds.

> This huge foreign debt which was floated in London between 1823 and 1898, when Greece faced economic ruin after wars with the Turks, has borne an average annual interest of 8.19% continually from April 1898 to 1942, when the Nazis occupied Greece. In those forty-four years the British Bankers have drained Greece of $1,441,440,000 in interest payments alone. It is this staggering debt and the usurious interest rate which is largely responsible for Greece's impoverishment and also explains, in some measure, Britain's stake in the country.[17]

While the above figures may be questioned, the author's point is valid. The British used the Greek foreign debt as a means of exerting financial, commercial, political, and military influence. British investors had vital interests in Greek banks, industry, utility companies, real estate, and the general economy. The Service Governments, which the British authorities implanted in Athens, were designed to serve the empire's economic, political, and strategic interests in southern Europe.

British armed intervention during the Athens Revolt had resulted in a temporary and hollow victory for Churchill and Britain's imperial interests because the United States ultimately emerged as the preeminently influential power in the Near East. From the beginning of 1945 until the end of 1946, London and Washington were engaged in a latent power struggle for hegemony over Greece and the entire Near East. It was certainly not evident that such struggle had been taking place until after the "Third Round," or the civil war of 1946–49 between the KKE-backed Democratic Army and the Anglo-American-supported right-wing regime in Athens. The preoccupation of the West during that period focused on the embryonic Soviet-American confrontation. Research has shown, however, that Moscow remained largely aloof from Greek internal affairs during the 1940s for reasons which will be analyzed in detail in the following chapters.[18]

The Anglo-American rivalry over Greece was articulated as follows by Bickham Sweet-Escott, British banker and author, in an article published in July 1949.

> In all this [U.S. intervention in Greece since the Truman Doctrine] the British have been taking something of a back seat rather further than our influence warrants. For unlike Americans, we have economic interests of a more permanent nature in the country. My own bank for instance, has been operating in Greece for 110 years, and it is the oldest British concern in the country. Much more important is the British-owned power station, which supplies electricity to Athens and the Piraeus, and which is the largest of its kind in South-East Europe. Then there is the Lake Copais Company which years ago drained the Lake and now farms or lets some 50,000 acres of what is probably the most fertile wheat and cotton growing in Greece.[19]

American investments in Greece were negligible indeed when compared with British interests. United States private investments in Greece amounted to $8.5 million in 1936, $9.6 million in 1943, and a mere $5.9 million in 1950.[20] What was important, however, was not the actual amount of investments during the 1940s when the country was in political turmoil, but Greece's geopolitical significance to the United States, which was committed to the containment policy.

To secure an Anglophile regime in Athens, it was necessary for the government in London to revitalize the Greek capitalist system by investing millions of pounds sterling. Such investment capital was lacking because the dollar replaced the British pound as the strongest currency in the world and New York replaced London as the center of the capitalist world economy. Although the transition from London to New York as the world's banker started at the end of World War I, the process was not completed until 1945. "It took another world war," wrote Harry Magdoff, "the devastation of Europe and Asia, and the financial bankruptcy of the other leading industrial powers to set the stage for the United States to take over the financial as well as military and political supremacy of the capitalist world." As the United Kingdom became financially and militarily dependent upon the United States after the war, it was impossible for the government in London to retain its prewar status in Greece, and indeed in other countries (colonies, semicolonies) where it exerted influence, without facing a challenge from the government in Washington.[21]

The catalyst of the transition from *Anglokratia* (British hegemony) to *Americanokratia* (American hegemony) in Greece was UNRRA. Edward Stettinius, United States secretary of state, informed MacVeagh on 6 January 1945 that UNRRA was ready to commence operations in Greece. British officials were initially reluctant to surrender the ML's functions to the American-dominated UNRRA and proposed a joint relief effort of the two organizations. The State Department categorically rejected the plan and the government in Athens supported UNRRA, although Prime Minister Nikolaos Plastiras, a center-leftist politician, owed his position to the British authorities.

The Greek minister of finance, George Sideris, informed General Ronald Scobie, commanding officer of the British Military Mission in Greece, on 26 January that the Service Government was unable to meet the vital internal expenses of Greece without financial help from the United Kingdom and the United States. He requested that the expenses of the armed forces, which constituted a major drain on the budget, must be paid by either the British or the Americans.

The ML agreed eventually to assist UNRRA in the transition process of relief functions, which started on 15 March 1945. The United States government insisted that once UNRRA commenced operations in Greece, American officials would also be appointed as advisers to the host government, but would act independently of the British. Greece was honeycombed with British advisers and military personnel after the Athens Revolt. Even after UNRRA's arrival in the country, the British remained actively involved in Greece's internal and foreign affairs. They were eager to have American collaboration in determining policy on behalf of the Service Governments, but the

State Department denied the request for Anglo-American concerted policy in Athens.²²

Churchill appealed personally to President Franklin D. Roosevelt for the formation of a joint Anglo-American committee that would have advisory powers in the Hellenic government. The prime minister added that despite criticism by the international community regarding British interventionist policy in Greece, the military mission was not prepared to depart Greece and the British Embassy was intent on continuing to offer advice to the host government. Roosevelt rejected Churchill's proposal and maintained that the United States would act unilaterally in Greece. That same policy was pursued by President Truman as well.

UNRRA finally started operations in Greece on 1 April 1945. The agency was delayed partly because of the disagreements with the British ML, but also because of some initial differences with the Plastiras administration, which wanted control of UNRRA supplies. UNRRA's policy was that the "Recipient governments were required to sell most of the supplies and to use the funds for UNRRA-approved rehabilitation projects." Theoretically, that policy was applicable in Greece, but the government used UNRRA supplies as part of an extensive patronage system that augmented the interests of corrupt officials and certain distributors. UNRRA supplies were also used as a weapon against the communists and communist sympathizers. It must be underlined that neither the Service Governments nor the UNRRA officials adopted any serious measures to distribute relief supplies on the basis of need. Consequently, UNRRA did not alleviate Greece's postwar problems but, as will be seen below, helped aggravate them to a large degree.²³

The Failure of Reform Under Varvaressos

The Greek government was eager to initiate a reconstruction program and reinvigorate the economy in order to quell the revolutionary elements and restore sociopolitical stability. Such a large-scale program, however, could not be carried out without Anglo-American endorsement because the Greeks looked to external financing as a means of carrying out reconstruction. In April 1945 the Hellenic government invited American and British financial advisers to form a Joint Policy Committee, JPC. There were American participants in the JPC, but

MacVeagh instructed them not to engage in bilateral sessions with their British counterparts.

Winston Churchill sent Harold MacMillan, minister resident Allied Force Headquarters, Mediterranean Theater, to Athens in April 1945 "to assist the British Ambassador there in 'advising' the Regent [Archbishop Damaskinos, a conservative Anglophile] on the formation of a new government." MacMillan's instructions were to aid Damaskinos in the appointment of yet another Service Government that replaced the Plastiras cabinet. The new British-appointed prime minister was Admiral Voulgaris, a Liberal republican who served as minister of air in the government-in-exile. The strong man in the Voulgaris administration, however, was Kyriakos Varvaressos, a professor of economics who had served as governor of the Bank of Greece and was also a representative to the UNRRA Council. He was an Anglophile who believed that Greece's laissez-faire system, which benefited the nouveaux riches after the war, needed to be checked by the state. Varvaressos was entrusted by the British with the task of reviving the anemic economy and was appointed minister of reconstruction and vice president of the council. He also had the right to oversee the ministries of Finance, Trade, and Commerce. Despite such concentration of power in the office of one man, his programs failed and he was forced to resign three months after he joined the Voulgaris cabinet.[24]

Before he assumed his duties in the government, Varvaressos went to Washington seeking assurances of extensive American financial aid for Greece. He met with William G. Clayton, undersecretary of state, and with Treasury officials to discuss various proposals for assistance. He also had a meeting with Wayne C. Taylor, president of the Export-Import Bank, to arrange a loan. United States officials assured the Greek delegation of some future aid, but there was no firm commitment and no agreements were signed. The Export-Import Bank had reservations about extending credits to the Greek government, but it was willing to finance some projects through the private sector. A State Department memo revealed:

> Bank officials indicated the strong possibility that credit could be established in the near future for the purchase in this country of materials to revive Greek industry; that the Bank would be willing to send two experts to Greece to study the situation; that the credits might be opened for certain Greek Banking institutions in Greece, not the Greek Government.[25]

Certainly that was not what Varvaressos, an advocate of Keynesian economics, had in mind when he asked for aid. In any event, it should be noted that the Export-Import Bank was founded by Congress in 1934 to stimulate America's foreign trade amid the Great Depression by extending credit to foreign buyers of American goods and services. The bank coordinated its lending policy with the State Department's foreign policy and extended credits to Third World countries for infrastructural and agricultural development.

The government in Washington was willing to strengthen United States-Greek financial relations, but not as long as the British continued to exert paramount influence on Greek internal affairs. Precisely because of such considerations, the Export-Import Bank and the Truman administration denied any reconstruction assistance to Varvaressos, a British-appointed administrator. Despite America's refusal to extend immediate economic aid to Greece, the vice premier designed an economic reform program based on the assumptions of forthcoming American aid and of tacit support on the part of the Greek bourgeoisie.

The minister's reform program was initiated as soon as he took office early in June. It was based on strict government regulation of the economy, but it was by no means a socialist program. On the contrary, it was designed to revive capitalism on firm foundations by rationalizing the system. Varvaressos asked the merchants and the industrialists to reduce commodity prices by 20 to 50 percent, while at the same time he recommended wage increases ranging from 50 to 83 percent. He imposed rigorous regulations on industry and agriculture and introduced tax increases on profits. As head of the Reconstruction Ministry, he was also in charge of distributing UNRRA supplies. To ameliorate sociopolitical tensions amid a postwar atmosphere of societal polarization, he ordered the swift distribution of relief supplies which were rotting away in warehouses.[26]

All of these measures were necessary, considering the exigent economic and political conditions of Greece after the Athens Revolt. Varvaressos realized that the free enterprise system, unchecked by the government, augmented the interests of the very few who controlled the means of production at the expense of the majority. Arguing in favor of his quasi-statist policies, he wrote:

> The result of lack of state control in this country is that one class in possession of the various commodities . . . succeeds in making a comfortable living and sets aside considerable profits whereas the great majority of wage earners and other small

income classes are scarcely able to keep themselves alive. It is evident that this class has been responsible for the great demand for gold and for causing the increase in the exchange rate of the sovereign. . . . depreciation of the drachma has been brought about by this class alone which demands huge prices for what it sells and collects the greatest part of the public's buying power only to invest most of it in gold. Thus while this class is highly capable of readjusting its income immediately to the rise in prices, living becomes more problematical day by day for the remaining classes.[27]

He went on to charge that the wealthy elite was responsible for the dwindling foreign exchange reserves in the nation's financial institutions and for the perpetual economic dislocation in Greece.

Varvaressos represented the old oligarchy and was opposed to the mobilization of the nouveaux riches, whose wealth emanated to a large extent from the war economy. He implemented a policy of heavy taxation on the wealthy classes and imposed price controls to limit the power of the new bourgeoisie. He did not propose, however, any tangible program for agrarian reform accompanied by industrial development to address Greece's structural economic problems. He opposed industrialization and the big bureaucracy which was based on a patronage system. His ultimate goal was to strike a balance between the old and new capitalist elites by imposing heavier taxes on the latter. The Greek version of the New Deal failed because it was an ephemeral measure designed to cope primarily with the problems of profiteering and speculation, rather than the systemic problems of the economy, by strengthening the state and initiating agrarian reform, public works programs, and development of the capital-goods sector.

On 17 August 1945 the vice premier disclosed to the public the part of his plan concerning the financing of the reconstruction program.

Today I am in the fortunate position of being able to announce that the question of foreign aid has been settled. The American government itself invited us to submit an official request for the granting of credits by the Export-Import Bank. The request has already been submitted for 250 million dollars and we are certain that it will be accepted. These credits will be used for the purchase in the United States of all items indispensable to the reconstruction of our economy. We have requested machines and materials for the reestablishment of our ports, of the Corinth Canal, of the railway network, of roads, of structures, of materials for the construction of cities and devastated villages, of rolling stock and other means of transport, of animals and agriculture, in other words everything which we need for our economic recovery.[28]

He concluded that UNRRA spent $300 million in Greece and that it would continue its assistance program for several more years.

In order to justify the ambitious program, which would have forced the country into financial dependence on the United States, Varvaressos argued that Greece planned to borrow $300 million from abroad—a small price to pay, considering that the entire outstanding foreign debt did not exceed that amount. He admitted privately, however, that the Export-Import Bank was willing to grant Greece only a $20 million loan, not $250 million as was announced to the press. Moreover, the minister believed that some manufacturers, importers, merchants, and bankers were bound to oppose his reforms, but the opposition would be counterpoised by popular support for reform.

The Export-Import Bank approved a $25 million loan for Greece, but only after Varvaressos resigned from office. Furthermore, UNRRA did not allocate nearly as much money for Greece as the minister expected. He estimated that relief assistance would amount to $1.9 billion: one billion for economic rehabilitation and 900 million for supplies. UNRRA's total contribution to Greece amounted to $416,252,800 from 1 April 1945 to May 1947.[29] The funds were expended on each item as follows:[30]

$186,344,800	Food
40,250,000	Clothing
11,856,500	Medical and sanitation
58,374,000	Agricultural and rehabilitation
53,935,000	Industrial rehabilitation
65,492,500	Miscellaneous
$416,252,800	Total

The United States provided $312 million of the total UNRRA aid to Greece, while other UN members contributed $104 million. The deputy premier, therefore, exaggerated UNRRA's actual contributions and overestimated America's predisposition to reinvigorate the Greek economy under an Anglophile regime. It is also quite possible that he did not consider seriously the profound long-term consequences of foreign aid for Greece's economic and political future.

The United States was willing to use aid as a tool of furthering its future economic, strategic, and foreign-policy interests. One indication that such was the case was a dispatch that MacVeagh wrote in November 1945. It stated:

> American contracting engineering firms should have every opportunity to bid with provision in Export-Import Bank credit for payment [of] their services in dollars. No organization exists in Greece qualified [to] execute large construction programs utilizing [the] amount of equipment requested. Unless US firms receive support [in] connection [with] Export-Import Bank credit, [the] latter [is] probably wasted [to a] large extent or utilized [for the] benefit [of] other foreign contractors.[31]

Such terms were moderate by comparison with those in connection with United States government assistance. Nevertheless, the Greek government, including Varvaressos, was willing to pay the price because it regarded foreign assistance essential to reviving the economy.

The Varvaressos reforms failed miserably, partly because of the counterproductive role that UNRRA aid played in the Greek economy. UNRRA imported, distributed, and sold supplies, many of which were produced locally. The Greek merchants and industrialists protested against the sale of inexpensive foreign-relief supplies which cut into their profits. The Voulgaris administration did not adjust the prices of UNRRA goods partly because Varvaressos was trying to bring inflation under control. As a result of that measure and because the government imposed high taxes on profits and rigid price controls, the industrialists cut back on production and stockpiled goods, and the merchants resorted to hoarding. Moreover, the farmers preferred to sell their products in the black market, which offered higher prices than the government-regulated market. The black market thrived, therefore, and undermined the legitimate economy.[32]

UNRRA's negative impact on the Greek economy was such that even the United States Embassy in Athens criticized its operations, though not for reasons already stated above.

> Its [UNRRA's] officials were often in a position to decide which factory would operate, which railroad line would be rebuilt and how retail trade should be conducted . . . even fully justified

decisions by UNRRA officials in Greece have been subject to reversal by someone in London or Washington, with effects upon Greek economy which no one at that distance could foresee. Both Greek Government agencies and private business frequently have found themselves in a helpless position before UNRRA juggernauts, with the resulting encouragement of an attitude of helplessness and irresponsibility.[33]

The embassy censured UNRRA because the prevailing attitude among United States officials was that the agency hindered the progress of free enterprise and Washington's foreign policy toward Greece.

The cost-of-living index jumped from 5.6 in June 1945 to 15.5 in September as a result of hoarding, which was a reaction to Varvaressos's reforms and UNRRA's role in Greece. Many factories either cut production or shut down completely in an apparent effort to force a change in policy. Wages declined precipitously, and unemployment and underemployment remained very high. Labor leaders, who were sympathetic to the leftist and centrist parties, organized strikes in protest of relentless economic dislocation. Since organized labor, farmers, merchants, and manufacturers opposed and actively undermined Varvaressos's reforms, he was forced to resign on 1 September 1945.

In April 1947 he blamed the nouveaux riches for the failure of his policies. "The conscienceless economic oligarchy," Varvaressos wrote, ". . . after collaboration with the enemy during occupation, took advantage of the shortages of goods after the liberation in order to accumulate riches." Although there were many mitigating factors that played a role in the demise of the quasi-statist reform policies, there can be no doubt as to the validity of Varvaressos's thesis.[34]

Greece was a nation of about 7,250,000 people after liberation, but it was controlled by a few thousand wealthy Athenians. Some belonged to the nouveaux riches group and had made their fortunes by collaborating with the Nazis. A report published by the British Economic Mission to Greece confirmed Varvaressos's allegation regarding the inordinate influence of the oligarchy in society. The report stated that:

> Although there are no titles and social distinctions in Greece, there are more or less 3000 exceptionally wealthy families who live primarily in or around Athens. The family members of this establishment, to which belong many of the country's politicians, live in great luxury. They have at their disposal gold sovereigns and they remain indifferent towards the high cost

of living, and since there is no income tax, according to the British notion of tax, they live essentially untaxed.[35]

It is interesting to note that during the protests against Varvaressos by the capitalist class, the banking community also sided with the antireformist elements, thereby undermining the government's policies.

The Voulgaris cabinet was also responsible for the inefficiency of Varvaressos's reforms because it did not support his fiscal measures. It must be pointed out, however, that governments in Greece since the War of Independence served the interests of the propertied classes, and only on rare occasions were economic reforms implemented to benefit the lower strata of the population. A political regime that would have been committed to social justice was needed if reforms were to succeed.

The Food and Agricultural Organization of the UN compiled a report on Greece which revealed how the government's fiscal policies perpetuated socioeconomic polarization as the burden of taxation fell upon the poor.

> Although there are some taxes on profits, rents and real property, direct taxes yield only 15 percent of the current national ordinary revenues, while customs, excise commodity, public monopoly revenues, and other indirect taxes make up the balance. In addition [most] local revenues [emanate] from commodity taxes. Over four fifths of the tax revenues thus come from taxes which either reduce incomes to producers (especially farmers), or raise cost to customers (mostly farmers and low income city workers). Less than one fifth of the taxes is of the type that bears primarily on the well-to-do persons receiving large incomes.[36]

The problem of the regressive tax structure had deleterious effects on the national economy after liberation, when the state lacked revenues to initiate a reconstruction program. For every 10 shillings per person collected in direct taxes, the government collected £2.10 in indirect taxes.

The Greek capitalist class virtually escaped taxation primarily because the government "looks to the rich industrialists and profiteers and to the hierarchy in the army as now constituted (the right-wing elements) as its domestic support."[37] The majority of the population lived at or below the poverty line and was much more sympathetic to the centrist and leftist political parties than to the foreign-imposed regime. Greece during the immediate postwar years, like other underdeveloped societies, experienced notable socioeconomic polarization. One scholar described the chasm between the poor and wealthy as follows:

> According to estimates by UNRRA and the Bank of Greece, 50 percent of the provincial populace and 30 to 35 percent of townspeople were living in misery and were unable to buy even the bare essentials, while merchants, professionals, and manufacturers, comprising 14.5 percent of the population were earning 77 percent of the money income.[38]

The politically entrenched wealthy elites resisted any policy changes that would have compromised their privileged position in society. The following chart provides a lucid illustration of the income levels and the distribution of wealth in Greece in 1947.

Families	Collective Incomes (in Drachmas)[39]
675,333	2,165,778
676,157	4,573,247
287,805	7,281,512
71,951	23,571,413
33,247	39,543,728
7,316	71,389,216
2,894	194,134,400

The polarized socioeconomic structure was a phenomenon that predated World War II. Its significance in the 1940s was that the country was undergoing a profound political crisis amid the ominous economic dislocation. Many manufacturers, merchants, bankers, and war profiteers seized the opportunity to "cash in" on the country's hard times, rather than assuming a more responsible role to revive the economy. Professor McNeill wrote that the industrialists "hated to put money into any productive enterprise unless it promised at least 40 percent profit of the investment, because they could make that much simply by manipulating their money in foreign exchange."[40]

As noted above, Varvaressos maintained that the capitalist class was the main cause of Greece's lingering and grievous recovery. The bourgeoisie diverted their resources from productive works into highly profitable gold and foreign exchange investments. The former minister of reconstruction wrote that production was low after liberation principally because of profiteering. He continued:

> Unfortunately, it began also to become apparent that some of those who take advantage of the present difficulties are not content to exploit the existing scarcity, but often increase it by hiding or by keeping production at a low level, and so hinder the revival of the economy, the disappearance of unemployment and the beneficial use of imported supplies.[41]

After he resigned from office, Varvaressos pointed out that there was gross misuse of credit funds that were intended for revitalization of the economy. Sixty percent of the loans earmarked for reconstruction were awarded to just seven concerns at a time when more equitable and fair distribution was essential for economic as well as political purposes.

The Bank of Greece, which was a government agency, granted over 5,872 million drachmas in loans to industry and 21,767 million to commercial banks for industrial loans in 1945–46. Because of the concentration of capital, the beneficiaries of those loans were a few industrialists and merchants whose wealth was in gold and foreign exchange and who supported the reactionary Service Governments.[42]

Sweet-Escott was so impressed by the concentration of capital and the virtual absence of competition in Greece that he remarked:

> the bulk of Greek production is in the hands of remarkably few people. In May 1945 six of the firms engaged in the chemical industry controlled 75 percent of the output, three of the firms engaged in woolen spinning controlled 60 percent of the production, and six of the cotton-weaving firms controlled 42 percent of the capacity. There can be little doubt that this concentration has led in several industries to something very like monopoly.[43]

Bodosakis Athanasiades, the mogul of Greek industry who rose from poverty to become the most prominent capitalist in the country, dominated the chemical industry and exerted considerable political influence after the 1930s. He had a number of political personalities on his payroll, including Prime Minister Voulgaris before he took office as well as General Napoleon Zervas, the notorious right-wing guerrilla leader who headed the National Republican Greek League, EDES, during the war and had close ties to the British government.

The Greek business community and speculators were not the sole obstacle to the success of Varvaressos's reforms. UNRRA and the United States were major hindrances to the recovery of Greece's postwar economy. Some aspects of UNRRA's counterproductive role have been already mentioned, but the connection between the relief agency, the governments in Washington and Athens, and the Greek profiteers must also be established. As far as UNRRA officials were concerned, the root cause of the relief problem was distribution of supplies. That process involved the Greek government, a clique of profiteers in Athens, and United States officials. The government awarded contracts to industrialists and merchants who bought relief supplies cheaply and sold them at very high prices. UNRRA and American officials in Athens knew about the profiteering that resulted from the government contracts, yet they allowed the situation to continue unabated. When the Labour government of Prime Minister Clement Atlee assailed the Greek capitalists for their counterproductive role in the country's economy, Lincoln MacVeagh defended the profiteers as "the most virile forward-looking sections [of the] Greek population."[44]

Fifty percent of the national wealth was in the hands of a mere 0.5 percent of the population. It was primarily that elite group which exploited the UNRRA program in the absence of American criticism and a sense of accountability on the part of the Service Governments. Meanwhile, the poverty-stricken peasants and workers were without medicine, shelter, and basic necessities for survival. In his perceptive critique of UNRRA and the Greek government, Howard K. Smith wrote:

> The Greek government's administration of UNRRA goods was nothing short of criminal. The bulk of the proceeds went into the pockets of private black market profiteers who were allowed to distribute the goods. When the American aid team arrived in Greece in the summer of 1947, it found tons of good American textiles, sent to Greece as gifts, rotting in warehouses, while the Greek people were in rags. The government had refused to distribute the cloth for fear it would bring down prices of domestic Greek textiles. While American UNRRA foodstuffs went via the black market to the rich restaurants and missions, UNRRA estimated that seventy-five percent of all Greek children were suffering from malnutrition.[45]

The American Mission for Aid To Greece, AMAG, reported in December 1947 that $75,000,000 worth of supplies and equipment sent by UNRRA and other relief organizations to Greece remained undistributed in the docks and warehouses. Many of the supplies included foodstuffs and medicine which were unsuitable for use after they were left to spoil.

The Greek parliament (Vouli) reproved the negative impact of UNRRA and subsequent American aid to Greece. The Deputies concluded in 1957 that "the waste of American assistance was outrageous. A great part of the supplies was stolen by the different groups and distributing committees, and most astonishing of all was that in the depredation were involved allies and Greeks as well as ladies of 'high society.' "[46] Vavaressos charged in 1952 that UNRRA was partly responsible for draining the country's revenues and contributing to the overall deterioration of the national economy.

The Greek government had arranged to manufacture and package, at the public treasury's expense, UNRRA materials, many of which were readily available in domestic markets. The funds spent for processing such materials could have been devoted to the reconstruction process. Moreover, after UNRRA's arrival in Greece the government adopted a complacent attitude and allowed the agency to assume responsibilities that ought to have been carried out by the state. Finally, Greece's commercial relations with the United States were expanded after UNRRA went to Greece. Greece enjoyed a favorable trade balance with the United States before the war, exporting $14,269,000 in goods and importing $6,683,000 for the period of 1936–38. Greek exports to the United States between 1942 and 1945 amounted to $153,000, while American imports totaled $30,291,000. The devastation of the European markets compelled Greece during and after the war to become a trade dependency of the United States. Greek exports to the United States in 1946 were $23,651,000, while American imports amounted to $143,826,000. Greek commercial dependence necessarily led to financial dependence, which was imperative for the country's foreign trade. Financial dependence, as will be seen below, led to military and political dependence.[47]

One final element that contributed to the failure of the Varvaressos policies and facilitated the transition of Greek dependence from Great Britain to North America was the fiscal blunder that persisted throughout the 1940s and 1950s. The state's expenditures between November 1944 and November 1945 amounted to 98,863 million drachmas, while revenues were 52,452 million, leaving a deficit of 46,411 million drachmas. Budget deficits were a chronic problem for Greece as they have been for most Third World countries. During the postwar years, however, amid economic dislocation the lower classes were victims of flagrant fiscal policies that encouraged waste and inefficiency. One contemporary economist, Professor Angelos Angellopoulos, analyzed the effects of the blundering fiscal policies as follows:

> Here we confine ourselves to note, that in just five months, from July 1945 until December 1945, the popular classes were taxed under the method of inflation by 92 billion drachmas. Though at the end of June the monetary circulation represented purchasing power of 2,425,000 gold sovereigns, at the end of November the circulation represented the purchasing power of 1,101,000 gold sovereigns. This dimunition of monetary value burdened the popular classes and especially the wage earners, where among them is found the paper currency and not, of course, the rich, who have their wealth in real estate and gold sovereigns. This inflation has produced and is producing the most unjust phase of taxation, which flagrantly strikes at the popular classes.[48]

The Service Governments and the elected right-wing regimes that followed during the late 1940s and 1950s were totally responsible for the grossly unfair taxation and income distribution.

One of the variables that aggravated postwar inflation and budget deficits was the burgeoning defense expenditures. At the end of October 1945 the notes in circulation reached 60 billion drachmas, 15 billion of which was expended for the Allied (British) forces in Greece and 33 billion for administrative costs. A total of five-sixths of the circulation went for consumption purposes, leaving practically nothing for economic development. The real burden on the state's finances and the national economy was the one-fourth of the circulation that was spent on the foreign forces. The British government had agreed to reimburse Greece for such expenses, but at the end of November 1945 the former owed the Greek government £12,500,000. The overall military expenditures of Greece in the 1940s absorbed about fifty percent of the budget. It was impossible under such conditions, therefore, for the Greek state to initiate the type of reconstruction programs that the North Balkan countries, which were building dynamic fiscal state structures, were implementing during the late 1940s.[49]

Kyriakos Varvaressos initiated reforms against insurmountable odds since indigenous and foreign forces worked against his efforts. His failure to revitalize the national economy by increasing the spending power of the lower classes and granting more powers to the state was due to the unwillingness of the capitalist class to support even the most essential reforms. The refusal of the United States to underwrite Greek reconstruction as long as the British played a major political and military role in the country was also a factor. Finally, UNRRA's counterproductive role, combined with the exorbitant defense spending that was designed to keep the unpopular Service Governments in power, was important to the demise of the ephemeral Varvaressos reforms.

The Anglo-American Struggle for Hegemony in Greece

After Varvaressos resigned from office, price controls were lifted and many commodities reappeared in the open market. The prices of UNRRA goods were raised to make them more competitive, and the government discontinued the costly processing of UNRRA materials. Custom duties were raised, but import regulations were eased and the Bank of Greece was once again permitted to provide the necessary foreign exchange for imports. The central bank also resumed unrestricted gold sales, which Varvaressos had curtailed. In short, there was a complete reversal of Varvaressos's quasi-statist policies and a return to laissez-faire, which was in accord with the spirit of the Bretton Woods system.

The effects of deregulation after 1 September 1945 were cataclysmic for the national economy and the lower strata of society. Within three days of the former minister's resignation, prices increased 40 to 50 percent and the cost-of-living index, which had been relatively stable for the first eight months of 1945, jumped from 10.0 in August 1945 to 100.3 in January 1946. The price of the gold sovereign soared from 18,000 drachmas to 240,000 drachmas during the same period under consideration. The state's financial status deteriorated precipitously. The Bank of Greece had the following assets in September 1945.

$116,000,000	Foreign Exchange in Pounds Sterling
26,000,000	Foreign Exchange in U.S. Dollars
28,000,000	Gold (coins and bullion)
$170,000,000	Total

Of the above assets, $80 million represented the unexpended balance of advances that the government in London made in the early part of the war. Greece needed to retain $60 million to cover its currency circulation, leaving the remainder for imports. There was nothing left, therefore, for reconstruction.[50]

Considering the state's precarious financial condition, the Voulgaris administration was eager to obtain foreign assistance. The premier wrote to Buel Maben, UNRRA chief in Greece, on 14 September 1945 that the government needed advice and support from the Anglo-American authorities to implement a feasible economic policy. A sense of profound fatalism had consumed the entire cabinet, which believed that it could not function without the advice of foreign elements.

Ernest Bevin, British foreign secretary, proposed that the State Department cooperate with the Foreign Office in advising the Voulgaris administration through UNRRA. He wrote to James Byrnes, United States secretary of state, that Anglo-American advisers in Athens "will be accused of excessive interference in Greek affairs." But since UNRRA supplied many of Greece's material needs, "they [foreign advisers] must inevitably exercise immense influence over the Greek government's internal economic policy." Bevin, who continued Churchill's imperialist foreign policy, was concerned about his government's inability to carry on in Greece without the backing of Washington.

Byrnes rejected Bevin's proposal for a bilateral agreement that would have blossomed into an Anglo-American policy committee in Athens. American officials believed that UNRRA, as well as the British authorities in Athens, had become obstacles to United States policy toward Greece. Ambassador MacVeagh had informed the State Department as early as June 1945 that the British were using UNRRA as a vehicle to exert influence on Greece's internal affairs. The Ambassador charged that the British dominated the Joint Policy Committee, which had an influential position in the Greek government's economic, financial, and political affairs. Moreover, he alleged that the British regarded UNRRA as an extension of the ML, and they had been deciding what ministers to appoint. Given those realities and the friction between London and Washington over policy in Greece, MacVeagh recommended that the State Department must "set up an independent advisory body in Athens which would be equivalent in every way to the British."[51]

UNRRA became very unpopular with the Truman administration as it was not perceived as an efficacious instrument of advancing

United States foreign policy. Ambassador MacVeagh recommended in October 1945 that UNRRA cease operations in Greece, so that the country would be compelled to import through commercial channels. He censured UNRRA because it obstructed the progress of Greek-American commercial relations and because it was not under the exclusive control of Americans. In the final analysis, the unilateral foreign policy of the Truman administration was incongruous to the functions of UNRRA, a multilateral agency.

R. G. A. Jackson, senior deputy director general of UNRRA, London Office, assessed the agency's relief efforts with a great deal of pessimism. He maintained that if UNRRA discontinued operations in Greece, "the basic condition of the country would be little better than it would have been if we had not come here." He blamed the government in Athens for the nation's deplorable economic situation and charged that profiteers behind the scenes had a decisive "influence on these Governments and whose main object is to make money quickly at the expense of the country." He went on to argue that despite its inability to carry out effectively the task of relief and rehabilitation, UNRRA had become a vital agency in the nation's politics and economy because Greece was totally devastated and looked to the agency for answers.[52]

The charges that Jackson and the American Embassy in Athens advanced against UNRRA were valid, but the agency could have played a constructive role if there had been a less corrupt and more accountable government in Athens. Moreover, UNRRA became a part of the decadent superstructure in Greece, which was sustained by the Anglo-American authorities, the indigenous capitalist class, and the armed forces. The Service Government of Prime Minister Voulgaris was utterly incapable of solving the nation's systemic problems and was helpless in advancing possible solutions after Varvaressos resigned from office.

A wave of labor strikes was staged by 3,000 bakers, 3,000 textile workers, and 4,000 general laborers in the fall and winter of 1945. They protested the rising prices and declining wages, but the foreign-backed regime remained oblivious to their demands. The daily wages for the average worker amounted to about 80 cents, but a loaf of bread was 40 cents, and olive oil—a universally used commodity in Greece—was $6 for two-and-three-quarter gallons. About 2,000 Greek employees of UNRRA and the British missions in Greece went on strike in September, demanding a 100 percent wage increase. The *New York Times* reported that there was widespread social unrest in Greece during September and that UNRRA was part of the problem, rather than the solution. Yet the host government was heavily dependent on the agency for advice.

Given the close relationship between UNRRA and the Greek government and taking into account the former's strenuous sociopolitical and economic developments after September 1945, Jackson proposed immediate economic intervention in the country by the West if future military intervention was not to be inevitable. He recommended to Herbert Lehman that a commission be established in Athens to "advise on the reconstruction of the governmental machine, and the economy of the country and to see that its advice is carried through by the Government." Jackson was an Australian national who, naturally, favored British policy in Greece. Therefore, his views regarding UNRRA's role in the country reflected those of the Foreign Office and not of the State Department. Nevertheless, he was fundamentally correct in prophesizing that the West would intervene militarily in Greece. The Truman administration was informed regularly by its Embassy in Athens about the prevailing social unrest, the increased leftist activity directed against the regime, the monumental economic problems, the profiteering and speculation by the capitalist class, and the general chaos that reigned after Varvaressos resigned. The American officials knew that if such conditions persisted, the British would have no alternative but to withdraw from Greece. American intervention was indeed inevitable, and the only questions of importance were when it would take place and in what form.[53]

The Voulgaris cabinet was dissolved in October 1945 after it was overwhelmed by a multitude of problems. Panayiotis Kanellopoulos became interim prime minister and lasted for only twenty-two days in office before the British removed him. Kanellopoulos was the leader of the National United party, which ran in the March 1946 elections as part of a right-of-center coalition known as the National Political Union party. He remained attached to the moderate conservative parties throughout most of his career. When he took office, Kanellopoulos appealed for aid to London and Washington, but his request was not honored. George Kassimatis, minister of finance, requested a short-term loan of 650,000 gold pounds in coin, which was intended to stabilize the drachma after the gold reserves of the central bank had reached the point of near exhaustion. He emphasized that unless his proposal was received favorably by the authorities in London and Washington, his economic policies were bound to fail.

Kassimatis reverted to price controls and moderate government regulation of the economy, but he too met with the same fate as Varvaressos. The interim government was so impotent in conducting policy that Regent Damaskinos confided in UNRRA officials "that he hoped Britain would intervene to reestablish economic order which he felt could not be accomplished by Greeks themselves." Damaskinos enjoyed the confidence of the Foreign Office, the United States Embassy in Athens, and the royalists. The regent, who owed his position to the British, went on to ask UNRRA "to appoint advisers who would have full power to act through dummy Ministers of Finance and Supply whom he would appoint."[54]

On 2 November 1945, the day Kanellopoulos took office, General William D. Morgan, Allied Commander Mediterranean Theater, admonished the British chiefs of staff that it was impossible for their government to cope with the "desperate" situation in Greece. He pointed out that the problems of unemployment, inflation, devaluation of the currency, and absence of reconstruction remained unsolved despite England's efforts. He also stated that UNRRA had not done a good job in Greece and that the country was confronted with the ominous threat of communism, both on the domestic and foreign fronts. In a telegram to London, the general concluded:

> Great Britain could not carry on alone. . . . [U]nless the United States decided to play a more active role in Greece, the British should get out and take their losses. . . . In any case if the US could not put troops in Greece perhaps it could station substantial air forces there. . . . [T]he British Government could not go on carrying the financial burden involved in Greece and the US could take some of this burden.[55]

General Morgan preferred an arrangement by which the United States and Great Britain would be on a 50/50 basis in Greece, but the State Department opposed any plan that involved sharing responsibilities with the British in Athens.

Two days after addressing the above telegram to London, General Morgan recommended to the secretary of state that he favored American control of UNRRA and a role of the United States authorities in Athens equal to that of the British. The idea of economic and military intervention was discussed well before the Truman Doctrine was enunciated and certainly before the civil war of 1946–49. It cannot be argued seriously, therefore, that the KKE alone provoked the government in Washington to intervene in Greece. American hegemony over Greece was decided as a matter of policy once the British and the American officials became aware that the United Kingdom was no longer in the propitious position of retaining Greece as a dependency.

After General Morgan's letter to the British chief of staff, the Labour government in London asked Washington to "share responsibility in Greece." Loy Henderson, director of Near Eastern and African Affairs at the State Department, reported to Secretary Byrnes that the situation in Greece warranted that the United States government must consider the British proposal seriously. Byrnes informed the president, however, that he favored unilateral financial aid to Greece and opposed joint action with the British.[56]

The Atlee government sent an economic mission to Athens in November 1945 to make recommendations to Regent Damaskinos concerning ministerial appointments and to formulate policy on behalf of the host government. The mission did not carry the financial aid package that Kassimatis had requested, but went to Greece simply to study the country's financial and economic conditions, so that it could determine a prudent future course of action. Greek and American officials in Athens resented the mission's resolve to dominate the government, especially since London did not offer immediate financial assistance. MacVeagh seized the opportunity to excoriate the British for their blatant intervention. He wrote to the State Department that the "British contemplate control of Greek economic life to an even greater extent than the Germans attempted during occupation." He recommended that Washington refrain from supporting the mission unless the United States was prepared to exert equal influence to that of England in Greece.

Hector MacNeill, parliamentary undersecretary of state for foreign affairs, headed the economic mission that was England's last desperate attempt to preserve its preeminent role in Greece. MacNeill had declared on 9 January 1945 that "Britain must not lose Greece as otherwise she would lose Italy and Turkey as well. British and Soviet ideologies clash at the Greek frontier." The domino theory, which the State Department advanced during the Truman administration and applied thereafter to dramatize the dangers of communist expansionism in the Third World, was actually entertained by the British government under Churchill. The clash of Great Britain and the USSR over Greece, however, never materialized, except in the most innocuous manner of protestations in the United Nations. London, on the other hand, did clash with Washington as the two governments endeavored to have influence in Greece.[57]

MacNeill's principal goals in Athens were to establish a new Service Government, the last before the first postwar elections of March 1946, and to provide Greece with a stabilization loan. Kanellopoulos was forced to resign on 20 November and a coalition of conservative and centrist elements, headed by the Liberal party boss Themistocles Sophoulis, was placed in power. Popular opinion in the country leaned heavily toward the center and left. Thus the government in London was compelled by Parliament to favor the formation of a more representative government than those that had been appointed hitherto. Moreover, the Foreign Office was anxious to reduce sociopolitical tensions in Greece because it wanted the Populist party, which was monarchist, to win the March 1946 elections.

After the economic mission designated the new Service Cabinet, John Winant, British ambassador in Washington, appealed to the State Department for the establishment of an Anglo-American mission in Greece. Dean Acheson, undersecretary of state and one of the chief architects of early Cold War policy, replied that the United States government, "although unwilling to take joint action with Brit[ain], is anxious to cooperate in all practicable ways to ameliorate Greek economic difficulties." Despite that statement, the State Department did not acquiesce to London's proposal for bilateral policy in Greece. From the British perspective, Anglo-American concerted policy in Greece was of the utmost importance, for it could have been extended to other parts of the world as well.[58]

White Terror and Profiteering

Ambassador MacVeagh informed the State Department on 15 December 1945 that the Greek Communist party, which was Stalinist and thus linked to the Soviet Union and the Balkan regimes, was the main cause of the problems confronting the country. He argued that although the Greek economy's failure to revive was due largely to factors unrelated to communism, fear of revolution was definitely a deterrent to productive investment. He continued:

> A combination of war damage, losses caused by civil strife of December 1944 and almost unprecedented drought of 1945, reduced Greece's farm and factory production during the past year to less than 50 percent of prewar levels; virtually nothing came into the country from abroad for industrial rehabilitation

until the middle of 1945, and then only in small quantities, while the effect of military and UNRRA assistance to agriculture will become apparent only after many months.[59]

Greece suffered in 1945 not only because of lack of goods, but also because of the government's failure to distribute the available goods and the apparent failure to implement a successful reform policy to redress the structural problems of the country.

The United States Embassy reported in April 1946 that UNRRA, Lend-Lease, and other relief programs had provided Greece with about $250 million worth of commodities in 1945. "Greece in 1945 consumed around 80 percent," wrote the United States chargé d'affaires, "produced 50 percent and received foreign aid to the extent of about 30 percent of a normal year's production or consumption." The foreign assistance that the country received could have compensated for the low production levels if it had been distributed more equitably. The more fundamental issue, however, had nothing to do with the economy, but was purely political. As long as the country was under the occupation of British troops that sustained unpopular right-wing Service Governments in Athens, the economic problems could not be solved.

The drought of 1945, which MacVeagh claimed as a major cause of food shortages, was a factor, but not a major one. The annual average of cereal production for the years 1936 to 1939 was 1,504,965 tons. In 1945 production plummeted to 672,000 tons, or 44.6 percent of the prewar level. Given the low productivity level and the hoarding by merchants, prices were bound to skyrocket. It should be stressed, however, that the price of practically all items increased in 1945 regardless of supply and demand. The failure of sound economic policy, therefore, especially after Varvaressos resigned, was the root cause of relentless economic dislocation.[60]

As the cost of living continued to increase, so did social unrest. Government employees went on strike in December 1945 to protest soaring prices. The leftist factions organized a massive rally in which 200,000 people participated in December 1945 to protest the deteriorating conditions in the country. In January 1946 a rally of 400,000 people was staged in protest of the dilapidating economic conditions and the repressive political regime. The Sophoulis administration was unable to deal with growing labor unrest because the nation's fate was determined primarily by Anglo-American advisers and the conscienceless oligarchy. The capitalist class remained adamant in its refusal to invest in productive enterprises that would have improved the national economy, quelled social tensions, and alleviated some of the deplorable conditions of the masses.

Commercial bank deposits totaled 23,453 million drachmas in 1938, and the notes in circulation amounted to 9,453 million. In 1945 the deposits totaled 8,600 million, while the notes in circulation reached 104,082 million drachmas. Many wealthy individuals and companies kept their investments in foreign banks, in gold and foreign exchange, and the government was unable to adopt any plausible measures to reverse the prevailing economic trends.[61]

Lincoln MacVeagh did not regard profiteering as the principal cause of Greece's economic dislocation and attempted to justify the practices of the indigenous capitalist class as follows:

> Fear for what the future may hold for them [entrepreneurs] in this regard is with them an obsession; for what assurances have they that British Labour Party preoccupation with Socialist dogma, or an American lapse of interest in Balkan affairs may not deliver Greece to Communism in much the same way as Yugoslavia? Therefore, it is scarcely to be wondered at if they are hesitant to take a long term view in utilizing what liquid capital remains to them in efforts to expand production. A small bag of gold, jewelry or foreign currency, held in readiness for sudden flight, would be worth far more than a large factory under conditions which many Greeks and others regard as by no means unlikely.[62]

MacVeagh's thesis that profiteering was symptomatic of the general sociopolitical instability rests on weak foundations, as a succinct examination of the following sequence of events will prove.

The threat of a communist revolution dissipated after the Varkiza Agreement was signed on 12 February 1945, and the British troops assumed policing powers in Greece. The EAM leadership asked the leftist guerillas to surrender their weapons to the Plastiras government and abide by the terms of the agreement. The KKE adopted a "legalistic" policy after Varkiza; that is, it wished to achieve legal status and was willing to work within the parliamentary framework. Nikos Zachariadis, secretary general of the KKE, as well as the majority of the party leaders, followed Stalin's directives and pursued the strategy of coalition after the Athens Revolt. The communists wanted minority participation in a democratic regime. The rank and file of the party were not enthusiastic about the new strategy, but there were only a few dissidents, including the legendary *Kapetanios* Aris Velouhiotis. Throughout 1945 the KKE endeavored to establish legality status, while the right-wing forces, with the tacit support of the British, unleashed a terrorist campaign not only against the communists, but also against communist sympathizers, socialists, and centrists. The British and the "Service Governments" assented to the "white terror" because they were eager to suppress the leftist opposition and the radical republicans who did not want the monarchy's restoration and demanded systemic reform. British officials in Athens permitted thousands of civil servants who had collaborated with the quisling governments during the war to remain in service. According to Bevin's calculations, there were 228 officers of the Security Battalions, a Nazi-organized paramilitary group of Greek terrorists, who held commissions in the army in 1946.[63]

A number of ultra-right-wing organizations collaborated with the Service Governments and the British after liberation for the sole purpose of eliminating the leftists from any positions of influence and monopolizing local and national government positions. Colonel G. Grivas, chief of the paramilitary organization X, was instrumental in the "white terror" of the 1940s. During the occupation, Grivas's commandos were armed by the Nazis and their goal was to liberate Greece from communists and socialists who constituted the bulk of the resistance movement. The "X" organization, which claimed 200,000 members after the war, worked fervently to capture and execute former resistance fighters.

The purpose of the Security Battalions was also to fight the resistance movement, hunt down and execute ELAS men, and in general help keep Greece in subjugation. After the Varkiza pact was signed, Security Battalion members were readily admitted into the gendarmes and into the British-trained Greek army. The government had vowed to purge collaborators, but instead targeted former resistance fighters for persecution. Government officials candidly admitted that the National Guard, which was also instrumental in the white terror, was composed of ultra-right-wing commandos.[64]

The strength of the extreme rightist elements, which enjoyed the support of the British missions and the Greek government, was felt throughout the country after the Varkiza pact. The Greek government failed to bring the war criminals to justice during the 1940s, while it launched an extensive campaign to eliminate the leftists. As Howard K. Smith put it:

In Greece governments are mere figureheads. They pass tax laws but cannot collect the taxes. They declare amnesties but cannot enforce them. Real power lies with the bureaucracy, the army and the police, and nothing has been done to purge these instruments even of the most vengeful pro-Nazis, not to mention the reactionary monarchists. At the end of the war the Greek government listed 22,000 Nazi collaborators for investigation. Of these less than half, some 10,000, were actually investigated. Of these only 7,000 were brought to trial. Of these only 3,000 were found guilty. Of these only 121 were sentenced to be executed. Of these, at the end of 1948, only 18 have been executed.[65]

The government arrested and convicted some 20,000 former resistance fighters between February and June 1945. That was a flagrant violation of the Varkiza Agreement, which granted amnesty to the guerrillas. Two thousand of the accused were condemned to death and the remainder were sent to prison. From February 1945 to March 1946, 84,931 leftists and centrists were arrested, 31,632 were subjected to physical torture, 6,571 were wounded in confrontations with the rightist commandos, and 1,299 were executed.[66]

The following excerpt from an official report, composed by a three-member British parliamentary investigating team, exemplifies the policy of the Service Governments toward the leftist and centrist opposition.

> Greece is rapidly becoming a fascist state. Behind the democratic facade a one-sided civil war is being carried on by the extreme Right against all democratic elements who dare to disagree with the government. Murders, illegal arrests, violent attacks and terrorism are the fate of thousands of victims. . . . If anyone has the courage to protest this state of affairs he is immediately beaten and imprisoned, frequently with neither indictment nor warrant against him and sometimes on a trumped-up charge.[67]

The reign of terror, which was institutionalized after February 1945, continued unabated throughout the 1940s and to a lesser degree during the early 1950s with the approval and encouragement of the British and American advisers in Athens. The "white terror" served the interests of the bureaucracy and the military, which wanted to preserve their positions, the interests of the capitalist class, which dreaded the possibility of a social-democratic (reformist) regime, and the interests of the West, which wanted to eliminate completely the influence of communists in Greece.

As the leftist elements were systematically demolished, the rightists regrouped and consolidated power under the auspices of the British Military and Police Missions. The British had 16,000 troops in Greece, which served as a constant reminder to the indignant masses and the leftist leadership that a future social revolution would be crushed as it was in December 1944. The KKE was unable to obtain any tangible assistance from Moscow because Stalin remained faithful to the Yalta agreement insofar as it pertained to Greece. The Soviet dictator recognized the bourgeois regime in Athens, though he did not approve of it. Ambassador MacVeagh, however, argued that Greece was unsafe for entrepreneurs to risk their investment capital for productive works. The principal reasons for those conditions, however, were the "white terror," the utterly incompetent regime, the presence of the British missions during peacetime, and the unscrupulous practices of many merchants, importers, financiers, and speculators.

Still more evidence must be presented to dispel the myth that the primary reason that Greek capitalists did not invest in the productive economy was the alleged unsafe conditions attributable to the communist threat. The Associated Press reported on 14 January 1948 that, according to the American Mission for Aid to Greece, AMAG, "large loans which were granted by the banks [in Greece] to industrialists for productive investment, were used for profiteering." The central bank's gold and foreign-exchange reserves were depleted in large part because of relentless profiteering, which neither the British nor the American authorities in Greece prevented. The above-cited case involved many wealthy Greeks, including prominent statesmen and government officials. One of the protagonists in the gold-smuggling operation was Alexander Kanellopoulos, an industrialist who headed the National Youth Organization, EON, a quasi-fascist paramilitary organization established by the Metaxas regime.[68]

Kanellopoulos and the others who were implicated in the scandal exported dollars to Switzerland and imported gold sovereigns. They purchased the sovereign at $8.50 abroad and sold it for $17 in Greece. After the scandal was uncovered, Kanellopoulos was sentenced to eight years in prison and one year in exile. For the most part, however, the government covered up the scandal because it was extensive and would have been an embarrassment for many political figures with ties to the monarchy. Profiteering and the reign of terror, therefore, were important factors in exacerbating the postwar volatile political climate and in debilitating the economy.[69]

The London Agreement

The Sophoulis government (November 1945–March 1946) was somewhat more successful in easing sociopolitical tensions than the previous Service Cabinets. The administration enjoyed more popular support than the previous unelected governments, but it was unable to produce any positive results in the economy and finances. The devaluation of the drachma continued, and the price of gold and the cost-of-living index soared between November 1945 and March 1946. Ambassador MacVeagh observed that a "reasonably good meal in a restaurant costs $50, eggs are $17 per dozen, cheese $11 per pound."[70]

The Greek Ministry of Finance informed the United States Embassy in Athens that "On 31st of December [1945] the cost-of-living index in drachmas stood at ninety-five times that of 1939, representing an increase for the month of 178 percent." The notes in circulation stood at 105 billion drachmas, and the price of the gold pound rose from 157 thousand drachmas to 190 thousand. Finally, the supply of the currency in the Bank of Greece was depleted by the end of 1945, causing considerable embarrassment to the government, which was unable to meet its obligations to its creditors.[71]

The task of improving the economy and shaping fiscal policy was entrusted to Emanuel Tsouderos, an experienced banker and politician who assumed the office of deputy premier and minister of Coordination in the Sophoulis cabinet. He consulted with British and American officials before disclosing publicly his reconstruction program and economic policy. The following were proposed as immediate steps to stimulate some movement in the economy.

> 1. That sterling equivalent of Greek advances to British troops can be utilized [to] purchase goods abroad. 2. That allies will discount [a] portion of reparations due Greece to [the] extent of forced loans obtained during occupation by Germans and Italians totalling 90 million dollars. 3. That the above sum (2) [the] Allies will turn over [to] Greece [as a] share of gold confiscated in Germany.[72]

The Paris Conference on Reparations had granted 4.35 percent of the total German reparations to Greece, but Greeks felt that more was owed. Occupation costs alone from May 1941 to September 1944 amounted to $210,606,400, and total damages were estimated at over $7,000,000,000. Those were exaggerated figures, as the United States Embassy in Athens was quick to point out. Nevertheless, Greece received less than its fair share of reparations because neither Great Britain nor the United States wished to burden Germany with inordinate reparation payments. Officially, the Greek government claimed $15 billion in war-related losses, but received only $100 million, which was not made readily available and thus did not have a significant impact on the recovery process.

Given the decision by the Paris Conference on Reparations, Greece was forced to borrow heavily from foreign sources for her reconstruction requirements. The mission, which Hector MacNeill headed, recommended to the Treasury in London in December 1945 that immediate aid for Greece must be allocated if a monetary crisis was to be averted. Tsouderos submitted a request for £6 million in reconstruction assistance for a five-year period. The governments in Athens and London reached an agreement to solve Greece's monetary problem by a British loan of £10 million.

The stabilization loan was payable in ten equal installments at no interest beginning in July 1951. The funds, however, were held by the Bank of England, whose approval was needed before the authorities in Athens were able to withdraw from the account. The British waived a claim on a £46 million loan that Greece contracted in 1941 as part of the loan agreement. But that was done on the proviso that the Bank of Greece free its funds for imports from markets designated by British and American officials. The government in London also presented "claims on account of prewar commercial indebtedness, settlement of which would require the use of foreign exchange that the Greeks want for other purposes."[73]

As part of the loan agreement, the United Kingdom made available for Greece products valued at £500,000. Those consisted primarily of textiles and household utensils which UNRRA and other relief agencies provided and which were readily available in Greek markets. Since those products were not essential to the Greek economic recovery, the aforementioned case can be categorized as "dumping." During the negotiations for the London Agreement, the Greek delegation insisted on assurances for continued aid beyond the termination of the UNRRA program. England was hardly in a position to make any such guarantees, but it promised to grant several merchant vessels and provide construction materials.

The London Agreement was a device that permitted greater British control in Greece's internal affairs. The British formed three separate committees that allowed them to manipulate Greek economic and financial affairs. First, the Currency Committee was headed by Tsouderos and included the Minister of Finance, appointees of the governments in London and Washington, and the governor of the Bank of Greece. The committee's purpose was to supervise the policy and practices of the central bank. Second, the Economic Consultative Committee advised the Greek government on financial and economic matters. Finally, certain advisers from the British Mission, which General John Clark headed, were appointed to ministerial posts as joint policymakers along with Greek administrators.[74]

The Greek government agreed to fix the rate of exchange to reflect the real value of the drachma, a move that was not in the best interests of Greece. Moreover, the agreement stipulated:

> The Greek Government will deposit as cover for the currency in the special account [of the Bank of Greece in the Bank of England] 15 million pounds from the foreign exchange reserves of the Bank of Greece in addition to the 10 million pounds to be contributed by the British Government.[75]

The Hellenic government was not empowered to decide how the £25 million would be allocated because that privilege was reserved for the Bank of England, the government in London, and the joint committees in Athens. The Sophoulis administration permitted the British to impose austere financial, commercial, and other types of controls in Greece, all ostensibly designed to stabilize the drachma.

The Atlee government had succeeded in imposing stringent controls upon the Greek economy and finances on the pretense that the United Kingdom sacrificed millions of its own currency to stabilize the drachma. According to Professor Angellopoulos, England owed £76 million to the Bank of Greece at the end of the war and an additional 50 to 60 million to Greek shipowners and seamen who were savings depositors in the Bank of England. Of those funds, £15 million was placed in a special account in the Bank of England as foreign-exchange cover for the drachma. The remaining funds could not be used outside of England due to the nation's banking and foreign-exchange laws. The £10 million stabilization loan, therefore, was derived from the £130 million which England owed Greek depositors.

Premier Sophoulis announced to the press on 26 January 1946 that his cabinet was grateful to the United Kingdom for its "new sign of friendship and sympathy." He went on to state: "As a result of the Agreement I can put into practice a detailed program aiming at the recovery of credit and at stepping up industrial and agricultural production." He failed to realize, or at least he gave no indication to that effect, that the country would sink deeper into financial chaos and economic disarray which would end with the inevitable dependence on the United States.[76]

The main beneficiary of the London Agreement was the United States, although the package was designed to preserve England's prominent role in Greece. The Americans benefited inadvertently from the Agreement because Greece lifted foreign-trade restrictions after January 1946 and the central bank was authorized to convert Greek currency freely into foreign exchange for imports and other approved purchases. Within a few months, the country's foreign exchange reserves, which totaled £63 million in January 1946, were exhausted. The bulk of the money found its way into the United States, which had become Greece's number-one trading partner. Consequently, the government in Athens was impelled to seek assistance from the United States since England also borrowed from the same source.

The Truman administration had some initial reservations regarding the London Agreement because the Currency Committee had an overbearing role in Greek monetary policy. Dean Acheson pointed out to Ambassador Winant that the Hellenic government should have been given the opportunity to stabilize the drachma without the committee's supervision and control. He charged that foreign representation on the committee constituted interference in the affairs of a friendly nation. The Truman administration did not wish to be associated with the London Agreement because it was solely a British project and its prospects of success were not very good since the loan was so small.

The State Department offered to send its own mission to Greece at Sophoulis's request, but it also declared publicly that "The United States has no intention of making Greece a forty-ninth state and is not willing to become involved in responsibility for Greek internal administration." Prime Minister Sophoulis agreed with the State Department's proposal concerning the viability of an American mission to Greece and hoped that Washington would commit itself financially after sending the mission.

The secretary of state informed Tsouderos on 10 January that the United States had permitted an American economist to serve on the Currency Committee. That was not indicative, however, of Washington's willingness "to provide funds for a currency reserve account" as the Greeks had proposed. Moreover, the Truman administration made it very clear to the Sophoulis government that it did not wish to share the responsibility for any of the committee's policies, practices, and results connected with such efforts. James Byrnes publicly praised the London Agreement on 26 January and expressed his appreciation for the Greek government's invitation of an American official to serve on the Currency Committee.[77]

The London Agreement permitted the British to establish the Anglo-Greek Trade Organization, whose purpose was to control Greek trade and allocation of its proceeds thereof. British officials actually decided with which nations Greece would trade. Furthermore, they decided that all foreign exchange emanating from commercial shipping and commerce ($85 million annually) would be converted into pounds sterling and deposited in the Bank of England. That was simply unprecedented control of a sovereign nation's economy by agencies of a foreign government.

Another calamitous effect of the London Agreement was the lifting of restrictions on the domestic gold market. The Bank of Greece was authorized to sell gold sovereigns "indiscriminately to any importer who applied for them." In 1946 the central bank sold $17.3 million in gold sovereigns as compared with $4.2 million in 1947 after the United States compelled the Greeks to restrict gold and foreign-exchange sales and to curb their imports. The British-imposed laissez-faire policies had ruinous effects on the Greek economy, which was in desperate need of more government controls. One economist described the effects of the London Agreement as follows:

> As a consequence [of the Agreement] gold and foreign exchange reserves of the Bank of Greece were reduced from $190 million on January 31, 1946, to 36.5 million on December 31, 1946. It was said that, owing to the slack measures considering the disposal of gold and foreign exchange, large quantities of gold were smuggled out of the country, and millions of dollars of Bank of Greece foreign exchange reserves were lost because

of fake invoices for improved goods that were either overcharged or never delivered.[78]

The London Agreement, therefore, exacerbated the existing abuses of gold and foreign exchange in Greece.

The Greek government authorized the sale of up to £100 per month after the London Agreement. The American representative on the Currency Committee, Gardner Paterson, argued against that practice because the country needed the foreign-exchange reserves for essential imports. He also charged that the Greeks discriminated in favor of the United Kingdom by authorizing the sale of sterling to British citizens. The Greek minister of finance was prepared to extend the same privilege to the Americans, but Paterson rejected the offer, arguing that "such a measure would result in unjustifiable flight of capital from Greece with small commercial advantage." Despite Paterson's sagacious advice on the matter, the Sophoulis administration and later the elected government of Prime Minister Constantine Tsaldaris pursued reckless laissez-faire policies until the central bank's reserves were depleted.[79]

Within a few weeks after the implementation of the London Agreement, it was obvious to astute political and economic observers that Greece's finances were deteriorating precipitously. Kyriakos Varvaressos, executive director of the International Bank for Reconstruction and Development, IBRD, wrote to Dean Acheson in March 1946 that "Great Britain is no longer in a position to *continue* the assistance which she has supposedly been granting to Greece since liberation." The former minister accused the British officials in Athens of tolerating and even encouraging financial mismanagement with total disregard of the needs of Greeks. In assessing the merits of the London Agreement, he wrote:

> Britain granted a 10 million credit in sterling to be used exclusively for the conversion of drachmas into sterling and not for imports or the purchases of dollars. Sterling, however, being itself an inconvertible currency, was not found an attractive investment by the holders of drachmas and there was no demand for it. The 10 million credit is therefore still intact. The result was that the program of stabilization was financed *exclusively* out of Greek resources.[80]

He went on to argue that since the £10 million was still intact in the Bank of England, the loan was not a burden to the British economy. The Bank of Greece, on the other hand, had made drachma advances to British authorities totaling about £20 million, of which England released only 5 million. He concluded that Greece needed real financial assistance from the United States in order to recover economically. Dean Acheson sympathized with Varvaressos's concern about Greece's economic predicament, but he refused to make a definite commitment for aid.

Varvaressos, who was a vehement critic of the Greek oligarchy, charged that the London Agreement augmented only the interests of the wealthy, while having long-term negative consequences for the national economy. "More than 150 million dollars were allocated for imports in 1946," he wrote, "but only 58 million dollars worth of goods actually entered the country. The rest of the money was transferred abroad by means of false payments and stretched invoices."[81]

The full impact of the London Agreement was not felt in Greece until the end of October 1946. Constantine Tsaldaris, leader of the Populist party (monarchist) and the first elected prime minister after liberation, presented an urgent note to the American Embassy on 2 November 1946 for immediate financial aid to save the regime from imminent collapse. "Today we have only 10 million dollars in freely expendable exchange," announced the prime minister, "and those dollars represent a recent loan from New York Federal Reserve Bank against our gold stock."[82]

The central bank's dollar reserves amounted to 25 million at the end of September 1946, but 18 million of that was outstanding in confirmed credits, 4 million covered the currency account, and 3 million was confirmed credits for imports of fertilizers, overcoats, and blankets. Thus the Bank of Greece had no dollar assets available. The gold stock was also dangerously low because $10 million of the $22 million in gold reserves was pledged for the New York Federal Reserve Bank loan. The sterling stock was also depleted. There were £24 million at the end of September, but that included the £10-million loan. By the end of October, Greece was left with a mere £3.5 million amid an ominous sociopolitical and economic situation. There can be no doubt that the depletion process of the gold and foreign exchange was hastened by the London Agreement.[83]

Greece was left in financial bankruptcy by the fall of 1946, and the government was confronted with a disgruntled population and a nascent guerrilla movement in the mountains, which was determined to finish the struggle that was started in 1943. As the political and economic situation became more ominous for the indigenous capitalist class, the bourgeois politicians and the army, the United States government was preparing to intervene in Greece and declare it the battleground between communism and democracy.

II

The Origins of Greek Dependence on the United States

The Twilight of British Influence in Greece and the Venizelos Mission

The European nations were largely dependent on the Lend-Lease program for material needs during the war. President Truman terminated the program abruptly on VE day, much to the dismay and shock of the Europeans who relied so heavily on American supplies. England was in a serious economic predicament at the end of the war and was adversely affected by the cessation of Lend-Lease. One recent study placed the United Kingdom's postwar financial position in the following perspective.

> Britain's dollar reserves had been exhausted early in the war. The nation's ability to earn foreign exchange was a mere fraction of what it had been in 1939. To sustain the war effort, 36 percent of British capital assets owned abroad had been sold between 1939 and 1945, and 33 percent of gold reserves expended. The value of exports had fallen to 40 percent of its prewar level. By December 1945 Britain's foreign debt totalled (pounds sterling) 3,567 m., an increase of some 750 percent since the outbreak of hostilities.[1]

The government in London commenced negotiations with Washington for a loan in September 1945 and reached an agreement by the end of the year. The loan was for $3.75 billion, interest-free for the first five years and at 2 percent annual interest for the fifty years thereafter. In return for the American loan, the British were obliged to abandon their neomercantile system of Imperial Preferences, which was established under emergency economic conditions at the Imperial Conference at Ottawa in 1932.

The British commercial concessions to the United States in return for the loan were indicative of the dollar's ascendancy in the world market and the sterling's demise. The dollar-sterling relationship was determined at the Bretton Woods Conference in 1944, where the principles of free trade, free flow of capital across national borders, and free enterprise became the foundation of United States foreign economic policy. While the Bretton Woods system furthered the interests of the United States, which was in the auspicious position of competing globally, the system was not favorable to the war-devastated countries in Europe or to the underdeveloped regions throughout the globe. State intervention to protect existing industries and markets and to stimulate the economies of the weak nations was essential after the war, but discouraged by the Bretton Woods system.[2]

The American loan to the United Kingdom provides an excellent illustration of the advantageous position of the United States in the world economy after 1945. The British government was obliged to accept a policy of free trade, rather than protectionism, during a very critical period in history. F. S. Northedge, who has studied the causes of Britain's demise as an imperial power extensively, has written the following regarding the impact of the American loan on the British economy.

> She [Great Britain] undertook to make sterling convertible into other currencies not later than twelve months after the Loan Agreement came into force; that meant the end of the Sterling area pool which limited the freedom of Sterling Area countries to spend dollars earned by exports. She also agreed not to apply quantitative restrictions discriminatingly against dollar goods, which implied that any British restrictions on purchases from the United States, applied in order to conserve dollars, would have to import from every part of the world. Thirdly, Britain consented to enter into negotiations with countries holding British sterling liabilities with a view either to scaling them

down or refunding them; from the American point of view this would have the effect of diverting to the dollar market the import demands of countries holding sterling balances which they might otherwise liquidate by purchases in Britain.[3]

British markets throughout the world became available to the United States with the penetration of the dollar into sterling areas, and many former British colonies became dependencies of the United States. The Labour government attempted to resist relinquishing its advantageous position in many Third World markets, but the dynamic American economy necessitated the new conditions. Clement Atlee, who was not particularly enthusiastic about the Loan Agreement, admitted that his government was hardly in a propitious position to negotiate better terms with the Americans.

The United States government approved the loan in July 1946 after some initial objections that the House of Representatives and the Senate raised over the issue. The loan had profound immediate and long-term negative consequences for the British economy. The American wholesalers raised their prices by 20 percent in 1947 and by another 27 percent in 1948, when Europe was experiencing economic dislocation and the Third World was engulfed in monetary and price inflation. Bevin charged that, as a result of the price increases of American exports, the United Kingdom lost $1 billion, or about one-fourth of the loan, in purchasing power. Moreover, the United States compelled the British to "ensure free convertibility of sterling to dollars by no later than July 15, 1947," which resulted in the depletion of England's foreign-exchange reserves by the time the Marshall Plan went into effect. Great Britain's balance-of-payments problem, therefore, was aggravated after the Loan Agreement and was not alleviated as the Atlee government had hoped.

Perhaps the most significant aspect of the American loan to the United Kingdom was that it marked the demise of diehard British imperialism as the process of decolonization began its course with the emergence of American supremacy in the non-communist world. The "New Deal" policies and the war economy, combined with the decline of Western Europe after 1945, accounted for unprecedented economic expansion in the United States. Great Britain, which had been declining since the end of World War I and finally faded in the shadow of Pax Americana after 1945, reluctantly allowed the United States to assume the leadership role in the Near East as well as in other areas of British prewar influence.

The United States replaced England's paramount financial influence in Greece after July 1946, and its political and military influence after March 1947. That was an inevitable development, considering that most of the direct and indirect foreign assistance to Greece since 1944 emanated from the United States. It must be emphasized, however, that 54 percent of all foreign assistance before the Truman Doctrine went for military purposes, while only 21 percent was actually spent on economic programs.[4]

A Greek delegation headed by Premier Tsaldaris went to London in July 1946 seeking financial assistance. Although the delegation was aware that the Atlee government had just contracted a $3.75 billion loan from the United States, Tsaldaris requested a $6 billion loan from the British, clearly a test indicative that the Greeks were not serious about the loan request. The funds were to be used as follows:

> a. A loan of $5 billion for reconstruction of material damage; the loan to be extended over an unspecified period. b. A loan of $600 million to cover shipments over 5 years, in decreasing amounts, of consumer goods, industrial products and raw materials. The loan appears to be essentially a continuation of the aid supplied by UNRRA; it is to meet the balance deficit which those essential imports would incur. c. A loan of $440 million to cover internal budget deficits for a five year period. d. An unspecified loan toward development over and above the prewar level of the Greek economy.[5]

There is no question that Greece needed some source of outside assistance to finance the reconstruction program that was imperative for stimulating the economy and creating political stability. The right-wing government of Prime Minister Tsaldaris, as well as the ostensibly center-right-coalition regimes that followed, relied totally on foreign aid, credits, and loans from the United States. Greece was in desperate need of progressive tax reform to strengthen the state's fiscal structure and allow the public sector to finance part of the economic-recovery program from domestic sources. Such remedial measures were also desirable to curb the excessive manipulation of the anemic economy by the Greek oligarchy.

The cost of living soared after January 1946 because the British loan to Greece did not have a stabilizing effect. One contemporary observer noted that "In terms of dollars the index of wholesale prices for all commodities, based on a 1939 figure of 100, stood by the middle of

1946 at 348 in Greece as compared with 161 in the United Kingdom." The rise in the cost of living during the 1950s was due in part to the worldwide price and monetary inflation caused by the war economy and the strength of the dollar against other currencies. Profiteering and hoarding, however, aggravated the problem in Greece, as well as in other Third World countries. Retail prices in Greece were marked up 100 percent in 1946 in comparison to markups of 30 percent before the war. The cost-of-living index in Athens jumped from 19.0 in 1945 to 145.2 in 1946. Given such ominous conditions, Tsaldaris followed the traditional practice of seeking foreign economic assistance to solve the multitude of economic, financial, and sociopolitical problems and save the regime from imminent collapse.[6]

The prime minister, the royalists, and some centrists—George Papandreou was the most notable example—were alarmed about the growing leftist forces that were preparing to resume their armed struggle after they had been demoralized by political and economic developments since the signing of the Varkiza Accord. Tsaldaris warned Greece's allies in an interview in Paris that

> Greece is surrounded by the occupying armies of communism and her internal economic and social structure cannot continue to exist without outside aid. . . . Unless the drachma is supported by aid from Britain, France or the United States, it will collapse with disastrous inflationary results.[7]

The rhetoric concerning the threat of foreign communist forces scheming to undermine the regime in Athens was a useful device to attract aid from the West. During his interview, Tsaldaris stressed that his administration was interested in working with "Allied economists on a plan to revive Greek industry and shipping until it reached prewar proportions." Greece needed to rebuild the shipping industry, but it was much more important to reform and modernize agriculture and initiate plans for the simultaneous building of the capital-goods sector.[8]

Prime Minister Atlee rejected the Greek loan request for $6 billion and the Foreign Office recommended that the Greek delegation seek assistance from the IBRD. Tsaldaris notified United States government officials that Greece was in dire need of aid, especially since UNRRA was scheduled to cease operations in the spring of 1947. The prime minister held a conference with James Byrnes in Paris and found the latter "receptive to his explanations of Greece's acute needs." Specifically, the Tsaldaris administration asked for $175 million in credits from the Export-Import Bank. The State Department did not consider that request because the $25 million loan that the Bank had approved in January 1946 had not been utilized by the Greeks. Furthermore, American officials were convinced that the government in Athens did not have any economic plans for the future, and the $6 billion as well as the $175 million loan proposals were simply made to test the reaction of London and Washington. Dean Acheson and MacVeagh agreed that the Tsaldaris government needed to initiate serious efforts to revive the national economy, without relying exclusively on foreign loans and aid.[9]

A Greek delegation headed by Sophocles Venizelos, the son of the legendary Liberal statesman Eleftherios Venizelos, left for the United States on 18 July 1946 to cultivate closer Greek-American commercial and diplomatic relations. American officials deemphasized the Greek mission's far-reaching accomplishments, which represented a major step toward Greek commercial/financial dependence on the United States. It was also the first clear indication that the Greek capitalist class looked to New York and Washington as the centers of power, rather than to London or Paris.

Such an indication was given when Demetrios Maximos, foreign minister in the Tsaldaris cabinet and former governor of the National Bank of Greece, proposed to MacVeagh on 14 December 1945 that American investors purchase either minority or majority stock of the Greek bank. The Bank was founded in 1840 and had a hundred branches in Greece and a number of offices in the Middle East and New York. It was the largest bank in the country and one of the largest in the Near East. It had the largest deposits of all Greek banks, it controlled approximately half of the country's industry, and it enjoyed considerable political influence as many of its former governors and top officers served in the government. Maximos confided in MacVeagh that "American participation in the National Bank, with its wide ramifications in the Near and Middle East, would be most useful in furthering American interests and influence throughout the area, which was a matter of growing importance to our [American] foreign policy." The political and socioeconomic elites in Greece had a propensity toward dependence on the United States, and that was the message which the Venizelos mission conveyed in the summer of 1946.[10]

The Greek delegation included the well-known Constantine Karamanlis, a pro-American Conservative deputy from Serres, Michael Ailianos, undersecretary of coordination, and Anastasios Balabasis, deputy from Rodopi. The delegates met with Export-Import Bank officials, but their loan request was denied. The mission then conferred with officials from the Departments of State, Treasury, Commerce, and Agriculture, but none wished to discuss the issue of loans. The prevailing attitude of the Truman administration toward Greece was that loans could not be extended until such time as the government in Athens showed firm intention to institute economic, financial, and tax reforms to put its own house in order.

Both the United States and Greece were willing to launch a new era of improved commercial and financial relations as a prelude to establishing close diplomatic and strategic ties. Consequently, an agreement between the two sides was inevitable. The government in Washington preferred to reanimate the Greek private sector, rather than support government-financed reconstruction. That was obviously not in the best interests of Greece's national economy, which needed a policy mix of state- and privately initiated development programs combined with sweeping land and tax reforms. In any event, the Department of Commerce expressed interest in Venizelos's proposal to export Greek tobacco to America. Henry A. Wallace, the controversial secretary of commerce who opted for coexistence with the Soviet Union in the late 1940s, promised to support the Greek mission's objectives. William Clayton, the State Department's top foreign economic policy expert, and the tobacco companies extended the same assurances as Wallace regarding Greek tobacco exports, which had no market after the war.[11]

The Greek delegation conferred with the National Advisory Council on 23 August to discuss a number of issues of mutual interest. Venizelos proposed that an American mission be sent to Athens to study the state of the economy and present its findings with recommendations on policy changes to the host government. United States officials concurred that such a mission would be sent to Greece. Clayton, however, seized the opportunity to excoriate the Tsaldaris regime for its inability to revive the national economy. He charged that Greece wasted gold and foreign-exchange reserves to the detriment of the national economy.

> We, furthermore, have some doubt that all possible measures had been taken in order to prevent profiteering during the postwar period of occupation and to tax those profiteers who had become prosperous during the period of occupation and

during the confused period subsequent to it. We also wondered if the tax structure in Greece corresponded to Greek economic needs of the moment.[12]

Despite the above criticism of the Hellenic government, the Truman administration did not take any decisive steps to compel the Tsaldaris regime to adopt sound fiscal measures.

Venizelos's most noteworthy acomplishment on behalf of the Greek capitalist class was to secure one hundred commercial vessels from the United States. The Marine Commission agreed to sell the ships at the request of the Greek government. The ships were of the type "Liberty" and averaged 14,000 tons each. The cost was $550,000, but the shipowners actually paid only 25 percent in cash of that amount, while the balance was spread out into twenty annual installments at 3.5 percent interest. The Greek government guaranteed repayment of the shipowners' debt, so they risked nothing.

The purchase of the "Liberties" was a laborious process that involved behind-the-scenes lobbying by Greek shipowners. Manolis Kulukundis, President of the Greek Shipowners Association in New York, was instrumental in persuading the Tsaldaris government to arrange the "Liberties" deal. When Venizelos went to New York, Kulukundis solicited his assistance for carrying out the scheme. It was not difficult to persuade Venizelos, for he represented an administration that was unswervingly committed to strengthening the strongest sectors of the economy. Both the Greek and United States governments shared the view that reinvigorating the shipping industry was essential for the process of economic recovery. If it were not for the reluctance of the shipowners, the Marine Commission was predisposed to sell as many as 150 vessels.

The "Liberties" deal was a constructive step, but not essential to the revival of the Greek economy, for it simply strengthened the sector that needed the least stimulation in the postwar years. The value of Greece's prewar shipping was estimated at £8,200,000. The Greek shipowners received £42,000,000 from insurance claims for the damages and losses that the commercial fleet suffered during the war. Many Greek shipowners who operated in North America had purchased 300 ships from Canada and the United States during the war. In 1948 the United States government granted Greece seven tankers of approximately 10,500 tons each, which were in turn sold to shipping tycoons. Moreover, the government in Washington arranged that part of the reparations owed to Greece be paid in commercial vessels. The Greek government received four such vessels from Italy in 1951 and sold them to two private concerns. Greece received a total of 36 ships in reparations, and all were sold to the shipping tycoons at 50 percent below cost.

The "Liberties" were sold to ten companies and twenty-two shipping families. The shipping interests had close ties to the conservative politicians and the Greek royal house. An indication of the shipowners' ascendancy in the political arena after the war was Tsaldaris's intention "to impose taxes of only 15 percent on the net profits up to $100,000 on each of these ships [Liberties] and none on the large profits which the private owners were expected to net above that figure."[13]

Most of the Greek merchant vessels flew foreign flags, even though the government in Athens had arranged the purchase of many ships sold to private owners and financed a great number of them. Bevin pointed out to Tsaldaris in 1946 that the Greek shipowners avoided taxation by flying foreign flags and thus did not contribute to the national revenues. The prime minister defended the shipowners, arguing that the seamen earned 50 percent more in wages than their foreign counterparts. Moreover, communist agitators were urging the Greek seamen to seek higher wages and benefits, so it was not profitable for the companies to fly the Greek flag. Even after the civil war ended and all remnants of communist influence in Greek society were thoroughly suppressed, however, Greek ships continued flying Panamanian, Liberian, Honduran, Costa Rican, and other flags during the 1950s and 1960s and refused to contribute to the Greek public treasury from which they benefited so lucratively. They were permitted to operate in that fashion, of course, because right-wing regimes tolerated such conditions.[14]

Paul Porter, an American official who headed a mission to Greece before the Truman Doctrine, reproved the parasitic role of the Greek shipping interests in September 1947.

> Shipping interests have also been run in a scandalous manner. The Greek merchant navy is now flourishing and shipowners are making immense profits, but the bankrupt Greek State gets nothing out of it. The sailors' wages return to Greece, but the shipowners send most of their profits to safety in foreign banks. Every enterprise should pay a substantial contribution to the State under whose protection it operates. This is doubly true of the Greek shipowners, whose biggest profits are earned

by the "Liberties" that were allocated to them by the American Shipping Commission under guarantee of the Greek State. Most of these shipowners are very charming people who speak good English. They are always eager to do anything at all for the American mission. But behind all that lies their wish to use the American mission to further their interests.[15]

The government in Washington, which sold the merchant vessels to the Greek government, must also share in the responsibility for not imposing conditions that would have made the Greek shipowners more accountable to the regime in Athens.

Besides completing the lucrative "Liberty" deal, Venizelos and his colleagues held meetings with Emilio Collado of the IBRD and with the chairman of the Federal Reserve Board, Marriner Eccles. The object of those meetings was to secure credits for Greece, but there was no commitment by either Eccles or Collado regarding future prospects of American credits to Greece.

Venizelos succeeded in inaugurating a new era of Greek commercial dependence on the United States. The State Department and the president publicly opposed United States interference in Greek internal affairs before the Venizelos mission. That policy changed, however, at the end of the summer of 1946. William Clayton informed MacVeagh on 7 September that it was "informally agreed that the possibility [of] sending [a] small top flight economic and financial commission to Greece in [the] near future if requested by Greek Govt would be presented to the National Advisory Commission." In December 1946 the Porter Mission was the first of a series of American missions to Greece sent to evaluate and report on all aspects of Greek society, especially defense and economic affairs, and to advise the host government regarding policy. In other words, the American missions carried out the same functions—and much more as will be seen below—as the British, whom President Roosevelt had criticized for interfering in Greece's internal affairs.

The Truman administration also reversed its policy regarding government assistance for Greece after the Venizelos mission left Washington. Averell Harriman, United States ambassador to Moscow and Henry Wallace's successor as secretary of commerce, confided to Venizelos that the United States intended all along to extend aid to Greece, but did not wish to make a public commitment "before the international situation is clarified and the Paris Conference ends." After the fall of 1946, when the Paris Peace Conference ended and the

British government relinquished its responsibilities in Greece, the Truman administration adopted the first concrete measures to incorporate Greece into the nascent American global economic and military network.[16]

The Soviet-American Confrontation and the Outbreak of the Greek Civil War

Greece constituted the western part of the "Northern Tier," which was a strategic belt that included Turkey and Iran. Greece was also the only Balkan country that was not assimilated in the embryonic Soviet bloc. The Truman administration adopted new and decisive measures after September 1946 to secure the Northern Tier as a permanent sphere of American influence. The area was vital not only for the obvious strategic considerations, but also because it was a buffer zone that shielded the Middle Eastern oil fields. Hence, it was of paramount importance that pro-Western regimes controlled Greece, Turkey, and Iran.

Soviet-American relations deteriorated in the course of 1946, and the UN became the arena of confrontation between the two superpowers. On 21 January 1946 Andrej Vishinsky, Russian representative to the UN, raised the issue of the British troops in Greece. He condemned the military occupation of Greece and argued that the government in London maintained the military mission in support of reactionary and unpopular forces in Greece. Vishinsky also charged that the presence of foreign troops in a country that was not at war constituted a threat to regional peace.

The Ukranian representative at the UN raised the Greek question before the Security Council once again on 21 August 1946. He accused the United Kingdom of backing Greek monarchists in power with the support of the military mission. Furthermore, he alleged that Greece posed a threat to the peace and stability of the entire Balkan region because the Tsaldaris administration was belligerent and entertained territorial ambitions at the expense of Greece's northern neighbors. Greek territorial ambitions were not satisfied because the country was hardly in a position to risk war with its communist neighbors, and the West did not support expansionist schemes that the conservative politicians entertained. Moscow's concern over Greece's territorial claims coincided with the preparations in Greece for the plebiscite, which ended the regency of Archbishop Damaskinos in September 1946 and restored the king to the throne. Since George II was a staunch Anglophile and had a history of backing the most reactionary political elements in Greece, the Soviet Union and its Balkan allies were apprehensive about the prevailing political trends in Greece and about the future of the KKE. The United States government, on the other hand, was suspicious of Soviet criticism of the British role in Greece, especially since Stalin had agreed with Churchill that Greece fell within the Western sphere of influence. Although the disagreements between the Russians and the Americans over Greece were part of a larger diplomatic war, the Truman administration was concerned that the volatile Tsaldaris regime could collapse in the face of such immense political pressures, coupled with economic difficulties.[17]

There were signs that the Tsaldaris regime would be short-lived precisely because the economy remained in perpetual dislocation and the state's finances were running dangerously low. The Hellenic government informed the Foreign Office in May 1946 that after "the provision of 240 billion drachmas ($48 million) for defense services—100,000 men, of whom 30,000 represented the gendarmerie and police—there would be a heavy deficit." The Populist regime expected England to provide 415 billion drachmas ($83 million) in military aid to Greece for fiscal year 1946–47. London, however, reduced the amount of Greek military assistance by 140 billion drachmas ($23 million) after January 1946. The reduction in military aid coincided with the London Agreement, which had adverse effects on the economy, as stated above.[18]

Greece was obliged to allocate a greater portion of the general revenues to the defense sector amid a period of declining gold and dollar reserves. Furthermore, the economic problems that plagued Greece were complicated by the rising sociopolitical tensions after the election of Prime Minister Tsaldaris. As the government prepared to restore King George II, persecutions of the anti-monarchist elements intensified. Hence the resurgence of the guerrilla movement was hastened, and it became a major concern for the regime and its allies in the West. The new resistance movement blossomed from the remnants of the old after Greece was reduced to a semi-police state by the Tsaldaris administration. In April 1946 there were about 950 guerrillas, in May 1300, in June 2700. By December 1946 the number soared to 9,285. The increase in the number of communist rebels was to be expected, considering that the Varkiza Agreement did not result in the amelioration of tensions between the left and the right and Greece was more authoritarian after the elections of March 1946 than before.[19]

The State Department regarded the political developments in Greece with increasing apprehension, partly because the Soviet Union's public opposition to Britain's military presence coincided with the strengthening of the rebel movement in the country. Moreover, Great Britain's demise as an influential power in the Near East created a power vacuum which the Soviet Union would have filled if the United States did not assume England's role in the region. The third option was for the United States to support a center-left coalition government for which there would have been a broad popular base of support. The formation of such a regime was not only plausible, but it was indeed desirable by most politicians during the interim period between the Athens Revolt and the civil war. Neither the British nor the Americans, however, wanted to gamble with the uncertainty of a democratic coalition that would have inevitably enjoyed more independence from the West than the subservient right-wing regimes that were installed in power.

Throughout 1946 the United States Embassy in Greece sent alarmist reports to Washington about the imminent collapse of the regime. The Food and Agricultural Organization reported in September 1946 that Greece urgently needed a minimum of $1 billion from foreign sources (Anglo-American) if it was to survive. The State Department's response to such reports was attentive once the Atlee government admitted that it was simply unable to defend the regime in Athens.[20]

The Truman administration was preparing a major foreign policy initiative toward Greece and Turkey as early as October 1946, but it was not revealed to the world until 12 March 1947. President Truman addressed a very confidential memo to Ambassador MacVeagh asserting that "the US Government regarded Greece as a country of vital importance to the United States." The memo continued:

> On October 18, 1946, the American ambassador presented the message to King George II and stated that the Americans were willing to help Greece's shattered economy. The President urged, however, that the government in Athens should help persuade American public opinion that the rulers of Greece did not constitute an oligarchy of reactionaries bent on exploiting U.S. aid in order to tyrannize their political opponents.[21]

Social unrest was so widespread by September 1946 that practically all sectors of the population were disillusioned with the Tsaldaris government. The regime was incapable of solving the country's economic problems and concentrated on eliminating the leftist and centrist opposition. Policymakers in the Truman administration were concerned that the United States would be accused of aiding an unpopular regime. It was important, therefore, for the Greek government to be more representative of all the anti-communist elements, not just the monarchists.

The State Department's concern over the quasi-authoritarian Tsaldaris regime notwithstanding, the Truman administration considered the threat of a communist-led social revolution much more perilous to America's global interests than a right-wing government. Given that policy assumption, Dean Acheson addressed a telegram to MacVeagh on 15 October, directing him to advise the host government on its internal affairs. Furthermore, the United States ambassador to the UN was instructed to defend Greece's position against charges by the Soviet-bloc countries. The Truman administration also decided to provide weapons for Greece since it was in the interest of American security to militarize the entire Northern Tier. Acheson noted that the United States government would initiate a media campaign to "inform" the American people about the administration's Near Eastern policy. On the issue of economic assistance, he suggested:

> Make available to Greece appropriate US financial and economic advice through advisers and technicians or through dispatch of US economic mission. [Take] appropriate US action when necessary to assist Greece in finding export markets and in acquiring essential goods in [the] US market.[22]

In the same telegram, he instructed MacVeagh to urge King George II and Prime Minister Tsaldaris to adopt more moderate measures toward all noncommunist political parties and to focus their struggle against communism.

The groundwork for the Truman Doctrine was laid in October, but it must be noted at this juncture that the economic and strategic interest of the United States in the Near and Middle East was expressed during World War II. Greece was the gateway to the region, but the country's economic dislocation, political volatility, and social strife compelled the American government during the Cold War to adopt an interventionist policy. A State Department internal memo articulated the issue as follows:

> The strategic importance of Greece to US security lies in the fact that it is the only country in the Balkans which has not yet

fallen under Soviet hegemony. Greece and Turkey form the sole obstacle to Soviet domination of the Eastern Mediterranean, which is an *economic* and *strategic* area of vital importance. [Emphasis added.][23]

While it is very difficult, if not impossible, to determine the Soviet Union's foreign-policy intentions during the late 1940s, it is quite clear that it would have been to Russia's interest to have satellites in the eastern Mediterranean. Josef Stalin, however, did not interfere in Greece's internal affairs and even discouraged the Greek Communist Party from pursuing a revolutionary course. On the other hand, President Truman was much more intransigent and confrontational in dealing with the Russians. That was a reaction not solely due to Soviet expansionism in Eastern Europe but also to social revolutionary movements in China, Korea, and Vietnam. Moreover, American Cold War policy was determined by the preeminent strategic and economic role of the United States in the world economy and was not necessarily a response to Soviet expansionism.[24]

The Soviet Union was eager to create a strategic buffer zone around its borders after the war, and there is no doubt about its blatant intervention in and Sovietization of Eastern Europe. But it is doubtful that the Russians entertained a global-expansionist foreign policy under Stalin since they lacked the means to carry out such a policy during the 1940s. George F. Kennan, former United States ambassador to the Soviet Union, author of the "containment" theory, and a recent advocate of coexistence between the superpowers, dispelled the myth that the Kremlin had a foreign policy based on interminable expansion during the 1940s.

> It was perfectly clear to anyone with even a rudimentary knowledge of the Russia of that day, that the Soviet leaders had no intention of attempting to advance their cause by launching military attacks with their armed forces across frontiers. Such procedure fitted neither with the requirements of the Marxist doctrine, nor with Russia's own need for recovery from devastation of a long and exhausting war, nor with what was known about the temperament of the Soviet dictator himself.[25]

The real threat to the status quo, argued Kennan, was social revolutionary movements with indigenous varieties of Marxists. That was true in Asia as well as Europe. America's resolve to suppress social revolutions in Greece and China was not necessarily a response to Soviet foreign policy. Albeit Stalin wanted the success of revolutionary movements, he was not prepared to risk Soviet interests to aid them. It must be stressed also that the State Department opposed social revolutions in the Third World, no matter how necessary it was to rectify deplorable societal conditions and to modernize archaic economic structures. The United States, therefore, found itself on the side of the most reactionary elements in the Third World and justified counterinsurgency operations in the name of preventing alleged Soviet expansionism.

Greece became the focal point of the Soviet-American confrontation during the late 1940s for several reasons. First, it was no mere coincidence that major United States petroleum companies reached an agreement, with the backing of the government in Washington, to construct a $200 million pipeline across the Arabian peninsula just as the Truman Doctrine was enunciated. Second, the United States relied rather heavily on certain strategic minerals in the Third World, which was the arena of East-West conflict. Finally, the nationalist and socialist tendencies of the Africans, Asians, and Latin Americans constituted a threat to the "outward-oriented" American-based transnational corporations which supported the institutionalization of President Truman's Cold War interventionist policies. As will be seen below, Greece was the testing ground for the implementation of the policy of containment militarism.[26]

Policy Antecedents to the Truman Doctrine

The Truman Doctrine had profound global reverberations, for it set a precedent for American intervention in Third World countries where social revolutions threatened the status quo or reformist regimes pursued economic and foreign policies incongruent to the interests of the United States. Greece, as well as China and Vietnam, were cases where social revolutions were a perceived threat to the geopolitical interests of Washington. Iran, Guatemala, and the Dominican Republic exemplify the resolve of the United States to prevent even reformist regimes from succeeding. The Central Intelligence Agency, CIA, overthrew Iranian Prime Minister Mohammad Mossadeq in August 1953 and President Jacobo Arbenz of Guatemala in June 1954. Juan Bosch, the only elected President in the history of the Dominican Republic, was forced out of his country by the landing of American marines in August 1965. All three leaders were nationalist reformists who were prepared to challenge foreign (United States) interests in order to gain greater control of their respective nation's domestic and foreign policies. It was not Soviet expansionism, therefore, but the Truman administration's foreign policy, tested in Greece, which left a legacy of American intervention directed against structural societal change in the Third World.

The Truman administration was well aware that the Greek economy was bankrupt, the parliamentary system debilitated by personal and factional struggles, and the level of social discontent on an ever-rising course. The State Department informed Tsaldaris on 16 Octoberr 1946 that an American mission to Greece was prepared to evaluate the country's foreign-aid requirements and to submit recommendations regarding long-term economic solutions. Paul Porter headed a mission that included experts in finance, engineering, and other areas. The mission left for Athens in January 1947, and its task was near completion by the time President Truman announced his aid package for Greece and Turkey.

The Greek government was obviously euphoric about the news of the American mission, for it entailed foreign military and financial aid as well as unswerving diplomatic support. The Tsaldaris government needed foreign support because it lacked a popular base. The rebel movement was helped immeasurably by the regime's incessant persecution of leftists and centrists and by the continuing economic dislocation. The government supplied arms to right-wing bands that raided villages and looted and assaulted guerrilla sympathizers as well as innocent peasants. The liberal newspaper *Vima* published the following account on 30 October 1946 regarding the activities of the right-wing forces.

> This tactic and policy [of terrorism] drives the people to the hills since no Greek is willing to be beaten without good reason only because he is an opponent of the party in power. . . . Even worse is the fact that the Army detachments and Gendarmes, unable and unwilling to repress the leftist bands, enter villages and arrest old people, women, babies and democratic citizens for allegedly helping the band, and send them to Lamia for deportation.[27]

Guerrilla bands, in some cases acting independently of the Communist party's directives, carried out hundreds of successful operations against the government and right-wing paramilitary forces in October 1946, thereby initiating the tragic civil war, or Third Round.

As the confrontation between the leftist guerrillas and the government troops intensified after October, Prime Minister Tsaldaris informed Bevin and MacVeagh that Greece needed immediate financial assistance to avert a total monetary crisis. The central bank's gold and foreign exchange reserves were nearly depleted and England was cutting back on aid to Greece. Bevin recommended that the government in Washington make an early announcement of its plan to send a mission to Greece, so that confidence would be restored in Greek financial circles. The announcement was made, but it did not produce the expected results. Ambassador MacVeagh presaged an inescapable financial collapse unless foreign aid was forthcoming. He wrote:

> Suggest this [aid] should be both in kind and cash, the former to follow termination of UNRRA supplies while cash grant (probably better than loan) should be made available without awaiting results of economic mission survey now scheduled to leave United States early January and impossible of completion till next spring.[28]

He added that the British Treasury also considered a loan proposal of £4 to £5 million to Greece, but the Labour government had not made a definite commitment on the matter.

Greece's finances reached their nadir in December 1946, prompting Prime Minister Tsaldaris to visit the United States for a personal appeal for foreign aid. He stressed that Greece's territorial and political integrity depended on such aid, and he was obviously correct since his government would have collapsed without foreign support. He estimated that the foreign-exchange reserves deficit was about $15 million a month and that $50 to $60 million in aid would be needed to meet the country's most immediate needs. He also asked for a cash advance from the Export-Import Bank and with "US Govt guarantee some banking firm could discount reparations in order to advance ready cash to Greece at this time." American officials promised to extend financial assistance to Greece, but the proposal had to go through Congress for approval.

The regime in Athens considered military aid much more essential and urgent than financial aid because the royalists wanted to increase the size of the armed forces to suppress the guerrillas in Northern Greece. Tsaldaris secured military aid from the British and the Americans. The Atlee government agreed on 28 November 1946 to support the existing Greek military force composed of 100,000 men. The Truman administration was more reluctant to grant any aid to Greece until the Tsaldaris regime accepted certain American conditions. The president and the State Department urged the Greek prime minister to form a coalition cabinet that would have included the centrist parties. The centrist party leaders—George Papandreou, Sophocles Venizelos, Themistocles Sophoulis, and Panayiotis Kanellopoulos—were vehement anti-communists, and their participation in, or support of, a broad coalition government was imperative for a successful anti-guerrilla drive.[29]

Tsaldaris naturally resisted the idea of a coalition government and rebuffed allegations that he was the obstacle to a more representative regime. He argued that the opposition leaders refused to cooperate with him because no one wanted to share responsibility for reconstructing the shattered economy.

> I would only be too happy if my desperate requests for economic aid to Greece and for a timely increase of the Greek armed forces had been acceded to. Thus, if adequate and well-equipped military forces had been put into the field, order would have been restored within a very short time so that no extraordinary security measures would be required, while the leadership of the Communist Party of Greece would not have taken the liberty of openly undertaking responsibility for rebellion.[30]

There is some merit to Tsaldaris's implicit charge that the United States and the United Kingdom were partly responsible for Greece's internal development because Anglo-American advisers had more influence in formulating policy than cabinet ministers. Moreover, the Truman administration knew of Greece's ominous situation, but did not act until a crisis point was reached.

The Bank of Greece borrowed $10.8 million in September 1946 from the Federal Reserve Bank of the United States and pledged its gold as collateral. The central bank, however, was unable to repay the three-month loan in December 1946, for it only had $9 million. The State Department intervened and granted the Bank of Greece a deferment, but financial difficulties persisted. The Ministry of Supply requested a $2.5 million loan in December to import wheat for the bread rations for the month of January. At the same time, it was discovered that Greece owed $700,000 to Anglo-American authorities in Germany for coal purchases from the Ruhr. The Greeks had assumed that the coal imports were part of the reparations and were shocked to discover otherwise. Furthermore, the central bank had no funds available to meet the government's needs.

The State Department had made recommendations to the Tsaldaris administration regarding economic policy, but the advice was hardly sound. The United States placed a great deal of emphasis on the stimulation of Greece's export trade. "Taxes on production, sale, movement or export of commodities should be reduced or removed," a State Department memo stated, "at least for a period sufficient for a substantial amount of exports to be made and to permit revision of the system of taxation." The State Department urged the Hellenic government to provide incentives for exporters and to recapture some of the prewar markets. The emphasis was placed on agricultural exports, rather than on the development of the industrial sector. The United States government, the IBRD, the IMF, and the Export-Import Bank encouraged Third World countries to pursue export-oriented growth policies, that is, to concentrate on the development of the primary sector of production. Obviously, modernization could not take place under policies that had a proven record of failure since the nineteenth century.

The United States urged the Tsaldaris administration to place controls on foreign exchange and limit its use to the "purchase of essential commodities or the payment for essential services." Gold sales, which contributed to monetary inflation and to the thriving black market, were also curtailed. The State Department recommended heavier taxation on the wealthy Greeks, especially the merchants and industrialists, but no meaningful reforms were implemented. The American officials urged that Greece needed to adopt a plan for the reconstruction of the basic infrastructure—roads, highways, electric power, railroads, ports, municipal waterworks, and other related projects. Finally, the State Department suggested that UNRRA spend $40.9 million to start a reconstruction program. UNRRA, however, had spent $53,935,000 for industrial projects in Greece with meager results because of rampant corruption among public officials, and because the funds were severely limited.[31]

The irony in the State Department's policy recommendations for Greece was that American officials recognized the oligarchy's counterproductive role in the economy, but relied on the latter for political considerations. The October 1946 policy memo stated:

It appears necessary for the merchants and industrialists to make greater efforts and to direct these toward production and distribution of goods essential to the Greek people. As there may be greater profit in the production of luxuries, it may be necessary, in these difficult years, for the Greek Government to press and enforce measures which will direct production toward meeting the basic needs of the Greek economy.[32]

There was an increase in the production and importation of luxury goods after 1945 in Greece as in many underdeveloped countries, especially in Latin America.

Colonel A. W. Sheppard, member of the Australian Imperial Forces, UNRRA staff member, and director of the British Economic Mission to Northern Greece, made the following observation concerning the luxury-geared economy of postwar Greece.

The Bulletin of the Greek Information Office in London shows that only in the luxury trades such as ceramics, rayon and beer has production equalled or exceeded prewar levels. Essential commodities such as edible oils and fats were only 15 percent; cement and building materials 32 percent; textiles 58 percent of the prewar output in May of this year [1948].[33]

He went on to ascertain that perfumes, ties, scarves, automobiles, and other such luxuries were imported despite protestations by the Currency Control Commission. Another contemporary study by a journalist arrived at similar conclusions. Besides the drain on the foreign-exchange reserves by the luxury-geared economy, there was wasteful spending by the state amid a financial crisis. The Exchange Control Commission concluded that 40 percent of the British loan funds, that is, $10 million, was wasted on six hundred missions which the Tsaldaris administration approved "for the most improbable reasons."[34] In view of the long-standing pattern of government corruption and the myopic role of the ruling class, the State Department's proposals for reform were simply inadequate to rectify Greece's systemic problems.

The Porter Mission arrived in Athens in January 1947, and Tsaldaris was compelled to resign as prime minister after his government had been subjected to vociferous criticism by the opposition as well as by the governments in London and Washington. Dimitrios Maximos, former president of the National Bank of Greece and a staunch pro-American, became prime minister in a new coalition cabinet. The new administration was composed of vehement anti-communists from the right and center-right parties. Tsaldaris remained in the cabinet, which included Stylianos Gonatas, a supporter of the Security Battalions, and Napoleon Zervas, an ultra-rightest who became minister of public security. Zervas emerged on the national scene as a resistance leader during the war. He was instrumental in the "white terror" during the mid-1940s, a further signal to the leftists that the regime was moving increasingly to the right. As soon as the government was formed, it became obvious to astute political observers that there were no real policy changes implemented by the new cabinet. Paul Porter informed the State Department that the Maximos administration "in fact represents only a coalition of the Rightist and Conservative elements of the population, to administer effectively the extensive reforms needed."[35] Porter and MacVeagh were convinced that economic, financial, political, and social reforms were unavoidable if the government in Athens hoped to score a quick victory against the communist-dominated guerrilla forces that organized under the banner of the Democratic Army.

Porter delineated the nation's most severe problems in a lengthy report in which he censured the regime for overtaxing the poor, while allowing the very rich to escape taxation.

> You may be interested in knowing that of approximately 1% of the national income, less than $8 million is collected by the government in direct income taxes. While revenues from this source would not be considerable in any event, and the Government claims that it has no machinery for their collection, there is no doubt in my mind that failure to require the majority of wealthy Athenians, merchants, and businessmen to bear their proportionate share of the cost of government creates a more fertile field for fomentation by the extreme left.[36]

It should be noted that Greece's regressive tax structure was a commonly shared problem of Third World countries. Societal modernization simply could not take place unless the fiscal problem was addressed, and that could not be done as long as the ruling parties primarily represented the interests of the indigenous elites that resisted systemic change.

The state's revenues for the fiscal year ending on 31 March 1947 amounted to $185 million, of which 40 percent derived from UNRRA supply sales and most of the remaining from consumption taxes that primarily burdened the lower classes. The deficit for the fiscal year was $87 million, which could have been covered if a progressive tax reform program were implemented when Tsaldaris took office.

Paul Porter became disenchanted after a few weeks in Greece and concluded that the wealthy Greeks were so powerful that no government could control their actions. "The profiteers, the merchants and the black market operator," he wrote, "are swimming in money and luxury and no government has been able to confront them effectively. In the meanwhile the popular masses are barely able to survive." The more extensive and protracted the profiteering and economic dislocation, the deeper Greece sunk into dependence on the United States, until the organs of the state fell under the control of American officials, as will be seen in the following chapters.[37]

During the first two weeks of February, the Greek Foreign minister, John Sofianopoulos, the only Socialist in the Maximos cabinet, visited Washington to discuss a number of issues, including Greece's economic and foreign policies. Sofianopoulos argued that a plausible coalition government in Athens must include all parties, otherwise the sweeping reforms necessary for reconstruction could not be implemented. The State Department insisted that the KKE must be excluded from government. George C. Marshall, secretary of state, reiterated the administration's policy that Greece needed to undergo certain reforms affecting the tax structure, monetary system, and civil service. That simply meant increased direct taxes, devaluation of the drachma, and decrease in the size of the civil bureaucracy to cut costs. In the absence of a center-left coalition government, however, even those innocuous reforms were difficult, if not impossible, because of the resistance to change by the politically entrenched groups.

During Sofianopoulos's visit in Washington, the Atlee government announced that the British economy was experiencing unprecedented difficulties. The Labour government issued a White Paper on 20 January 1947, disclosing the nation's dire financial predicament. The immediate effect of the White Paper in the domain of foreign affairs was that "Britain would have to cut her military commitments at home and abroad." There were 1.5 million men in the British armed services, and the work of another 500,000 people was required to keep them supplied. The United Kingdom was no longer in a position to grant loans or aid to its dependent countries. The Atlee government was confronted with the exigent problems of severe shortages of raw materials, lack of capital, acute unemployment, and rapidly deteriorating foreign trade.[38]

Ambassador MacVeagh informed the State Department on 7 February 1947 that England planned to withdraw from Greece. He recommended immediate American action by Washington. Throughout the month of February, American officials in Greece were apprehensive about the impending collapse of the regime. MacVeagh believed that the Democratic Army was capable of taking over the country in the absence of immediate foreign aid. As he noted:

> If nothing but economic and financial factors were considered, full collapse from Greece's present position might take several months. However, deteriorating morale both of civil servants and armed forces, as well as of [the] general public, owing to inadequate incomes, fear of growing banditry, lack of confidence in Government, and exploitation by the international communists creates [the] possibility of much more rapid denouncement.[39]

He added that Paul Porter conferred daily with Greek officials in pursuit of a plausible economic and fiscal policy, but it was clear that unless Washington approved immediate aid, the regime was bound to fall.

The Communist Threat

MacVeagh's observations regarding the foreboding situation in Greece were largely valid. There is no evidence, however, that international communists were responsible for the events that unfolded in the country before the promulgation of the Truman Doctrine. A succinct examination of the KKE's decision to launch a guerrilla war will shed some light on the issue. Representatives of the Greek Communist party's Central Committee met with Yugoslavian and Bulgarian officials to discuss the prospects of reviving the guerrilla movement in December 1945 after it was clear that the regime in Athens had resolved to obliterate the communists. Yugoslavia promised to support the KKE, but only within the former's borders. Bulgaria was more hesitant about becoming involved, and Albania, with its severely limited resources, could not do very much for the KKE. Nevertheless, all sides assumed that Stalin would back the KKE's struggle. When Dimitris Partsalidis, a member of the KKE Central Committee, met with Soviet leaders, they urged that Greek communists abandon their struggle and operate within the parliamentary system. Such was the policy advice which Moscow gave to all communist parties in the world during the 1940s. The Greek communists, however, deviated from the Soviet Union's directives, as did the Maoists, and urged revolution after cooperation proved impossible.

The KKE's decision to embrace guerrilla warfare, just before the enunciation of the Truman Doctrine, was made on the basis of a number of factors. Economic conditions in Greece had not improved since liberation, the bourgeois government in Athens supported the "white terror" to eliminate the leftist opposition, and the democratic parties refused to reach a negotiated settlement to end the escalating civil war. There was also the desire on the part of many among the rank-and-file, as well as KKE leaders, to capture control of the government by revolution. While it is true, however, that the KKE planned to engage in guerrilla war as early as December 1945, there were only sporadic clashes between the rebels and the army before the Truman Doctrine. Meanwhile, the Greek Communist leadership endeavored to end the armed struggle by compromise. That was especially true after the Soviet dictator informed the KKE that the United States planned to intervene militarily in Greece, making the guerrilla war a futile effort, a fait accompli.[40]

There is no doubt, of course, that Albania, Yugoslavia, and Bulgaria provided limited assistance to the Democratic Army once the civil war was in full swing and that the Soviet Union defended the KKE at the UN. That took place, however, after the Truman Doctrine made any compromise between the communists and the regime in Athens impossible. The decision to carry out a guerrilla campaign was not made by the Soviet Union or her Balkan allies. Although it may be argued that the Soviet Union would have benefited from a KKE victory, it cannot be argued that Stalin in any way encouraged the revolution. The decision to launch an insurgent movement was made by the inept and adventuristic KKE leadership, especially Nikos Zachariades, general secretary of the party, who failed to appraise correctly the domestic as well as international conditions. Therefore, the argument that international communist forces were responsible for the Greek civil war is not entirely true.[41]

The real concern of the Foreign Office and the State Department was to secure a pro-West regime in Athens. The Greek right-wing politicians appeared much more accommodating to the nascent Western bloc than either the centrists or the socialists. This was due in large part to the rightists' vehement anti-communist rhetoric and activities as well as to their support of the monarchy, which had been England's sentinel in Greece since the nineteenth century.

Lord Invarchapel, British ambassador to Washington, and Dean Acheson informed the Truman administration on 21 February 1947 that the government in Athens faced monumental problems as the foreign-exchange reserves were exhausted and the state was bankrupt. Both diplomats warned of the possible collapse of the Greek government. Paul Porter painted an equally pessimistic picture of Greece in one of his reports.

> Food prices up 4 percent this week, Govt deficit hit new high for last reporting period, imports mere trickle, food supplies exhausted. This has resulted in widespread unrest which causes Govt to fuse serious labor crisis. Pending immediately are demands of merchant marine seamen for 110 percent wage increase, Piraeus dock workers for double present wages, threatened textile strike, mill workers [strike] and repetition of last month's [January] civil service strike.[42]

Social revolution was inevitable given the KKE's apparent lack of alternatives and its determination to gain a legitimate role in the political arena after it had contributed so much to the resistance movement. Intervention by the United States was also inevitable given the breakdown of the Greek government and the geopolitical significance of the country to the West. George C. Marshall delivered the first major public address on 22 February 1947, which served as the ideological prelude to the Truman Doctrine and the Marshall Plan. The secretary of state indicated that foreign aid was to be used as a means of supporting pro-Western regimes against actual or potential social revolutions that furthered the Soviet Union's interests directly or indirectly. Two days later, on 24 February, Acheson, Kennan, and Loy Henderson deliberated with a special committee that studied the question of Greek-Turkish aid. The committee recommended United States assistance for both countries, although Turkey was by no means in a position analogous to that of Greece. On the same day, the State Department requested that the Departments of War, Navy, Treasury, and State confer jointly on the Greek-Turkish question and submit their reports to the president. The State Department issued the following directives, which brought the Truman Doctrine closer to reality.

Appropriate legislation [should] be drafted and presented to Congress at the earliest possible date which would enable the United States Government to extend large credits or grants to Greece and Turkey in amounts and under conditions which would enable their utilization under American supervision for strengthening the economy and promoting the stability of these countries.[43]

Specifically, the department recommended that the United States provide the two countries in question with military assistance and sufficient funds to meet their foreign-exchange requirements.

The policy preparations for the Truman Doctrine were hastened partly because Bevin announced to the Labour party on 15 February that British troops planned to withdraw from Greece on 1 March 1947. At the same time, Lord Invarchapel informed the State Department that Greece needed $250 million in foreign exchange to survive in 1947 and an additional $280 million for civilian and military requirements. England was predisposed to aid Greece, but the former suffered a £450 million deficit in 1946 and imported 42 percent of its food and raw materials from the Western Hemisphere, while exporting only 14 percent to the latter.[44]

It was under such ominous economic and financial conditions in Greece and the United Kingdom that the Foreign Office addressed a memorandum to the State Department asking that "the United States will agree to bear the financial burden [in Greece] of which the major part has hitherto been borne by His Majesty's Government." The Atlee government advised the United States to "supervise the utilization of funds made available to the Greek Government and to give the Greeks advice in the field of economic reconstruction" through an American mission.

The State Department invited Paul Economou-Gouras, Greek chargé d' affaires, to attend preliminary deliberations regarding the formulation of the Truman Doctrine on 26 February. Loy Henderson confided in the Greek chargé that the administration wished to project the impression that the Greek people were inviting American involvement in their country and that the United States was not inheriting England's legacy in the Near East. That was a decidely salient issue because world public opinion, including that in the United States, had denounced British intervention on behalf of the Greek royalist forces. A veneer of democratic ideals and anti-communist propaganda was essential, therefore, if American intervention was to appear justified.[45]

George C. Marshall was the key spokesman of early Cold War policy in the Truman administration. Before leaving for the Fourth Session of Foreign Ministers in Moscow, he addressed a note to the president concerning the impending foreign aid to Greece and Turkey and its significance to United States foreign policy. He maintained that

> the situation in Greece is desperate; that the collapse of Greece would create a situation threatening to the security of the United States, and that we should take immediate steps to extend all possible aid to Greece and on a lesser scale to Turkey.[46]

President Truman recalled in his *Memoirs* Marshall's recommendations with regard to Greece and Turkey and described the entire affair with a sense of idealism that was typical of the president. The United States, according to Truman, was the leader of the "Free World" and had a duty and an obligation to protect the weaker nations from international communism and Soviet expansionism.[47]

Truman was also a realist who appreciated the material benefits accruing to the United States from an expansionist/interventionist foreign policy. He placed the issue in a historical framework when he wrote:

> I knew from my study of American history that this country was developed by the investment of foreign capital by the British, the Dutch, the Germans and the French. These countries invested immense sums in the development of our railroads, mines, oil lands and livestock industry. After two world wars in each of which the United States was used as a source of supply for munitions and materials by the European countries, the invested funds in the United States of Britain, Holland, Germany and France were depleted. If the investment capital of the United States could be protected and not confiscated and if we could persuade the capitalists that they were not working in foreign countries to exploit them, it would be to the mutual benefit of everybody concerned.[48]

Foreign capital played a role in the economic development of the United States, but only after the country was developed and the prospects for further growth were unmistakably clear to European investors. The development of the American economy, however, occurred only after the country had undergone a political revolution. Moreover, the structural development of the American economy was carried by the efforts of indigenous capital that enjoyed the protection of a strong state. Finally, the United States entertained an expansionist policy that strengthened the capitalist class after the War of Independence. Truman's thesis that foreign-capital investment leads to development cannot be substantiated by the facts because no country in the world has transcended underdevelopment through the injection of foreign capital alone, that is, diffusion of technology and consumerist values. On the contrary, numerous studies have shown that foreign-capital penetration in the Third World has been the principal cause of the perpetuation of the process of underdevelopment, or at best of dependent development. The case of Greece certainly bears this out, as will be seen in the following chapters.[49]

The Truman Doctrine

In an interagency meeting held on 24 February 1947, Hubert F. Havlik, chief of the Division of Investment and Economic Development of the State Department, argued that "the financial part of the problem [with regard to Greece and Turkey] be approached on a global basis, urging that it must be presented to Congress as part of a world-wide program." Another department official added that the aid program "could be presented to Congress in such a fashion as to electrify the American people." The consensus among policymakers was that public opinion must not be taken for granted and that the issue must be universalized. Procedure, therefore, was just as important as substance in this case.

The prevailing thinking in Washington was that the situation in the Near East would be "watched all over the world as a manifestation of whether the rest of the world could look hopefully to us or would have to turn to Russia." That bipolar foreign-policy approach was the quintessence of the Cold War mentality that prevailed in Washington. James Forrestal, secretary of the navy, and Clark Clifford, the presidential aide who was instrumental in formulating the Truman Doctrine, regarded the Greek-Turkish question as part of an East-West conflict. "Which of the two systems currently offered the world is to survive," Forrestal asked rhetorically, "and what practical steps need be taken to implement any policies that the government may establish?" He and the other Truman administration officials did not consider the unique systemic conditions that gave rise to revolutionary movements in each country. Instead, they believed that each regime in the world had either a choice of following the Soviet bloc or the American camp.[50]

William Clayton returned from Europe in the early weeks of 1947 and provided the following observations concerning the growing Soviet-American confrontation:

> the reins of leadership are slipping from Britain's hands. They will be picked up either by the United States or by Russia. If by Russia then the balance of power will turn against America and war will be likely within a generation. Communist movements are threatening established governments in every part of the globe. These movements, directed by Moscow, feed on economic and political weaknesses.[51]

Dean Acheson entertained similar views, comparing the confrontation between the two superpowers to that of ancient Rome and Carthage.

Senator Arthur Vandenberg was also a contributor to the early Cold War propaganda. Like President Truman, the senator preferred to apply the Greek question to a nebulous universal framework, rather than dwelling on the specifics involved. He wrote:

> I am frank in saying that I do not know the answer to the latest Greek challenge because I do not know the facts. But I sense enough of the facts to realize that the problem in Greece cannot be isolated by itself. On the contrary it is probably symbolic of the ideological clash between eastern communism and western democracy.[52]

George F. Kennan, who knew the facts better than most politicians, drew similar conclusions about the case. He admitted that the Russians and their allies were "poorly set up to take responsibility either for the governing of Greece or for the support of the Greek economy." Nevertheless, he dreaded the consequences of a possible communist victory in the absence of a strong American response in Greece. Like other diplomats, Kennan emphasized the importance of Greece to the strategic interests of the United States. Counterinsurgency measures, therefore, enjoyed broad support within the administration as well as in Congress.[53]

Dean Acheson conducted a meeting with other department officials on 28 February to discuss ideas that were later incorporated into the president's speech concerning Greece and Turkey. The essence of Acheson's report was that United States policy was designed to avoid war and "to portray the world conflict between free and totalitarian or imposed forms of government." Acheson proposed that congressional approval be granted for Export-Import Bank funds to Greece and Turkey. He also advised that a law be passed "authorizing American government personnel to supervise the expenditure of these funds." On the same day that Acheson held a staff meeting, Truman conferred with congressional leaders to brief them about his Near Eastern policy. The legislators promised bipartisan support and the stage for the Truman Doctrine was set.[54]

The Maximos government submitted a formal request to Washington for American advisory personnel and material assistance. That request, which came at the State Department's suggestion, delineated Greece's economic and military needs, specifying reconstruction projects, foreign-exchange funds, and overall civilian and defense requirements deemed essential for the regime's survival. George C. Marshall assured the Hellenic government "that all foreign exchange costs of military will be met by outside assistance." He added that American administrative, economic, and technical personnel would be sent to Athens to plan and supervise the entire foreign-aid program.

A few days before the promulgation of the Truman Doctrine, Tsaldaris asked Ambassador Norton of Great Britain whether it was prudent on the part of the Greek government to accept preferred foreign aid from the United States, while giving up fairly sweeping powers to American officials. Norton replied that under the circumstances the Greek government did not have much flexibility in the matter. The price for the regime's survival was subservience to the American missions.[55]

During the first few months of 1947, Britain's future in Greece received a great deal of attention in Washington because the Truman administration did not want the British troops withdrawn from Greece before the foreign-aid program was fully implemented. Lincoln MacVeagh argued that it would be a mistake to efface British influence in Greece completely, even after the American assistance program was implemented. He suggested that it was preferable, from the public-relations point of view, for the United States to extend credits to the United Kingdom and allow the latter to continue its role as Greece's protector under Washington's auspices. Replacing British military troops in Greece with American military personnel was politically risky as far as MacVeagh was concerned. He was also concerned about the possible repercussions in world public opinion regarding American aid to an unpopular regime. "Greatest care should be taken," he wrote, "to avoid giving [the] impression that [the] US aim [is] . . . financing [a] Greek 'civil war' or maintaining in power an essentially reactionary government incapable of developing sound economic principles." MacVeagh candidly acknowledged that the regime in Athens was unpopular and that it represented only rightwing elements. His proposal of having Britain as America's proxy in Greece was certainly sound, but it did not find a sympathetic ear in the State Department.[56]

A few days before President Truman went before Congress to announce his doctrine, MacVeagh reminded the State Department of the political risks to the United States if public opinion misconstrued the foreign-aid program as support for the reactionary regimes of Greece and Turkey. Acheson disregarded all aspects of MacVeagh's advice and emphatically stated that

> any aid extended to Greece is in the interest of world peace and US security and is not to assist carrying on any Brit[ish] policy in Greece. Therefore, we shall not hesitate to give aid in military equipment direct to Greece.[57]

The British did not remove their troops from Greece until 1950, that is, after the civil war ended and the threat of social revolution dissipated. As the United States assumed the protagonist role in the Western world, England and the other Western European countries accepted the role of junior partners.

President Truman summoned his cabinet on 7 March to discuss the Greek-Turkish issue before delivering the long-awaited speech. He stated that the Greek government was not satisfactory to the United States and that "it contained many elements that were reactionary." Forrestal reiterated the well-known bipolar foreign-policy theme during the meeting, and the entire cabinet concurred with the president that the United States must support Greece despite the conspicuous shortcomings of the regime.

President Truman delivered the speech on Greece and Turkey before a joint session of Congress on 12 March 1947. It should be noted that he had rejected the original version of the speech, for it lacked the idealism and universal overtones which were essential to make it more appealing to the public. "The writers had filled the speech with all sorts of background data and statistical figures about Greece," he wrote in his *Memoirs*, "and made the whole thing sound like an investment prospectus." Clark Clifford was one of the speech writers, along with Dean Acheson and Joseph Marion Jones. They emphasized the broad implications of foreign aid to Greece and Turkey and the "request of the Greek government for American administrators, economists, and technicians and the great importance of American supervision of the funds."[58]

Truman asked Congress to appropriate $400 million for Greece and Turkey, as Acheson had recommended. He stressed that the two nations needed foreign assistance if they were to remain free. He dwelled on the ideological struggle and the divergent ways of life that separated East from West. The essence of the doctrine reflected foreign-policy trends that had been established since the London Conference of Foreign Ministers in September 1945. Those trends were articulated in a general fashion and were presented succinctly to Congress without any mention of the political, social, and economic realities of Greece since liberation.[59]

One scholar summarized the significance of the president's speech as follows:

> First, it bypassed the United Nations and announced a unilateral American approach to matters considered vital to United States interests. Second, it proclaimed the now familiar containment thesis against radicalism in general and communism in particular. Third, it invoked the domino theory, though not by specific name.[60]

Behind the veneer of idealism and rhetoric about democratic principles implicit in the Truman Doctrine, there was the reality of tangible American strategic and economic interests in Southeastern Europe and the Near East. American unilateral action to demolish (contain) social revolutions necessarily entailed that the United States set a precedent for intervention anywhere it perceived a threat to its interests.

The domino theory, which has been applied in Europe, Asia, and Latin America since the Truman Doctrine, has been an important component of United States bipartisan foreign policy. Gabriel Kolko summarized the significance of the domino theory as follows:

> In effect, just as the United States in the 1920s learned it had to make economic investments in the Third World to control raw

materials, so in the revolutionary world context of the postwar epoch it increasingly understood it had to make political and military investments to sustain the specific environment in which the neocolonial economic system could operate. The domino theory was simply an articulation of this counterrevolutionary assumption, yet its cost was one American leaders could never estimate in advance, thereby laying the seeds of their undoing.[61]

Acheson was one of the chief proponents of the domino theory, but the concept received broad support primarily because it was an effective way for the government in Washington to dramatize the danger of Soviet expansionism to world public opinion.

Many Greek politicians admitted that the Truman Doctrine was motivated neither by democratic principles nor by a moral conviction about the need to help the people of the Near East. The centrist and leftist elements in Greece were especially critical of the doctrine. The Liberal newspaper *Vima* maintained: "With the Truman Doctrine the country is transformed into a dependency and an organ of a foreign power." The defunct Central Committee of EAM also denounced Truman's foreign policy on the grounds that it violated Greece's sovereignty. The KKE's Central Committee charged that the Truman Doctrine was "an imperialist meddling which anticipates [saving] . . . monarcho-fascist Greece, which is not in the position to face conditions because it has to confront the people. With the Truman Doctrine Greece is converted into a military stepping-stone against the Democratic Balkans and Europe." The leftist and centrist press assailed the doctrine for representing blatant United States intervention in Greek internal affairs. Even certain conservatives admitted that behind the humanitarian veil of Truman's foreign policy there were concrete American interests. With the exception of the leftists, however, the other factions desired foreign aid from the United States. They objected vehemently only to the conditions that such aid carried.[62]

Reaction to the Truman Doctrine in the United States was by no means all favorable, despite the euphoria projected by the State Department. Among the more prominent opponents to the administration's foreign policy were Senators Claude Pepper, Robert A. Taft, and Glen Taylor. They objected to a number of problems that the doctrine raised. The most controversial issue was the president's total disregard for the UN as an instrument of global peace and multilateral policy. Furthermore, the senators were adamantly opposed to the

American militarism implicit in the administration's foreign policy. The opposition to the Truman Doctrine, however, constituted a minority, and it did not have an impact on changing the direction of United States foreign policy during the early Cold War.

The most important issue that the president's opponents raised concerned the UN. It was indeed ironic that the administration bypassed the UN, especially considering that the United States enjoyed a voting majority in that organization between 1945 and 1953. Moreover, a UN commission was sent to Greece on 30 January 1947 to investigate allegations that the Greek guerrillas were receiving assistance from communist-bloc nations. Warren Austin, United States ambassador to the UN, argued that the administration should have waited for the commission's report before enunciating a unilateral policy. The commission was pro-American, and its findings and conclusions would have strengthened United States policy objectives in Greece. President Truman and his advisers, however, chose a course of unilateralism, which was really started with the abandonment of Lend-Lease and was indicative of America's strength in the world.[63]

Certain segments of the American press and intelligentsia criticized the Truman Doctrine not only because it undermined the UN, but also because American taxpayers were asked to support a foreign-aid program designed to sustain in power semi-authoritarian regimes in Athens and Ankara. Henry Wallace, the former vice president and secretary of commerce, was among the most outspoken critics of the administration's foreign policy. He argued that Washington should have pursued a course of economic cooperation and coexistence with the USSR that would have averted the polarization of the world into two opposing camps. He charged that the government in Washington embarked on a bellicose trend toward the other superpower and that growing militarization of the two superpowers did not serve the interests of either side. Wallace's prophetic words did not find much support among the voters who were mesmerized by the anti-communist rhetoric and enticed by the ideals of freedom and democracy behind which the Truman administration veiled its interventionist policies.[64]

The Truman Doctrine inaugurated a new era of American dominance in the West and provided the ideological framework for interventionism and counterinsurgency. As Richard J. Barnet put it:

> The American experience in Greece not only set the pattern for subsequent interventions in internal wars but also suggested the criteria for assessing the success or failure of counterinsur-

gency operations. Greece was the first major police task which the United States took on in the postwar world.[65]

The success of American interventionist policy in Greece and Turkey led to the specialization of bureaucracies that dealt with military- and economic-aid issues. Moreover, counterinsurgency administrations were established that specialized in suppressing revolutionary movements and defending authoritarian regimes in the Third World.

The National Security Council codified the policy of "containment militarism" in a secret policy memo, NSC–68, which endorsed a global strategy of containment by military means in 1950. The Committee on the Present Danger, which was behind NSC–68, advocated an intensive arms buildup, dealing with the Soviet Union from a position of military superiority and intervening in the Third World militarily to prevent the success of regimes that were either unfriendly to the West or whose policies were contrary to American interests. Although the doctrine of containment militarism was adopted after the Soviet Union successfully tested its first atomic bomb in 1949, the successful American intervention in Greece was an impetus for that policy, which lasted until the end of the Vietnam War. Containment militarism was resurrected by the Reagan administration in 1980 in an attempt for the United States to reaffirm its hegemony in the West.

The far-reaching impact of the Truman Doctrine was not confined to American intervention in Greece, but affected Cold War policy in general, including the Vietnam War and intervention in Central America. As one Cold War critic observed:

> Greece was the Vietnam of the 1940s in more than a rhetorical sense. She was the first major battlefield of anti-communist containment. In Greece as in Vietnam, the nature and history of a National Liberation Front were clouded by deceptive talk of 'aggression from the North.' There too, the United States came to the aid of a set of fragile and repressive governments whose ambit was the great cities, while the countryside was in revolutionary turmoil. On Greek soil some of the earliest notions of counterinsurgency, 'pacification' and containment were tested, and American arrogance rewarded, with the future desolation of Vietnam as its direct consequence.[66]

Although there were distinct differences between the revolutionary situations in Greece in the 1940s and Vietnam in the 1960s, the important point is that the Truman administration established a long-standing pattern of interventionist foreign policy camouflaged with the propagation of democratic ideals, anti-communist rhetoric, containment, and domino theories and the use of massive military aid designed to prevent social change in the Third World. The question is whether there is a direct correlation between the policy of American interventionism and the inability of Third World countries to transcend their underdeveloped status in the world economy. The following chapters examine this issue as it applies to Greece.

III

The AMAG and United States Ascendancy in Greece, 1947

Conditions for United States Aid to Greece

The Maximos government, the right-wing elements, and the business community in Greece were euphoric about the new era of Greek dependence on the United States. For many in the armed forces, the bureaucracy, the business community, and politics, the Truman Doctrine signified that Greece's fate was inexorably linked with the West and would not be abandoned by it. The initial optimism, however, evaporated quickly when the price of American assistance became fully known.

The Porter Mission conferred with Premier Maximos, and the Currency Committee on 21 March and submitted a number of proposals to Washington and Athens concerning Greek economic and fiscal policy. The most important recommendation revolved around the need for rigorous trade controls under the authority of a centralized Foreign Trade Administration, which the Americans eventually controlled. Second, United States officials insisted that foreign exchange and gold sales by the central bank must be curtailed, for they had detrimental effects on the economy. It should be noted that gold sales ceased entirely after 12 March 1947 and the currency was relatively stable for a few months until they resumed. Finally, Porter urged the

Hellenic government to impose strict price/wage controls as one plausible method of controlling rampant inflation.

Porter underscored the need for a permanent American mission that would be authorized to postpone or withdraw aid and "exercise general supervision and participate in the development of fiscal policy." Moreover, the mission would also supervise surplus property, Export-Import Bank loans to Greece, and private as well as governmental imports. Prime Minister Maximos agreed to comply with Porter's recommendations, which were fully implemented after July 1947 once Marshall approved them. The secretary of state insisted that American officials must control the Foreign Trade Administration, and he requested that the government in Athens publicly acknowledge America's generosity as manifested in the Truman Doctrine.[1]

After some considerable debate, the United States Senate approved the Greek-Turkish Aid Bill by a vote of 67 to 23 and the House of Representatives followed suit, approving the bill by 287 to 107. The amount of aid was $400 million, and the bill became Public Law 87 of the 80th Congress after the President signed it on 22 May. During the ceremonial signing, Truman stated that "the United States is helping to further aims and purposes identical with those of the United Nations." He went on to maintain: "Our aid in this instance is evidence not only that we pledge our support to the United Nations but that we act to support it." Truman's rhetoric regarding America's steadfast commitment to the UN was prompted by clamorous opposition to the administration's unilateral foreign policy. Senators, congressmen, and influential journalists, the most important of whom was Walter Lippman, assailed Truman's disregard for and undermining of the UN.

The irony in the president's ostensible public support of the UN was that it contradicted the State Department's policy toward the organization. In May 1947 the Maximos administration requested that the UN assign a liaison to the American mission as an observer. The State Department categorically rejected the proposal just two days before Truman signed the Greek-Turkish aid bill. Loy Henderson wrote: "I feel it would be unfortunate for us to make any move to encourage U.N. observers to watch over our activities." The appointment of a UN observer would have mitigated the criticism of the American mission to Greece and played a positive role in checking abuses by the mission.[2]

The Agreement of Greek Aid was signed on 31 May by the government in Athens, thereby formally designating the beginning of *Ameri-*

canokratia. The agreement was drafted by American officials and submitted to Greek officials for their approval. It subjected the country to unprecedented controls because the twelve articles of the agreement granted AMAG virtually limitless authority over all facets of government. Article VI was the key to AMAG's comprehensive military and economic functions in Greece. It stated:

> The Govt of Greece will permit the members of the American Mission to observe freely the utilization of assistance furnished to Greece by the U.S. The Govt of Greece will maintain such accounts and records, will furnish the American Mission such reports and information as the Mission may request for the performance of its function and responsibilities.[3]

The agreement permitted AMAG to control the organs of the state, which was a flagrant violation of the nation's sovereignty. Such was the price, however, that the regime reluctantly paid to sustain itself in power and preserve the status quo that the Democratic Army threatened.

Every social sector was thoroughly permeated by the ubiquitous influence of the American mission. Professor William McNeill, who approved of foreign aid as part of the solution for Greece's complex problems, described AMAG's infiltration of Greece as follows:

> Advisers had been installed in the Ministries, field representatives had been stationed all over the country to check upon actual performance and when things went wrong or failed to conform to American ideas, vigorous efforts were made to alter the situation through 'advice' that often took on a peremptory tone.[4]

Initially, American ascendancy in Greece was confined to military and financial matters, but gradually every sector, from labor to education, was affected.

The Agreement of Greek Aid extended such comprehensive powers to AMAG that it had the effect of rendering the host government "unable to take any important decision without their [AMAG] approval." Once it became known that the mission enjoyed sweeping powers in the country, Greek newspapers of all political affiliations expressed strong disapproval of the preconditions for foreign aid. The rightist and some centrist factions continued to praise the Truman

Doctrine as a positive measure, leaving the center-left and the left to carry on the vociferous anti-American campaign. The Democratic Organization of Greece, a communist group, placed the Agreement of Aid in the following perspective.

> The most powerful factor in the direction of the Greek economy, including production, finances, trade, wages, etc. is neither a branch of the Greek Government nor any organization of Greek citizens, but the American Mission for Aid to Greece. Not one economic law, not one governmental measure can be finally adopted without the previous 'approval' of the Americans. The national budget is drawn up under the supervision of the American Mission and is not presented to Parliament without their previous approval.[5]

Greece had been subjected to foreign financial control during the nineteenth century when it defaulted on its loans. There was never, however, such blatant and extensive control of the economy and the armed forces as AMAG enjoyed during the 1940s. It must be underscored that the American officials in Athens exercised more prerogatives in directing the country's destiny than prescribed by the Agreement of Aid as they became impatient with Greek politics and overzealous about their own functions.

Protracted Economic Dislocation, Refugees, and Guerrillas

The optimists in Greece as well as in the United States had hoped that foreign aid would be the panacea for the beleaguered country. The immediate effect of the Truman Doctrine in Greece uplifted the morale of the army, the government, and the business community, but it did not result in any significant changes in the economy. Economic dislocation was accentuated, thousands of peasants were uprooted forcibly by the government in the struggle against the Democratic Army, and the guerrilla movement continued to gain strength.

When the American mission arrived in Greece, the government's most immediate problem was the depleted finances. The central bank's gold stock stood at $4,000,000, the dollar reserves amounted to a mere $150,000, excluding currency cover of $3,000,000, and the sterling reserves were down to 3,500,000, also excluding currency cover. All dollar-import applications were denied because of the bank's precarious position. The Atlee government extended a £2,000,000 loan to Greece as cover for the foreign-exchange requirements in April 1947, but that was not sufficient to counterpoise further financial debasement.[6]

In the spring of 1947 there was a maritime strike that had a crippling effect on the country's food imports and other essentials such as fuel. The labor strike coincided with the suspension of UNRRA operations. The United States Embassy informed the State Department that Greece was facing an imminent danger of famine and disease with cataclysmic consequences for the prospects of economic recovery.

A principal factor in the low productivity rate in Greece was that about 30 percent of all manpower was either engaged in the military and the gendarmerie, or was part of an ever-expanding refugee population. Colonel A. W. Sheppard argued in his study of postwar Greece that between 1945 and 1947, the period of considerable foreign assistance and British intervention, unemployment jumped 11 percent in the urban sector, the drachma was devalued from 600 to 20,000 per pound sterling, and the cost of living soared 34 percent between March 1945 and December 1946. The national income in 1947 was 62.6 percent of the prewar level, and the per-capita income was 59.6 percent of the prewar level. The average income per head was $52.8 annually in 1947 as compared to $90 in 1938, measured in 1938 value. Clearly, therefore, foreign aid and advice between the Athens Revolt and the Truman Doctrine had exacerbated, not alleviated, Greece's problems. Again, this is not to say that aid per se was responsible for the above-mentioned conditions. Its application, however, under Greece's political economy in the late 1940s, accounted for its negative results.[7]

Ambassador MacVeagh suggested to the authorities in Athens in June 1947 that they needed to purchase $500,000 in petroleum products to meet the immediate civil and defense needs. Furthermore, the government purchased $2 million in food supplies to avert a food-shortage crisis, but the Treasury lacked the funds for other extensive essential imports. The United States Embassy estimated that Greece's balance-of-payments deficit would rise to $8.4 million if the most essential supplies were purchased for the month of July only. In view of such calamitous developments unfolding against the background of growing sociopolitical polarization and escalating civil war, dependence on the United States was a matter of life or death for the regime and the upper classes. It must be emphasized, however, that even the popular classes were optimistic about the prospects for a reinvigorated economy and sociopolitical harmony after the promulgation of the Truman Doctrine. There was a perception among large sections of the population that United States aid would solve the country's problems. By 1950, however, that sense of optimism was replaced by the belief that emigration to America or one of the other advanced countries was the panacea.[8]

One of the principal reasons for the protracted economic dislocation was the refugee problem that was symptomatic of the civil war. The refugee problem was aggravated after the Truman Doctrine as the right-wing elements in Greece were encouraged by Washington's foreign policy and became more intransigent toward the Communists who were still hoping for a political solution. The government had at its disposal 160,000 men, including the paramilitary organizations, while the guerrillas numbered about 10,000.[9]

The armed forces did not confine their attacks to the Democratic Army, but were given carte blanche to eliminate the regime's opposition regardless of political tendencies. Sheppard noted that the Greek government was as authoritarian as the army and the paramilitary groups, which were overzealous in their quest to expunge the leftists and their sympathizers from society. He continued:

> Greece today is a police state. . . . In every hotel and large block of flats, every large factory or place of employment and in every street, there was a security officer who was responsible to the Minister of Public Security or his representatives. It is a little known fact that the Gendarmerie have been under [the] command of the Military Forces for the past 12 months, but martial law has not been declared.[10]

Many former Nazi collaborators had been assimilated into the regular army and the gendarmerie. Behind the veneer of representative government, under the center-right coalition of Maximos, and beneath the ostensible humanitarianism of American aid to Greece was the reality of continued "white terror" directed not just against the Communists, but all those who were suspected of assisting communists and were anti-royalists.

It was against such a background during the winter of 1946–47 that the government launched a major relocation program of peasants who were deemed to be an actual or a potential hindrance to the military's anti-communist campaigns in Northern Greece. The Democratic Army was confined primarily to the north, where it enjoyed greater popular support and where it had ready access to friendly borders. The government relocated 200,000 villagers, primarily in the northern areas, in the first half of 1947 and planned to continue as long as the struggle persisted.

The American consulate in Thessaloniki informed the State Department that some peasants had been relocated to refugee camps for safety and others had gone voluntarily. The majority of them, however, were forced to move by the army. At the beginning of 1947 there were 20,000 refugees in Thrace and Macedonia, and by October of the same year their number reached 310,000. The army relocated about 15,000 peasants a month to "security camps" where the population was under the care of the state. The number of refugees soared to 517,135 in March 1948 and peaked at 700,000, or about 9 percent of the entire population, in 1949 when the civil war ended. Professor L. S. Stavrianos estimates that if the servicemen and the people on welfare were added to the refugee population, the total number of unproductive people was 2,402,864, or 32 percent of the population. The tragedy of the refugee problem was not only the effects it had on the GNP, but also the fact that it was exacerbated by AMAG and was not rectified until 1951.[11]

The White House announced on 5 June 1947 that Dwight Griswold, former governor of Nebraska, was appointed chief of AMAG. Before departing for Athens, the government in Washington briefed Griswold about the functions and purpose of his mission. In an interagency meeting, government officials resolved that AMAG would recognize the Greek government but dismiss any Greek official who did not assent to the mission's directives. To avoid public criticism of United States policy toward Greece, James Forrestal suggested that Griswold "have a frank talk with such persons as Sulzberger of the *New York Times*, Roy Howard of the Scripps-Howard papers, and the heads of United Press and Associated Press."[12]

On 10 July 1947, five days before Griswold commenced his duties in Athens, George C. Marshall addressed a memo to him concerning AMAG's policy. He opened the three-page instructions with the following statement: "The situation in Greece today should be viewed against the background of a world-wide communist effort to subvert governments and institutions not already subservient to the Soviet Union." It must be kept in mind that General Marshall had spent most of 1946 in China in an attempt to prevent the success of the

Maoist revolution. He was personally engrossed, therefore, in the politics of counterrevolution before assuming the leadership role in the Department of State. He was deeply suspicious of the communists and shared the same views regarding the Soviet Union as other Cold Warriors.[13]

The secretary of state's comments regarding the Greek civil war warrant some analysis at this juncture since they were based on false premises. First, Josef Stalin had not lost complete confidence in the policy of coexistence with the West and in the UN as a viable institution of ameliorating relations between the Soviet bloc and the United States. Such a policy simply served Soviet interests much more than a policy of confrontation. Second, the Soviets severed relations with Greece in April 1947 in protest of the Truman Doctrine, not because the Kremlin had suddenly decided to back the Democratic Army. Finally, the thesis that the Soviet Union led a global communist crusade in the 1940s is simply exaggerated. One recent study concerning the Soviet dictator's leadership arrived at the following conclusion about the Truman administration's assessment of alleged Soviet global revolutionary schemes:

> In retrospect we may see flaws in Western reconstruction of Soviet motives. The Chinese and Yugoslav Communists were not under his [Stalin's] control and in 1946 acted against his advice. Even the Greek Communists disregarded his warnings against civil war and pursued an independent policy.[14]

Andrej Zhdanov and V. M. Molotov, Stalin's closest advisers and the most influential Politburo members, made it quite clear to the embattled KKE that Moscow had recognized Greece as a Western sphere of influence.

During the Eleventh Congress of the French Communist party, which was held in Strasbourg on 27 June 1947, further evidence was provided of the growing rift among European communists. The KKE defied the complacent Western European Communist parties, which advocated working within the parliamentary framework, and opted for armed rebellion as the only means of destroying Anglo-American imperialism. Certainly the Strasbourg Congress proved that there was a lack of cohesiveness, to say the least, among European communists. There is no doubt that Moscow endeavored to shape the embryonic communist regimes in Eastern Europe and force upon them a Soviet-style system. Despite the blatant manipulation of East Europe, which was of strategic importance to the Russians, the Kremlin exerted far less influence on the communist parties of most noncommunist countries. It was each country's unique historico-structural developments that determined the course and policies of European as well as Asian and Latin American communist parties—not the Soviet Union as the American government argued.[15]

The embattled Greek Communist party entertained an ambiguous policy that stemmed from the divergence of opinions within the leadership. The KKE Politburo publicly advocated armed struggle against the regime and its imperialist supporters, but at the same time it was secretly negotiating a political settlement with Sophoulis to end the civil war. MacVeagh informed his superiors in Washington on 23 July 1947 that the KKE submitted the following terms as a basis for a political, rather than a military, solution.

> 1. Resignation of the present government. 2. Dissolution of Parliament. 3. Formulation of "pure center government" under Sophoulis with [the] cooperation of such [Liberal] leaders as Tsouderos, Plastiras and Mylonas. 4. Agreement between [the] new government and KKE on [the] basis of Sophoulis' policy of appeasement, i.e. general amnesty to those laying down arms, and [the] promise of new elections on [the] basis of revised electoral lists.[16]

The communists were faltering about their armed struggle and had the propensity to resolve the conflict by political methods. Sophoulis rejected the KKE's compromise proposal and denounced the guerrilla movement. The reasons for Sophoulis's rejection were twofold. First, it served the interests of the centrist parties to eliminate the communists from the political arena by scoring a military victory against them. Second, it was very clear to all politicians that American aid to Greece was contingent upon the eradication of communism. Pressure from Washington, therefore, made it impossible for any noncommunist political party to succeed in heading the government unless it adopted a hard anti-communist and pro-United States policy. Griswold and Loy Henderson chose Sophoulis to head a new coalition cabinet three months after the latter had rejected the KKE's proposal.

The Greek Communist party abandoned all hope for a negotiated settlement and dedicated its efforts to the armed struggle thereafter. The tragic Third Round, however, could have been avoided if the United States had been predisposed to accept a political rather than a military solution. A climate of compromise was simply impossible once American assistance was guaranteed to the regime in Athens, for such assistance carried with it an anti-communist policy that was the catalyst of inexorable hostilities between the guerrilla bands and the American-backed army. Finally, the KKE leadership's strategy of engaging its followers in a vain struggle which was a fait accompli, as the Soviet dictator presaged, was a most tragic mistake with dire consequences for the party and the entire nation.[17]

AMAG's Preeminence and the Failure of Foreign Aid

The Greek government knew that AMAG would have preeminent control of Greek affairs. What was not known, however, was the degree of the mission's powers and the effects of its policies on the country's economy and finances. When AMAG formally commenced operations in the middle of July, it was organized into a number of departments attached to the Greek ministries and public agencies. American experts in the mission included military officers, agronomists, engineers, industrial technicians, experts in the areas of finance, welfare, transportation, and labor relations.

AMAG placed under its supervision all branches of the Greek government and gave priority to the armed forces. One State Department memo ascertained that

> its [AMAG's] advisory services cover all segments of the Greek economy, including such matters as governmental administration and procedure, internal budgetary and fiscal controls, control of all foreign exchange resources, programming and control of imports . . . .[18]

The Mission was in the paramount position to exert all-embracing influence on Greek affairs because the Aid Agreement allowed for American officials to dominate the Currency Committee, the Foreign Trade Administration, and the Central Loan Committee, all vital networks in setting monetary, fiscal, and commercial policies.

The Counterpart Account was one of AMAG's most powerful tools in determining the financial policy of Greece. The drachmas derived from the sale of goods under the aid program were deposited in a special fund at the Bank of Greece. The mission had jurisdiction over those funds that were initially designated for reconstruction and economic-development projects. Eventually, the Counterpart funds were absorbed by the immense budget deficits, or they were blocked by AMAG in an attempt to halt inflation. C. A. Munkman, former UNRRA and AMAG official, has written that the Americans used the Counterpart Account to manipulate Greek financial policy.

> The policy of the government and of the Bank of Greece in turn was completely subordinated to the actions taken by the American Mission in making essential imports available to the economy. . . . However, apart from the policy control [enjoyed by the Currency Committee] the American Mission, through the counterpart account, was by far the largest depositor with the Bank of Greece and consequently was able to influence the credit situation by manipulation of this account.[19]

The Greek banking system was divided into agricultural and commercial banks whose function was to extend credit to the private sector. With the exception of the National Bank, the other banks had only limited deposits after the war. Thus they relied on the Bank of Greece for funds. The central bank was the state's official agent, and its most important function in the 1940s was to extend credit to the government to cover the budget deficits.

The first shipments of American assistance arrived belatedly in August 1947, just as the State Department entertained serious doubts concerning the prospects of an early recovery in Greece. Congress approved the Greek-Turkish Aid Bill with the understanding that the program would end in June 1948; there was no mention of a permanent United States presence in Greece. The State Department argued in August 1947 that "accomplishment of our economic objectives would be difficult under any circumstances, and continuation of adverse conditions in all important security and political fields will make their attainment impossible."[20]

The monumental task of reconstruction was indeed impossible in just a year's time, especially considering that military aid absorbed most of the funds earmarked for economic aid. Such reallocation of funds was carried out by AMAG with the recognition that Greece suffered immense wheat and other foodstuff deficits in the summer of 1947. Moreover, the mission restricted imports and tightened monetary policy in order to curb inflation. Such deflationary policies had an adverse effect on the economy, as was to be expected. Finally, the enunciation of the Truman Doctrine and the aid accompanying it had an ephemeral impact on the Greek business community. Neither the businessmen nor the politicians believed that a mere $300 million was sufficient to secure long-term monetary stability, especially since most of the funds were spent for defense. As a result of this lack of confidence, inflation was running at the rate of 50 percent annually and currency circulation increased from 537 billion drachmas in 1946 to 970 billion in 1947, indicative of the continuing trend of devaluation. Moreover, there were 100,000 unemployed workers in Athens alone with no immediate prospects of finding work. Finally, the cost-of-living index in the capital soared from 145.2 in 1946 to 174.6 in 1947.

The precipitous rise in defense expenditures after March 1947 resulted in greater budget deficits, which were in turn covered by funds that could have been devoted to economic revitalization. This process obviously prolonged economic dislocation. Reconstruction appropriations in fiscal 1946–47 were less than one-tenth of military and public security appropriations. In the same fiscal year, 35 percent of the budget was incorporated into the ministries of Army, Navy, Air Force, and Public Security. The central bank advanced 510 billion drachmas to the state in 1946 to cover the deficit and 882 billion ($176.4 million) in 1947. Given the state's immense defense expenditures and the regressive tax structure, the prospects of a speedy economic recovery analogous to that of Yugoslavia and most of the other North Balkan countries was unlikely in Greece.[21]

The American Mission for Aid to Greece accomplished very little in stimulating the civilian economy because it concentrated its efforts on the more exigent military problems. Consequently, agricultural production was 85.2 percent of the prewar (1938) level and industrial production was 67 percent of the 1939 level. There was a direct correlation between the low productivity rates and the incessant rise in the cost of living. The cost-of-living index jumped from 20,473 in August 1947 to 23,047 in November. The central bank's reserves had dwindled even further, reaching $5 million in September 1947. AMAG, therefore, had not inspired confidence in the economy, as was expected, and its policy advice had not yielded any positive results.

The Greek government informed the mission in November that $46 million of the $55 million of Greece's surplus property in the United States had been used, and the remaining $9 million was intended to cover future purchases. The Truman administration planned to allocate an additional $40 million to Greece for foodstuffs as conditions in the country degenerated further with the rise of the refugee population. Griswold maintained that increased economic and military assistance to Greece was necessary not only for strategic, but also for political considerations. Governor Griswold and Loy Henderson had become personally entangled in the formation of a new coalition government in which centrists, headed by Sophoulis, and the rightists, led by Tsaldaris, shared power. More aid was imperative to give the Americans in Athens more leverage with the precarious center-right coalition.[22]

The AMAG chief requested an additional $15.3 million in economic aid because import prices in foreign exchange had increased 10 percent since April 1947. He also asked for $50 million in relief costs for fiscal 1947–48. The refugee problem was politically sensitive for obvious reasons, and the mission pointed to it as one of the pernicious consequences of the civil war. The cost of the refugees to the state was enormous and, according to the American consulate in Thessaloniki, it constituted a major drain on the Treasury. The Consulate's report stated:

> The Greek Government has been spending recently 8.4 billion drachmas monthly for the care of displaced persons, equivalent to $1,680,000 at the rate of 5,000 drachmas to the dollar. For the care of 284,812 needy displaced persons from October 1, 1947 through June 30, 1948, the Greek Government has estimated that it will require 241,415 billion drachmas, the equivalent of $48,283,000.[23]

The American mission concluded in November 1947 that unless the military situation improved in favor of the national army, the refugee problem would "assume proportions as to threaten the national economy and stability of the government."

The national army was strengthened after November 1947, but the rebels were difficult to subdue, as is often the case in guerrilla warfare, partly because they enjoyed the assistance of the peasants and Greece's Balkan neighbors. Meanwhile, the civilian population was indignant toward the regime because the civil war took precedence over economic problems. The American Foreign Relief Program reached the following conclusions in its Second Report to Congress.

> In addition to the 430,000 refugees, the Ministry of Welfare, in November 1947, reported that 1,617,132 persons were certified

as indigent, yet of this number only 1,124,179 persons, substantially half a million fewer persons, were entitled to receive free rations. Only those indigents in communities [of] less than 3,000 received supplies free. Persons were defined as indigent if they had a monthly income of $6.25 in some localities to $15 in others.[24]

Despite the inability of foreign relief and aid programs to redress such conditions in Greece, Griswold believed in the efficacy of aid and went so far as to claim that AMAG had a record of numerous accomplishments. He maintained that construction was started on 1,647.1 kilometers of highway; on the Corinth Canal and the harbors of Thessaloniki; on two major railways (Brallo Tunnel and Gorgopotamos Bridge) and on five major airfields, all under the auspices of the Americans.

The rebuilding of the basic infrastructure was certainly an important part of the overall reconstruction process, and its value should not be underestimated. The construction projects that were undertaken under AMAG's auspices, however, were concentrated in northern Greece—the core of the Democratic Army's operations—and in the capital due to political and strategic considerations rather than economic. AMAG-sponsored projects, therefore, were mostly military-related, and practically all economic aid under Public Law 87 was devoted to such projects. From a total of $350 million, which Greece received in American aid during fiscal 1947–48, $82 million was expended on the rebuilding of the military-related infrastructure, while the rest went directly to defense and administrative expenses.

The mission's most serious shortcoming, by its own admission, was in the housing sector. An AMAG report stated: "The housing program exclusive of the provisions of refugee shelter, calls for the reconstruction of a total of 12,500 units by June 30 [1948]. As of February 29, 3620 units had been completed." The favorable results AMAG claimed pertained to refugee housing. Under its program, there were 1,381 temporary huts built and 6,250 rooms in war-damaged buildings which housed 6,404 families. The number of refugees, however, exceeded 500,000 by spring 1948, and the mission's program provided for only a fraction of that population.

AMAG's annual report (1948) maintained that the mission would revive the Greek industrial and agricultural production to surpass the prewar levels; that it would assist in the stimulation of exports while helping to reduce the nation's dependence on imports; that it would eliminate the wasteful and cumbersome bureaucracy; that it would strive toward a balanced budget, stabilize the currency, and strengthen the national economy. Every year that passed after that unduly optimistic report was compiled, the size of the government bureaucracy—the product of political patronage—increased, budget deficits burgeoned, the public debt soared, the economy was dominated by foreign capital, and Greece was left more dependent on the advanced capitalist countries.[25]

The Greeks remained largely unconvinced by the mission's promises and optimistic outlook on the economy. Both the liberal and conservative press disapproved of AMAG policies, though for different reasons. Spyros Markezines, an ultraconservative politician, charged that Washington did not provide sufficient assistance, particularly military, for Greece. He and others in the rightist camp assailed Greek officials who followed the advice of the Americans blindly regardless of the soundness of that advice. They argued that if the coalition government was unable to convince foreign advisers of their policy errors, then the entire cabinet must resign. A deep sense of nationalism coupled with the disillusionment with foreign aid prompted the conservatives to criticize AMAG policies.

Much of the criticism leveled against the mission was also due to the overbearing role of Governor Griswold in Greek politics. In October 1947 he approved sweeping tax increases which some conservatives opposed. One newspaper, *Nea Alitheia*, charged that United States officials and the Sophoulis/Tsaldaris administration did not have the "power to hit the pockets of the mighty and privileged [in approving Griswold's tax reform plan] so they found easy recourse of making up the deficit" by burdening the poor with additional consumption taxes.[26]

One critic, who had originally supported the Truman Doctrine, published the following article on 31 October 1947, denouncing Griswold's shortsightedness regarding fiscal policy.

> The complete disclosure of the inadequacy of the aid voted and of the ineffective handling has been brought about by the insistence of the American Mission to cover regular and extra public expenses by pitiless indirect taxation, which necessarily pushes prices upward, i.e., it leads straight to monetary inflation, and salaries will have to follow the rising cost of living. The 150 percent increase announced in customs duties, on the very day when [the] 23 countries that met in Geneva under the United

States' leadership signed 123 trade agreements [General Agreement on Tariffs and Trade, GATT] which inaugurated the worldwide American endeavor to obtain a lowering of import duties, is particularly unbelievable, as it will cause the already high Greek prices to soar even higher. It would have been infinitely better to have left the state budget unbalanced. The Greek public would have believed blindly in an American promise that aid would be continued in the future.[27]

The above article reflected the sentiments of many Greek capitalists and conservatives in the political arena who were opposed to any tax increases. It is interesting to note that the State Department urged Latin American countries during the late 1940s to remove trade barriers and accept the General Agreement on Tariffs and Trade, GATT, principles. Greece's case was so desperate, however, that even the laissez-faire-minded Americans realized that the state needed to be strengthened if it was to survive at all. The criticism expressed in the above article had some merit because the mission approved astronomical tax increases on essentials while leaving luxury items and income taxes untouched. That was indeed an irresponsible measure, for it accentuated hyperinflation after October 1947.

Considering AMAG's shortcomings in economic and financial matters, liberal political circles in Greece began casting doubts about the role of the Americans in the country. The liberals argued that a stringent monetary policy, combined with higher indirect taxes that affected the lower classes, retarded economic growth. By the end of 1947, therefore, there was only a small minority that gave tacit approval to the American mission's accomplishments in the country. In addition to the dissatisfaction with AMAG's policies, there was considerable resentment in the political arena and the bureaucracy toward Griswold, whom many considered a pretentious authoritarian. The pugnacious governor was a controversial figure because he was entrusted with comprehensive powers that left him in the prominent position of determining policy. The *New York Times* characterized him as "The Most Powerful Man in Greece" in a complimentary feature story published on 12 October 1947. The article depicted the Governor as diligent, pertinacious, and flamboyant. It emphasized that hardly any major decision in Greece was made without his approval.

Griswold was characteristically candid about his mission's paramount influence in Greece and about the role of the United States in that country's affairs. "It is my considered opinion," he wrote, "that it would be wrong for AMAG or for the US Government to attempt to present to world opinion that AMAG does not have great power or that it is not involved in Greek internal affairs." He went on to justify his Mission's exorbitant powers on the basis of endeavoring to administer American aid to Greece successfully. He denied, however, that he and his staff enjoyed "unlimited authority" as the press alleged.[28]

Secretary Marshall generally concurred with Griswold's line of reasoning, but he deplored press criticism of United States foreign policy in Greece. "While we agree it is necessary [that] US influence and control over funds be recognized in Greece," he noted, "we hope this can be accomplished through direct contacts of proper officials with Greek authorities and doubt that articles in [the] American press [are] useful in this respect." He warned that Western press reports alleging that America "had taken over Greece" were more injurious to the administration's foreign policy than any Soviet or communist propaganda.[29]

One year of AMAG policy directives and economic development initiatives left the United States with a preponderate role in Greek affairs, but did not result in better conditions for the people or for the national economy. Under AMAG there was no long-term reconstruction program; there was continued financial bankruptcy and the value of the currency plummeted; the capitalist class continued to invest in gold and dollars; the refugee problem was exacerbated and life for the masses deteriorated. American aid to Greece under AMAG had few constructive aspects, for it was designed to offer a military solution to a political problem that was caused by economic factors, social injustice, and an unrepresentative and brutal regime. The most noteworthy achievement of AMAG was that it laid the foundations for American ascendancy in Greece.

IV

Greece Under the Marshall Plan

The Marshall Plan, Greek Finances, and the Defense Budget

George C. Marshall delivered a historic speech on 5 June 1947 at Harvard University, thereby formally initiating the well-known Marshall Plan or European Recovery Program, ERP. Dean Acheson and George Kennan were the chief architects of the Marshall Plan, which was in some respects an extension of the Truman Doctrine and the prelude to the North Atlantic Treaty Organization, NATO. The ERP was necessitated by postwar economic and sociopolitical developments in Europe and the United States and was not designed simply as a reconstruction program.

The ERP was multifaceted, with the strategic and economic aspects assuming precedence. World War II left the European economy totally decimated, and the strategic and sociopolitical ramifications of the continent's economy had far-reaching consequences for the United States. European economic dislocation coincided with the emergence of communist regimes in Eastern Europe. These were linked to the Soviet Union politically, strategically, economically, and culturally. Moreover, the Maoist revolution was a fait accompli by the time Marshall announced his plan, and the tide of communist revolutions was sweeping across Korea and Vietnam. Such developments had a negative impact on the outward-looking American economy, whose continuous expansion depended to a large degree on securing markets and raw materials overseas. The markets of Eastern Europe and most of Asia were closed or severely limited, while Western Europe had reached its economic nadir during the late 1940s as its trade with the United States was negligible. American exports to Europe amounted to $14 billion in 1947, $3 billion in 1948, and a mere $.5 billion in 1949. The aggregate American exports to the world in 1947 amounted to $16 billion while the aggregate imports were half that amount. The state had to take decisive measures to stimulate foreign trade and strengthen Western Europe.

Prominent businessmen and political leaders in the United States were apprehensive about the possibility of a depression due to the dislocation of the world economy. A solution to the problem of the international economy was imperative for the survival of Western European capitalism. The State Department estimated that Europe's balance-of-payments deficit was $5 billion annually, excluding food and fuel supplies. To reestablish long-term equilibrium in the world economy, the Truman administration maintained that it was essential to provide the Europeans with $5 to $6 billion in aid annually for four years. The ambitious Four Year Plan under the ERP cost the American taxpayers $13 billion. It served the dual economic purpose of reviving European capitalism while providing markets for American goods and services.[1]

The Marshall Plan also served the geopolitical and strategic objectives of the United States. First, the Truman administration reaffirmed its unilateral foreign policy by initiating the Marshall Plan, for it bypassed the UN and multilateral agencies. Second, France, Italy, and Greece had dynamic communist parties with considerable popular support. The governments in those countries were politically vulnerable primarily because of economic dislocation. Ambassador Kennan and other policymakers in the Truman cabinet argued that Moscow would have benefited ultimately if Western Europe fell into an insoluble economic predicament with no prospects for recovery. Social unrest and political turmoil would have been the logical consequences of incessant economic dislocation, and the communists would have seized power. The Soviet bloc, therefore, would have been enhanced considerably, according to Kennan's scenario, by the inaction of the United States. The strengthening of the Western European capitalist economy was indispensable for the containment of communism and the survival of bourgeois regimes.[2]

Another aspect of the ERP, which can be categorized as both strategic and economic, involved the issue of raw materials and particularly minerals that North America lacked. The ERP was used to stockpile minerals from Europe's colonies and semi-colonies. The minerals were then transferred to the United States for its civilian and military needs. After the implementation of the Marshall Plan, Europeans were obliged to open their own markets, as well as those of their dependencies, to American corporate interests. One historian noted:

> Unless aid recipients contributed raw materials from their own colonies to the United States to offset the transfer of American goods to Europe, the Marshall Plan would inevitably hasten the already advanced depletion of United States resources.[3]

European colonies in Africa and Asia provided the United States with vital raw materials for domestic use and export, while Latin America served both as a supplier of raw materials and a market for American manufactured goods, surplus military hardware, and investment capital. The Third World, in other words, contributed directly and indirectly to Europe's postwar recovery and to the continued growth of the American economy.

Finally, there was a purely strategic factor in the ERP that was conducive to the triumph of American supremacy in the Western world. The Economic Cooperation Administration, ECA, the agency established to administer ERP aid, required that each member nation "set aside local currencies equivalent to at least 5 percent of aid received in United States dollars for the American government to buy strategic materials." The ERP recipients were obliged to meet America's defense quotas in Europe as part of the containment strategy designed to police the communist bloc.[4]

The strategic objectives of the United States were realized due to the phenomenal success of the Marshall Plan. General James Van Fleet, commander of the Joint United States Military Advisory and Planning Group in Greece, informed the State Department in November 1949, when the Greek civil war ended, that America's strategic aims in Europe had been achieved. He wrote:

> To further its long range strategic concepts, the US has established a solid belt around Western Europe and through the Mediterranean area including Norway, Holland, Belgium, France, Italy, Greece, Turkey and Iran, and it appears that Yugoslavia is

about to be absorbed into this belt. The US is financing the program necessary to mold this belt of nations into a unified whole. Thus the US must hold the preponderate position on all fronts in the establishment of policy inasmuch as the US provides the funds and the equipment for implementation.[5]

The Marshall Plan, which the United States projected to world public opinion as a humanitarian program designed to save the destitute European continent, was a complex plan that was intended to secure, above all, American strategic, economic, and political interests in the West. Nevertheless, it had a positive impact on Western Europe as it resulted in its recovery and led to economic integration that was essential for the region's competitive position in the world economy.

Andrej Vishinsky argued that the Marshall Plan was designed to place "European countries under the economic and political control of the United States and direct interference by the latter in the internal affairs of those countries." While that was certainly true for the duration of the Four Year Plan under ECA, the Western European nations managed to retain a great deal of their independence in many areas ranging from commerce to foreign policy. The United States was unable to exert a preponderate influence in European affairs as it did in inter-American affairs partly because the Western European countries already had advanced economic structures. Contrary to the official Soviet position on this issue, Western Europe could not be manipulated as easily by the aid donor as Third World countries. Greece, on the other hand, which was one of the sixteen ERP members, was an underdeveloped country that was reduced to an American satellite and succumbed easily to pressures from Washington. Furthermore, Greece was engulfed in a civil war whose fate was decided largely by the United States.[6]

The Marshall Plan was adopted in Greece when the Greek-American Economic Cooperation Agreement was signed on 2 July 1948. The AMAG relinquished its functions to the ECA/G, which was accountable to the Paris-based ECA. The American mission was reorganized and its functions centralized under the authority of Ambassador Henry F. Grady, who assumed MacVeagh's and Griswold's duties.

One of the principal objectives of the ERP was to stimulate European exports and raise foreign exchange so that the balance-of-payments deficits would be eradicated or at least reduced. While that goal was largely achieved by 1951 in most European countries—the United Kingdom and Italy suffered notable trade deficits under the

ERP—Greece lagged far behind Western Europe in almost every sector, and it had the lowest standard of living in Europe. Greece's trade deficit amounted to $1,199,651,000 between 1948 and 1951, indicative of the dismal failure of foreign aid as a stimulus to an underdeveloped economy. The United States, which was Greece's principal trading partner, imported an average of 16.9 percent of Greek exports under the ERP, while during the same four-year period Greece imported an annual average of 36.6 percent of its aggregate imports from the United States. Since American officials were responsible for the direction of Greece's foreign trade, they obstructed the country from pursuing a multilateral foreign-trade policy that would have served its best interests.[7]

Legislative Decree No. 588 was one of the legal devices which the American mission used to apportion considerable authority to itself under ECA/G. Under that law, the Currency Committee determined the procedure and supervision of all credit allocation. The state was ultimately responsible for formulating credit policy, but the state was acting under the advice of the American agencies in Athens. Charles Coombs, AMAG financial expert and former Currency Committee member, devised Law 588. The object of that law was to centralize the nation's credit network so that the United States mission would be in a propitious position to implement a financial program more efficaciously and without becoming exposed to public scrutiny.

The law required the National Bank of Greece to deposit 15 percent of its total deposits with the central bank. The other commercial banks were obliged to deposit 5 percent with the Bank of Greece. The National Bank had 263 billion drachmas, or 75 percent of the total deposits of public organizations. The United States Embassy argued that the National Bank "has won an incomparable position in the Greek banking system and is seriously handicapping other commercial banks." The National Bank had 346 billion of the total 506 billion drachmas of the aggregate banking capital in October 1948. Because of its monopolistic position and the restructuring of the banking system under the aegis of the Americans, the National Bank was compelled to strengthen the central bank, whose policy was determined by the mission.

There were many nuances to Law No. 588, some of which warrant further elucidation since they affected the country's economy. First, the mission wanted to immobilize a sizable sum of the bank deposits in order to create a deflationary effect on the economy. That was achieved with relative success, but only at the expense of sluggish economic growth and widespread suffering among the working class and peasantry—hardly the most prudent policy option for an anemic economy. Second, the mission hoped that the banks would be discouraged from extending large credits to the private sector without adequate reserves, especially since a sizable portion of the loans were directed toward speculative ventures. Third, the law required the commercial banks to submit monthly statements of their business loans to the Currency Committee, which was the overseer of Greece's financial network. Finally, the banking system became rigidly centralized under the Currency Committee's authority because Greece's finances were enhanced to a limited degree by the stimulation that American aid provided.[8]

The second paragraph of Article II of Law No. 588 vividly illustrates the regimentation of Greece's financial network under the Currency Committee.

> The Currency Committee shall determine from time to time by its decisions the details of the financing of each branch of production, the total amounts of credits to be granted and the terms and preliminary conditions under which they are to be made available by banks, other credit organizations or any other kind of public law organization whatsoever, either out of their own funds or out of funds made available to them by the Bank of Greece.[9]

The Currency Committee enjoyed more comprehensive powers in Greece than any other public or private entity. The destiny of Greece's finances/economy, therefore, rested in the hands of American officials.

C. A. Munkman noted that between 1948 and 1952 "all expenditures of capital development, directly or indirectly, were controlled by the American Mission." The American officials in Greece enjoyed such unprecedented authority over Greek financial affairs partly because of two key agreements that were signed in 1948. The National Mortgage Bank of Greece, the government, and the AMAG signed an agreement on 30 March 1948 that provided $3.9 million for the development of the mining and manufacturing sectors. The second agreement, which the government, the mission, and the Agricultural Bank of Greece signed on 5 May, provided $7 million to stimulate growth in agriculture and fisheries. Considering that American foreign assistance to Greece between fiscal 1947–48 and 1950–51 amounted to an incredible $1,672.6 billion, the funds allocated for mining, agriculture, manufacturing, and fisheries were negligible. Furthermore, it was a small price to pay for the United States government, whose mission regimented Greece's economy.[10]

The Currency Committee continued to regulate the operations of the banking system throughout the civil war. In January 1949 the commercial banks were compelled to hold 22 percent of their resources in reserve for the demand-and-time deposits of public organizations and 10 percent for all other deposits. "A year later reserve requirements increased once again; this time banks were required to hold in reserve 25 percent of the demand and time deposits of public agencies and corporations and 12 percent of all other demand and time deposits." As the banking system became more centralized under the auspices of the mission, the Bank of Greece assumed more authority in the country's financial structure.[11]

The American Mission enjoyed as much influence in Greece's fiscal policy as it did in monetary and credit policies. The AMAG initiated a program of increased indirect taxes, a wage/salary freeze across the board, and credit controls in March 1948. Governor Griswold anticipated that such measures would reduce inflation, stabilize the currency, and generate more revenues to cover the chronic budget deficits. The mission authorized a 25 percent increase for cigarettes and an 8 percent increase for bread. Such policies were extremely burdensome to the lower classes and stifled development. Nevertheless, Ambassador Grady estimated that revenues generated from indirect taxes would reduce the prospective 1948-49 budget deficit by 600 billion drachmas, and the money saved would then be devoted to reconstruction projects.

Unfortunately, the precipitous rise in taxes, which coincided with price increases, proved inflationary, and the budget deficits soared as the defense expenditures burgeoned amid the civil war. Consequently, the mission's fiscal policy was unpopular, for it failed in its purpose. Organized labor, whose leadership was sympathetic to the regime and the mission, objected vehemently to the wage/salary freeze policy because prices were allowed to rise and income taxes, as well as business taxes, were not considered as alternative methods of raising revenues. Moreover, the actual budget deficit for 1948-49 was grossly underestimated by the American officials in Athens, leaving the politicians seriously concerned. The national budget, which was prepared under the mission's supervision, was submitted to Parliament on 28 September 1948, three months after the previous fiscal year had ended. The reason for the long delay was that Ambassador

Grady actually vetoed the administration's bloated budget in July as it did not conform to his directives.[12]

An Indian newspaper excoriated Grady's veto and questioned the stipulations that Washington placed on all foreign aid. The article explained Grady's overbearing role in Greek internal affairs as follows:

> Dr. Grady sends a strong note to the Greek Government vetoing the Greek Budget on the ground that it contains expenditures other than agreed upon between the Greek Government and the American Mission. . . . The important point is that, wise or foolish, good or bad, it is the Budget drawn up and agreed upon by the Greek Government and vetoed by an American Ambassador. And a country's budget is the expression of its policy in the exercise of its sovereignty. Where then does the sovereignty of Greece lie? Until this question is fully elucidated, there will be some uneasiness in debtor nations and the would-be-borrowers will become more cautious.[13]

The United States government justified its inordinate powers in Greece on the grounds that American aid kept the regime from collapse and the country from falling under communist control.

Appropriations for defense expenditures totaled 1,974 billion drachmas and nonmilitary appropriations amounted to 1,949 billion. The projected deficit for fiscal 1948–49 was 700 billion drachmas, but 500 billion would have been covered by foreign aid. Hence, the estimated deficit was 200 billion drachmas. The fiscal planners assumed that the civil war would end in 1948 and had not calculated the extraordinary defense expenditures in the budget. Military and relief expenditures were estimated with a 25-percent reduction rate in the first half of the fiscal year to be followed by a 50-percent reduction in the second half. Since the guerrilla war ended in October 1949, the military and relief savings were not realized and supplementary expenditures for those sectors were required, thereby resulting in still higher deficits.[14]

The conservative and liberal press assailed the government in Washington for not providing sufficient assistance for Greece and driving the country deeper into debt. One newspaper, *Kathimerini*, maintained that, according to the report of the Supreme Council of Reconstruction Committee, the prospective budget deficit would be one trillion drachmas, not 200 billion as the mission estimated. Other newspapers pointed out that ERP funds were unjustly transferred from vital reconstruction programs to the defense budget.

The ECA/G authorized the Greek government to divert 500 billion drachmas from the reconstruction program to cover the budget deficit for fiscal 1948–49. The total expenditures for the fiscal year amounted to 4,387 billion drachmas, leaving a 937 billion drachma deficit. To avert a possible wrecking of the state's finances, American officials hastily recommended raising direct taxes, while at the same time they imposed drastic reductions on nondefense spending. The government adopted the above measures and reduced the deficit to 622 billion drachmas, which was covered by the Counterpart fund.[15]

Budget deficits persisted throughout the postwar years partly because of the regressive tax structure and the ever-rising defense spending. Military expenditures absorbed 47 percent of the budget, or 9.4 percent of the entire national income, between 1948 and 1952. The net indebtedness of the state to the Bank of Greece continued to soar after the Truman Doctrine. The following chart illustrates the trend of government borrowing in billions of drachmas.[16]

1947	1948	1949	1950	1951	1952
882	1,097	2,861	3,549	5,577	6,057

Since the defense budget grew progressively higher after the civil war ended, it cannot be argued that exigent conditions merited such exorbitant spending.

The Organization for European Economic Cooperation, OEEC, an agency responsible for European economic integration created after the enunciation of the Marshall Plan, concluded in its 1952 report that the defense budget of Greece absorbed a great percentage of the GNP. It stated:

> The increase in defense expenditures will absorb, between 1951 and 1953–54, about 22 percent of the increase in the gross national product at factor cost; the percentage of the gross national product absorbed by the defense expenditure will rise from 8.6 in 1951 to 9.3 in 1953–54.[17]

To place this issue into a broader perspective, the following chart provides a lucid comparison of the defense allocations of six NATO countries in fiscal 1952–53. The chart shows the percentage of the budget allotted by each country.[18]

Greece	42%
Turkey	33
Italy	23
France	32
Holland	27
Belgium	23

The conservative governments in Athens, which the United States backed, opted for a strong defense, especially as relations between Greece and Turkey were strained over the Cyprus issue. Ultimately, however, responsibility for the disproportionate defense spending lies with Washington, which provided Greece with military assistance and policy advice on strategic affairs.

The American mission announced in 1952 that the United States government had decided to discontinue subsidizing the Greek budget. The government of Prime Minister Alexandros Papagos, which was installed by the Americans, retaliated immediately. As Munkman put it:

> The impossibility of establishing budgetary equilibrium without cutting military expenditure is obvious. Consequently the Greek Government and press stated that unless the United States supported the budget by a definite grant, the army establishment would be cut. As a result a specific grant (described as for military aid) provided to meet the 1953–54 deficit of 750 million drachmas increased to 1,050 million in 1954–55 estimates ($1 = 30 drachmas).[19]

The United States retained its preeminent influence on the Greek military establishment and exerted more control over the country's defense policy than did the indigenous military high command. It was possible to do so because of American military aid to Greece. Finally, it must be stressed that since 1947 Greek defenses were designed to suit the United States global policy of containment militarism, rather than Greece's regional requirements. There has been a consensus in Greece on this issue that has developed regardless of political affiliations and ideological leanings. The first attempt to redirect the defenses to meet the country's own requirements was made in 1981 by Prime Minister Andreas Papandreou.[20]

After the termination of the civil war, General Van Fleet concluded that American strategic interests in Greece were designed not simply to eliminate the threat of communism, but also to install a permanent presence in the country that would police the menacing communist bloc. According to Van Fleet:

> The geo-political position and military strategic position of Greece remain unchanged from the time [the] "Truman" doctrine was announced. However, it appears that the strategic control of the Mediterranean area by [the] US has increased since that announcement. Greece offers an important base for the collection of strategic intelligence. US year to year policy must be changed to a long term policy. *The US is here to stay.* Greece can be [a] secondary front to Soviet diversion in [the] event of war. Also, its strategic position has greatly increased. Greeks will fight, are a good investment. [Emphasis added.][21]

Eventually, Athens became one of the major centers of Central Intelligence Agency operations and Greece the host of American military bases. Greece, Turkey, and Iran—the Northern Tier—became part of an American regional strategic network, subordinating their own national security interests to those of the United States.

The Four-Year Plan in Greece

Ambassador Grady delivered a speech on 28 November 1948 on Athens radio regarding the relevance of the Marshall Plan to Greece. He emphasized that the ERP was above all a humanitarian program and added that the United States was resolved to emphasize the revitalization of the devastated European economy for the sake of peace, prosperity, and the containment of communism. He then introduced the Greek Four Year Plan, stressing that it was purely a "Greek plan, drawn by your Ministers and technicians after long and careful study of the many complex problems which the country faces today." He admitted that the Greek officials "worked closely with their American colleagues," but he did not point out that members of his embassy and mission were the chief architects of the plan.

Stefanos Stefanopoulos, minister of coordination, also delivered a speech on the virtues of the Marshall Plan and the Four Year Plan. He did not divulge the specifics of the program because the OEEC had not approved it. He stressed, however, that "the economic problem of Greece is characterized by inadequacy of cultivable land and shortage of capital equipment in the country on the one hand and by a rapid increase of the population on the other." The minister of coordination maintained that unemployment and chronic underemployment must be eliminated if the nation was to experience substantial economic recovery.[22] The general objectives of the Reconstruction Plan were outlined as follows:

> 1. Execution of large projects for a speedy industrialization of the country. 2. Exploitation of hydraulic energy to secure cheap electric power and development of solid fuel (lignite) in the country to develop power in Greece are set as basic prerequisites for industrialization. The exploitation of hydraulic energy will also facilitate the progress of agriculture, a revival of the countryside and a checking of movement of rural dwellers toward the cities, in combination with execution of hydraulic and land improvement projects on a large scale.[23]

According to the minister's estimates, 40 percent of the total investment under the plan was to be spent on industrial development.

Hydroelectricity was given priority as the foundation for rebuilding the infrastructure and eventually for industrializing the country. Industrialization, however, as defined by the plan, entailed the exploitation of minerals. There were no plans to build new industries in locations other than the capital, which was already overpopulated. The development of waterpower took precedence because it would reduce the nation's dependence on expensive imported fuels while making possible the rise of agricultural output, flood control, and drainage works. It is interesting to note that the United States entertained a general policy of fostering the development of the infrastructure and agricultural sectors of Third World economies. Projects similar to those of Greece, for example, were underway in many Latin American countries during the same period and were financed by North American credits and loans.

Stefanopoulos predicted that by 1950 industrial production would rise to 115 percent of the prewar level and agricultural production to 119 percent of the prewar level. He expected a 10 percent reduction in imports of consumer goods and a 70 percent increase in imports of construction materials. Exports were expected to rise 26 percent above prewar levels, and an additional 280,000 jobs would be created by the Four Year Plan. Finally, the minister accurately predicted that the balance-of-payments deficit would not be eradicated by the program because Greece was not expected to reduce its debt and foreign trade deficit.[24]

The Four Year Plan was doomed to fail from its inception for several reasons. First, it required immense United States economic aid on a long-term basis "whereas it was the practice of Congress to vote appropriations to ECA for one year ahead only." Second, it was inadequately funded because the governments in Washington and Athens reduced reconstruction expenditures at various intervals during the program. Third, there was gross abuse of funds by Greek administrators. Fourth, the plan emphasized the development of infrastructure and the primary sector of production with no mention of the capital-goods sector. Finally, fund-appropriation authority for all projects rested with the mission, not the Greek government. Consequently, American officials made decisions to finance projects they deemed necessary for the country, rather than allowing the local authorities to make such decisions.

The question regarding the plan's financing is most perplexing because funds that were originally earmarked for economic aid were transferred to defense, and economic-aid funds that were earmarked for industrial projects went for agriculture or other sectors. The internal cost of the program was estimated at $600 million on the basis of the Greek 1948 price level at 6 trillion drachmas. The mission estimated the cost of the plan at $546 million, of which $343 million emanated from American aid and $203 million from Greece's own resources. For fiscal 1948–49 the ECA/G approved $67.4 million for reconstruction and development and for the uncovered dollar deficit. Of the above sum, $3.1 million was in dollar aid, $46.3 million was in ERP drawing rights, and $18 million was to be contributed from the Greek sterling resources that constituted part of the British war debt. Of the total annual aid package amounting to $390.6 million for fiscal 1948–49, only $49.4 million was allocated for reconstruction and development, and a substantial part of that was cover for the country's dollar deficit.[25]

Greece financed part of the Four Year Plan from the $105 million reparations settlement with Italy. According to the Greek-Italian Agreement, which was signed on 31 August 1949, the reparations were discharged in five annual installments in the form of industrial machinery and tools, several ships, and consumer goods. Greece also received an additional $10 million in reparations from Germany and it, too, was devoted to the reconstruction program. Its own resources, however, were still insufficient to finance the Four Year Plan.

120   Intervention and Underdevelopment

The ECA in Paris did not fully endorse the Greek plan, and the ERP administrator, Paul Hoffman, an American businessman, did not believe that the program would be completed on schedule. In the spring of 1950 the original plan was revised because very little had been accomplished hitherto. In the revised program communications and electrical power were earmarked for 23.5 percent and 14.3 percent, respectively, of the total program expenditure. Agriculture and fisheries were to receive 13.2 percent, while industry was earmarked for 17.9 percent. The remainder of the designated $663.5 million reconstruction package was for housing, public health, land reclamation, mining, sanitation and water-supply projects, education, refugee rehabilitation, and tourism. The Four Year Plan had proved unsuitable for the country's needs and, as will be seen below, even the plan that was finally implemented ended in failure.[26]

The Failure of ERP in Greece

The basic infrastructure of Greece was largely completed by the end of the Four Year Plan, but industrialization, which was not one of the objectives of the American planners, was not achieved. The object of the reconstruction program was to foster the primary sector of production and retain Greece as an exporter of raw materials and an importer of manufactured goods and capital. Furthermore, the reconstruction plan was designed to pave the way for direct foreign investment. "Under the initial AMAG program continued under the ECA," wrote Munkman, "groups of American contractors moved into Greece to rebuild the Port of Piraeus, open the Corinth Canal, repair the damaged railways, and build or repair principal strategic roads."[27]

Some construction projects were defective because of rampant corruption and lack of proper supervision. Ambassador Grady noted in June 1949 that the civil authorities in Patras were accused of misusing ECA funds that were appropriated for work-relief projects. A State Department report revealed in September 1949 that "the Greek highways rebuilt under American construction program were breaking up already due to poor engineering or materials, hasty construction during winter weather for military reasons, etc." There were considerable repairs on faulty road construction that contributed to the overall cost overrun of the reconstruction projects. Commenting on the abuses of the reconstruction program by contractors and public officials, Professor Stavrianos wrote:

Roger D. Lapham, the ECA chief in Greece, disclosed on April 19, 1951, that two American highway construction advisers were asked to leave Greece. A dozen Greek contractors and members of the Ministry of Public Order were being investigated concerning irregularities involving $500,000, and the Greek Government was asked to rebate $100,000 mispent on one road project.[28]

It is interesting to note that American firms had a reputation of defective and costly work and of dealing with corrupt public officials in many underdeveloped countries. There was a big scandal in Ecuador, for example, involving an American construction firm charged with the task of building the Quevedo-Manta Highway during the mid-1940s. There, too, American funds and advisers were used to help build the country's infrastructure. There was indeed a pattern of abuses involving American aid or loans to the Third World, American businesses, and local public officials.

The American officials in Athens were in a paramount position to help launch Greece into the age of industrialization so that it would be able to compete effectively with the other European countries. Instead the mission chose to keep Greece on the periphery of the world economy. This was accomplished by the manipulation of the credit network as well as by the fiscal and monetary policies for which the American advisers were responsible. The Central Loan Committee, which was dominated by American officials and which enjoyed veto power over every loan, initially financed eight loans totaling $9,133,700. By July 1949 the committee had approved twenty-five loans amounting to $17,540,524. The British-owned Athens-Piraeus Electricity Company was the recipient of the largest loan, while companies manufacturing chemicals, cement, copper, paper, and other essential materials were also granted loans.[29]

Long-term loans for the revitalization of private businesses amounted to $12,987,000 in 1949 to be spent abroad and 33,343 million drachmas to be spent domestically. The amounts increased to $40,343,000 and 260,000 million drachmas, respectively, in 1950. The above funds emanated from foreign aid and the Counterpart Account. The Central Loan Committee guaranteed $80.5 million during its existence between 1948 and 1954. All loans were repayable in dollars and were allocated as follows: "52.4 percent to manufacturing, 14.7 percent to agriculture and fishing, 13.4 percent to mining, 12.4 to power, 5.4 percent to communications and transportation and 1.7 percent to tourism." The aggregate bank credits to the economy from 1949 to 1952 were 18,988 billion drachmas, of which 3,125 billion were devoted to industry. The value of industrial production showed a significant recovery under the Marshall Plan, but that cannot be attributed to the ECA's plans to industrialize Greece since only light industry experienced growth. Thus, there was vertical expansion—established industries benefited—rather than horizontal development—new industries—in the secondary sector of the economy. In any event, industrial production was 87 percent of the 1939 level in 1949, while in 1951 it reached a peak at 125 in comparison to the prewar level. Thereafter, industry experienced a period of stagnation because economic aid was severely limited and the banks were compelled to curtail credit allocation to fight inflation.[30]

Neither the indigenous capitalist class nor the government made any genuine efforts in the late 1940s and early 1950s to industrialize Greece to levels comparable to those of most East European countries. The American mission, therefore, was not solely responsible for the lack of Greek industrial development. The private and public sectors invested the lowest percentage of the national income in comparison to other European nations, as the following chart indicates.[31]

Greece	8.5%
West Germany	23
Scandinavia	30
Western Europe	15–30

The statistics in the previous chart are applicable for 1952, but Greek investment in productive works remained the lowest in Europe throughout the 1950s and never exceeded 10 percent of the national income. The next chart delineates the percentage of public investment in the various sectors of the economy between 1948 and 1952.[32]

Transportation	36.9%
Housing	17.0
Electrical power	8.6
Agriculture, forestry, fisheries	16.8
Mining and manufacturing	1.7
Public administration	18.8

The state devoted most of its investment capital to the infrastructure and the primary sector of production at the expense of investment in heavy industry. That policy was in accord with the American advice since 1947, but the Greek state and capitalist class were resigned to the fact that structural development would be unrealistic for a country with limited capital resources, technicians, and scientists.

Andreas Papandreou, who served as director of the Center for Economic Research in the early 1960s, wrote in 1962 that the Four Year Plan (the 1950 version) had not achieved its own objectives of "development of resources, a reduction of unemployment and the achievement of a tolerable standard of living." He argued that Greece's monumental economic problems could have have been rectified only by the development of the secondary sector of production.[33]

Industrialization was possible under the ECA program, but it was deliberately precluded for a number of reasons. Greece received $648 million under the AMAG program, but only $119 million was actually allocated for economic assistance. Under the ECA plan the government received $550 million in economic aid, but only $150 million was spent on reconstruction and economic development. The remaining $400 million was used to cover the budget deficits and the balance-of-payments deficits. Defense spending and the financing of American imports, therefore, absorbed the capital resources that could have been devoted to economic development.

The Counterpart Account funds were sufficient to enhance the financing of the Four Year Plan, but the mission blocked them. In 1948 there were 219,801 million unused drachmas in that account, while in 1952 the amount soared to 7,446,362 million. Those funds were ostensibly intended for agricultural and industrial development, but the United States officials in Athens did not release the funds for a number of reasons. First, the circulation of such an immense amount of money would have created even higher monetary inflation in the volatile economy at a time when the mission's primary goal was to bring it down. Second, the funds were held back to cover the budget and balance-of-payments deficits. Third, the Counterpart Account, as Munkman noted, was the key to the mission's control of Greece's monetary policy. Finally, United States foreign economic policy was designed not to foster the industrial development of underdeveloped countries, but to perpetuate the export-oriented segment of those economies.[34]

Before elucidating fully the precise method that the mission adopted to prevent Greece from industrializing, it should be pointed out that the country's commercial dependence on the United States was one of the factors in the former's inability to industrialize. The government in Athens and the ECA/G deliberated on the balance-of-payments issue in June 1949. They proposed the following measures: "a. flexible subsidies to be obtained through corresponding import levies, b. multiple exchange rates for imports and exports, and c. general revaluation of the drachma to a more realistic rate." Greece imported at the rate of $450 million annually and exported at the rate of $150 million in 1949. The above measures were designed to redress the gross trade imbalance that American and Greek officials attributed to overpricing Greek products in the world market, the inflated drachma, and the loss of prewar markets, especially Germany and Eastern Europe. The State Department and the IMF gave similar advice to other Third World nations that were dependencies of the West. Devaluation of the currency, curtailment of government spending on development projects and social programs, liberalization of trade, restriction of credit extension, and extension of lucrative terms to foreign investors have been the prescription that the IMF and the United States government passed on to underdeveloped countries since Bretton Woods in 1944. The results have been greater dependence on the United States by the periphery countries and inability to foster independent industrial development.[35]

The responsibility for the balance-of-payments deficit rested particularly with the Foreign Trade Administration, FTA, which was headed by an American official. The FTA's policies were designed to stimulate the export sector and perpetuate the consumer-oriented economy of Greece. The balance-of-payments deficit before the war was 16 percent of the total foreign payments, and the country's exports covered 60 percent of the imports. In 1952, under *Americanokratia*, the exports covered only 28 percent of the imports, and the balance-of-payments deficit was 55 to 60 percent of the aggregate foreign payments. The OEEC report of 1952 stated: "The deficit in the balance of payments on current account, which was about 60 percent of external expenditure from 1948 to 1952 and will remain very high in the coming years, is certainly the most urgent problem for the Greek economy."[36]

The United States government assistance program subsidized a large percentage of Greece's balance-of-payments deficit for the duration of the ERP. It was precisely that process which led to foreign trade and financial dependence on the United States once aid ended and was replaced by trade. The table below compares the per-capita trade of Greece with that of other OEEC members in 1951, and it shows that the former remained a net importer while the latter recovered much faster under the Marshall Plan.[37]

Country	Imports	Exports
Greece	$52.39	$13.38
France	106.92	98.25
Germany	69.40	68.80
Italy	45.33	34.86
Turkey	19.20	15.00

The next table compares Greece's imports which were financed by exports against those of other ERP recipients and shows the degree to which the former lagged behind those of other countries.

Greece	28%
Turkey	78
Italy	77
France	92

It is important to emphasize that 90 percent of Greece's foreign trade during the early Cold War was with North America and Western Europe. Trade diversification, which was absolutely imperative for the country's economic as well as political interests, was precluded by trade dependence on the West. The government in Washington prevented Greece from engaging in regional economic integration by discouraging commercial relations with Eastern Europe, the Soviet Union, and, to a lesser extent, the Arab world. Given Greece's geographical proximity to the aforementioned countries, it was contrary to its interests not to have extensive relations with them.[38]

The American mission had publicly vowed to make Greece self-sufficient through the aid program. Although self-sufficiency should not be misconstrued as autarchy since that is impossible in a world of interdependence, the general idea was that Greece would attain a balance in its foreign payments. The ECA country report of 1949 concluded that Greece could not achieve peace, financial stability, reconstruction, and development without foreign aid. Upon the termination of the ERP, the nation was less self-sufficient and had not achieved the reconstruction and development goals that the ECA/G set for itself. One critic of American intervention in Greece wrote the following concerning the results of foreign aid.

> For all the grandiose talk about reconstruction there has been no reconstruction in Greece. Both industrial and agricultural

levels of the country are still [in the middle of 1950] below prewar levels. General William A. Methany, former chief of the Air Section of the U.S. Military Mission in Greece, told a *Christian Science Monitor* reporter (on September 8, 1949) that only 15 percent of the many millions of dollars we have poured into Greece during the past two-and-a-half years have gone to help the economic recovery of the country. All the rest has gone for direct and indirect army expenditures.[39]

Military expenditures, as stated above, took precedence over economic-development programs. Based on the Greek government's records, American economic aid to Greece for fiscal 1947–48 and fiscal 1949–50 was earmarked at $760.7 million. The military got $476.8 million.

Of the cumulative aid amounting to $1,237.5 million for the three-year period under AMAG and ECA, only $232 million was actually spent on reconstruction and economic development. Indubitably, aid did stimulate economic growth, but it did not contribute to Greece's structural development. One economist drew the following conclusion concerning appropriation of aid funds to Greece.

> During these two years (fiscal 1948–1949 and 1949–1950) economic aid (earmarked at $530.5 million) was used either directly or indirectly for military expenditures and also for purposes of keeping the economy going on a day-to-day basis. So while other countries were using aid to reconstruct their economies and build a solid basis for later growth, Greece had to spend her share on purposes far removed from economic development.[40]

Unlike other members of the Organization for European Economic Cooperation, Greece was immersed in a costly civil war. Damages to property resulting from the guerrilla war have been estimated at $250 million and military expenditures at $750 million. An unofficial source calculated that the civil war absorbed 84.7 percent of the cumulative foreign aid that Greece received to the end of 1949. The total foreign aid amounted to $2,138 million, of which $1,812 million accounted for losses sustained as a result of the guerrilla war. The bulk of American aid, therefore, was devoted to the military and not to economic development.[41]

Despite the enormous cost of the civil war, it was possible for Greece to initiate industrial development under the ECA/G. The American mission, however, as noted above, did not have such plans. The ECA and the State Department had decided that Greece did not have an industrial base or the technical personnel to industrialize, as did Western Europe. It was decided, therefore, that Greece must develop its mining, agricultural, fishing, and consumer-goods industries—in short, the established sectors. Paul Hoffman reflected this view in a 1949 ECA report. In proposing the most efficacious method to alleviate underemployment in the countryside, he stated:

> New and expanded food and other processing, manufacturing, and [the] mining industry can provide the basis for this employment. Essentially Greece needs to look to the development of industries requiring a relatively large percentage of employment per $1000 of product and *not the development of heavy industries requiring large investments per worker.* [Emphasis added.][42]

The above formula was in fact a prescription for perpetual underdevelopment; a number of contemporary Greek officials and scholars disagreed with the view of Hoffman and the State Department regarding Greece's industrialization.

The secretary general of the Supreme Reconstruction Council, S. Agapitides, argued in an article published in 1950 that industrialization was the only possible solution for reducing Greece's unemployment and structural underemployment. He maintained that 60 percent of the rural population was far in excess of the labor force required to cultivate the land. Even with the modest modernization of agriculture, which promised to make more land available for cultivation, there was still 20 percent surplus labor in the countryside. "Only industrialization," wrote Agapitides, "could absorb the country's surplus manpower."[43]

Studies conducted under the auspices of the Center for Economic Research in Athens during the early 1960s arrived at the same conclusion as Agapitides. Professor Angellopoulos estimated that in 1953 one million of the four million people in the labor force were idle as unemployment and underemployment among peasants stood at 40 percent. The OEEC Report of 1952 corroborated the figures and conclusions that Angellopoulos reached. Urban unemployment, according to OEEC, was about 150,000, while rural unemployment and underemployment was 1,000,000. Yet there was nothing but promises in the Four Year Plan to redress this catastrophic problem, which plagued Greece throughout the 1950s.[44]

The country's valuable mineral deposits, especially bauxite, which was in abundance, were part of the answer to the question of industrialization. Hugh Seton-Watson noted in his illuminating study on Eastern Europe:

> Greece more than any East European country needs a programme of planned industrialization. Its foundations can only be the mineral resources and water power of the country. Instead of exporting minerals, Greece must work them in her own industry and export the more valuable semi-finished products.[45]

Land, mines, and labor were all underutilized—partly because the American advisers discouraged central planning along the lines followed by the communist countries or even a policy mix of state and privately initiated industrial development.

All Eastern European countries had introduced short-term recovery plans by 1948 and long-term development plans by 1950 once the communist regimes had consolidated power. The purpose of the reconstruction plans was to meet or exceed prewar production levels in most sectors and to begin laying the foundations for structural development. That entailed sweeping land reforms, nationalization of industry and the financial apparatus, and the monopoly of foreign trade by the state. Almost invariably, the emphasis of the long-term programs was on the development of heavy industry, rather than on agriculture and light industry, as was the case in Greece. The results of the short-term economic plans were most impressive, as the following chart indicates.

INDUSTRIAL OUTPUT, 1938–50[46]

Country		1938	1939	1945	1946	1947	1948	1949	1950
Gross output									
Albania	(—)		100	24	97	159	254	306	395
Bulgaria	(1939)		100	106	97	102			
	(1956)			100			203	268	309
Greece	(1939)		100	106		56	71	77	93	117
Romania	(1938)	100	102	56					
	(1955)	100							147
Yugoslavia	(1955)		100	106	(32–37)	84	113	159	177	182

Commenting on the progress of Eastern Europe's centrally planned economies during the late 1940s and early 1950s, Seton-Watson noted:

These far-reaching plans strike the imagination. Even a foreign observer cannot fail to be affected by the enthusiasm and optimism of the planners. Moreover it is certain that large-scale industrialisation, public works and mechanisation of agriculture are the right remedies for the rural over-population and poverty, and the lack of manufactured goods, which were so striking in the old Eastern Europe. It is also understandable that the new regimes should wish, from a general feeling of patriotism, to diminish their countries' economic dependence on foreign countries.[47]

There is no doubt that the Eastern European people had to make sacrifices for long-term structural development, and the region was ultimately dependent on the Soviet Union. But the Greek people, too, made enormous sacrifices, and their country was dependent on the United States. The difference between the North Balkan countries and Greece was that the former—with the exception of Albania—established firm foundations for long-term development and were able to elevate the standard of living without mass emigration.[48]

Despite the progress that most Eastern European nations made by undertaking the structural development of their economies by central planning, Greece failed to emulate her neighbors due to political as well as socioeconomic considerations. The American mission was the major obstacle in that regard. It rejected the Greek government's proposal to exploit the coal deposits of Central Macedonia. The bauxite mines fell under the semicontrol of the Americans since it is well-known that bauxite is one strategic mineral that the United States lacks. The rich mineral resources were not utilized as the basis for industrial development because that would have entailed statist policies, which the American advisers vehemently opposed. It would have also meant sweeping agrarian reforms and agricultural modernization to create a mobile labor force, combined with drastic changes in the consumer-oriented economy. Such dramatic changes were simply impossible given the existing power structure and its ties to the United States.

The German government offered Greece a steel mill as part of reparations payment in 1949. Paul Porter used his veto privilege to prevent Greece from engaging in steel production. Consequently, the country was compelled to purchase steel as well as other metals from the developed countries. That case exemplified the manner by which the American officials in Athens obstructed the progress of Greece.

As already stated, however, the State Department entertained the same policies toward Third World nations in general. When the government in Colombia endeavored to build a steel mill in 1948, an IBRD mission to that country advised against it and rejected funding for the project. The mission maintained that it was cheaper for Colombia to purchase steel from the United States than to produce it locally. In many cases, therefore, foreign aid and loans were designed not to help the development of the Third World, but to prevent it.[49]

The Greek representative at the OEEC was convinced that the United States and Western Europe prevented Greece from industrializing in the late 1940s and early 1950s. He maintained:

> Industrialization met with certain reaction mainly because of its effects on the foreign trade of the interested countries, but also largely because of the economic self sufficiency of Greece, which would have resulted from it in a few years' time. Thus it was commercial, economic and political interests that imposed on the countries an unqualified hostility towards all plans for industrialization.[50]

The bulk of American exports to Greece consisted of surplus agricultural products, but there were also exports of dubious use to the mass consumer. Finally, it should be noted that after 1953, when economic aid was gradually phased out in favor of trade, American exports to Greece consisted of consumer goods that the host government did not deem indispensable to the economy.

The more serious short-term failures of the ECA/G were in connection with the refugee population and the taxation issue. The American mission had assumed the responsibility of assisting with the refugee problem, but was unable to accomplish a great deal. Ambassador Grady informed the State Department in June 1949 that there were 600,000 people in security camps who were in dire need of housing, jobs, farm equipment, and other means to enable them to start over again after the guerrilla war. Many farmers returned to their homes only to discover that their property was destroyed. Others went to the cities seeking employment at a time when there were very few jobs for unskilled labor.[51]

After the civil war the refugee population was gradually reduced, but its remnants lingered on throughout the early 1950s. Constantine Karamanlis, minister of coordination and future prime minister, disclosed the following information in September 1949 concerning the condition of the refugees.

> The misery of the countryside is immense. Moreover, of the evacuated peasants, 1,033,000 are paupers receiving assistance. Eight hundred and eighteen thousand are receiving financial assistance from the state. Thirty-four thousand orphans are dependent on the state. A hundred and fifty-eight thousand peasant families are far from their homes and many of them have lost all their property.[52]

Despite the government's efforts to mitigate the refugee tragedy, there were still 450,000 people in that predicament in the summer of 1950, and the effects of the refugee phenomenon were felt for many years thereafter.

The effects of Anglo-American intervention are lucidly discernible in the standard-of-living index during the early Cold War. From 1945 to 1953, the years when Greece received billions of dollars in foreign assistance and was subjected to foreign intervention, the cost-of-living index jumped from 1,895 to 41,280, while the notes in circulation increased from 104 billion drachmas to 2,971 billion. It was during that period that Anglo-American advisers exerted enormous influence on Greek internal affairs. British and American advisers were in a propitious position to introduce a sound tax structure for Greece, especially considering the incessant criticism from London and Washington on this issue. Yet there was no fundamental tax reform, and the low-income families continued to bear the burden of taxation.[53]

Direct taxes in fiscal 1948–49, according to the Greek government, accounted for 17.3 percent of all revenues, while in fiscal 1951–52 direct taxation was equal to—in constant drachmas—the 1938–39 level. Total revenues for fiscal 1951–52 were on a par with those in fiscal 1938–39. Wray O. Candilis has written:

> But as incomes in 1951 were higher than prewar ones, taxation became consequently lighter. Incomes of businessmen and corporations were at least double in 1951 compared to 1938, while taxes were approximately the same; this meant that their burden was half of what it was. Furthermore, tax evasion was widespread, especially among high income groups, and no measures were taken to establish a tax system that could be

both effective and simple and would provide the necessary incentives for investment and economic development.[54]

There were tax reforms under the missions's initiative, but they affected indirect taxes, which were regressive. Few adjustments were made in income taxes, and the lower classes continued to bear the brunt of taxation under an archaic tax structure. Although the Greek regime must ultimately assume responsibility for failing to rectify this problem, the American advisers behind the regime played a significant role in the government's fiscal affairs.

The numerous shortcomings of the ECA/G had a far-reaching impact on contemporary Greece. The American mission was concerned principally with the geopolitical importance of Greece and reduced the country to a military satellite and an economic dependency on the advanced capitalist countries. The military establishment, the bureaucracy, the conservative and centrist politicians, and the capitalist class were responsible for collaborating with the United States government in a desperate attempt to prevent a possible change in the patronage system, the power structure, and the status quo in general. Consequently, Greece failed to make economic progress comparable to that of either its Eastern or Western European neighbors during the Cold War and to solve the issue of social justice, which had been one of the primary causes of social revolution in the 1940s.

From Foreign Aid to Private Investment

American government aid, Export-Import Bank and IBRD credits, as well as other forms of economic assistance, have been used invariably by Republican and Democratic administrations in Washington since President Theodore Roosevelt to stimulate the expansion of American businesses. Greece had a limited potential as a market and as a supplier of raw materials in comparison to larger Third World countries such as Brazil, Chile, Iran, etc. However, the United States mission laid the foundations for the eventuality of massive foreign capital penetration in Greece.

The transition from aid to trade and foreign-capital investment took place in the early 1950s as American aid was almost exclusively military after Greece was inducted into NATO. United States officials informed the government in Athens in February 1951 that Greece must restrict commercial credit, restrict the distribution of basic foodstuffs, which were either given away or sold at reduced prices, and revise the Recovery Program to allow for the enhancement of military projects. All of the above measures were recommended to prepare the government to cope without foreign assistance. The Greeks complied with the austere policy recommendations that resulted in sluggish economic growth during the early 1950s.

In 1951 the United States government cancelled all Greek reconstruction-program aid projects that had not already started. Economic aid was reduced from $181 million in fiscal 1951–52 to $21.3 million in fiscal 1953–54. Paul Porter explained that the drastic cuts in economic assistance were designed as "punishment" for the Greek government, which refused to seek out tax evaders and curtail budgetary spending. There can be no doubt that the Greeks were guilty of those charges, but there is no correlation between the foreign-aid reductions and the remiss conduct of the pro-American regime in Athens. Once the Greek Communist party was thoroughly crushed and the country was firmly in the Western sphere of influence, there was no need for the United States to continue economic assistance to Greece. Foreign aid undermined private trade and was not in accord with the principles of the Bretton Woods system.[55]

American businesses started investing in Greece gradually after the end of the civil war and escalated such activity after 1953. Paul Porter assured a group of American investors on 10 November 1949 that Greece was a lucrative area for investment because wages were low and were not likely to rise. After 1949 American firms gained control of major construction and waterworks projects and invested in mining and industry. The government signed an exclusive contract in June 1949 with the International Telephone and Telegraph Company, an American-based transnational corporation, granting the company a monopoly of the country's communications network. The Greek News Agency in London reported on 4 August 1950 that

> American-owned firms are replacing Greek firms, while American capital is securing a controlling position in many companies, nominally Greek. The International Telegraph Company announced on June 21, 1949 that it had assumed control of all communications in Greece through an autonomous company free from all governmental or ministerial control.[56]

The Greek government, acting on the advice of the American mission, extended lucrative incentives to foreign investors. Prime Minister Alexander Papagos devalued the drachma on 9 April 1953 from 15,000 drachmas to 30,000 to the dollar. At the same time, he abolished special import taxes and export subsidies. Those measures were adopted at the insistence of the American government, which gave similar advice to other Third World countries during the postwar years. The minister of coordination, Spyros Markezines, admitted publicly on 4 September 1953 that the Papagos administration was impelled to implement the above measures because of pressure from the American mission.[57]

A State Department memorandum, dated 4 August 1949, revealed that a staff of seven American policymakers planned "the future path of [Greek] economic development and capital investment in Greece without the advice or consent of the Greek authorities." The policymakers discussed plans for reducing aid to Greece, which had a negative impact on the standard of living. Large-scale emigration and direct foreign investment were recommended as options to counterbalance the negative impact of cutting economic aid. Finally, the policy memo candidly stated: "Greece will achieve economic viability at some level, and *we do have to decide what that level will be.*" [Emphasis added.] The country's fate rested to a large degree with policymakers in Washington because they found various elements in Greece that were eager to collaborate.[58]

The transition from aid to foreign private investment was completed in October 1953, when the government in Athens enacted Law No. 2687, which dealt with the creation of advantageous conditions for foreign-capital penetration. The law was based on the following principles:

> 1. Guarantees against any kind of compulsory acquisition or government interference with foreign ownership enjoying the protection of the law; 2. The unchangeability of terms and conditions agreed upon; 3. The fixing of terms for repatriation of capital, profits and interest in foreign exchange; and 4. Creation of an especially advantageous system of taxation in favor of protected foreign capital.[59]

Under the new law, foreign investors were permitted to export profits up to 12 percent of the amount of imported capital. They had the option of receiving foreign exchange from Greek lending institutions and of discharging the service on their loans contracted abroad "and for payment of interest up to 10 percent annually." As foreign capital pervaded the Greek economy and took over key sectors during the 1950s, indigenous capital fled to the metropolis, seeking higher profits and more secure investments. Capital flight is a general characteristic of Third World countries, and it has been one of the key factors in the process of underdevelopment.[60]

The incentives and guarantees that the Greek government extended to foreign-capital investors in 1953 were quite similar to those which authoritarian regimes in Colombia, Cuba, Peru, Taiwan, South Korea, and other countries in the periphery sector of the world economy extended during the Cold War when the United States was at the zenith of its power. Although Greece was part of the European community, during the early Cold War she had a great deal in common with other Third World countries that were military, political, and economic dependencies of the United States. In the last analysis, the unique characteristic of Greece was its strategic position in the eastern Mediterranean, which made it an invaluable member of NATO.

V

The American Mission and the Greek Labor Movement

United States Infiltration of the Greek Labor Movement

Although trade unionism in Greece became prevalent after 1918, with the formation of the General Confederation of Labor, GSEE, its origins date back to the early 1880s. Organized labor went through a tumultuous period during the 1920s and 1930s when Greece experienced economic and political instability. Leftist trade unionists were persecuted and free-trade unionism was abolished in 1936 by the quasi-fascist regime of General Metaxas. Trade unions during the dictatorship were co-opted by the state and restructured on the basis of the Italian corporativist model. During the Axis occupation of Greece, the leftist resistance forces established the Workers' National Liberation Front, EEAM, an organization that enjoyed popular support, but that was forced to dissolve after the Varkiza Agreement.[1]

Organized labor in Greece, as in most countries, was immersed in politics. At the conclusion of the Athens Revolt, the communists and the socialists dominated the majority of the trade unions. The royalists and other conservative elements, which were commonly referred to as "reformist" since they rejected the class-struggle principle, did not enjoy much support among the working class but competed vigorously with the leftists for control of the labor movement. The dichotomy between left and right in the political arena was also manifested in trade unionism as there were two GSEE executives representing the opposing camps. The reformist group, however, enjoyed the support of the British authorities in Athens and the Service Governments. Hence it was in a far more auspicious position to win control of organized labor than the demoralized and persecuted leftist forces.

The British government endeavored to end the rivalry between the two labor camps in Greece and to bring organized labor under the control of the regime. Sir Walter Citrine, the secretary general of the Trades Union Congress, TUC, was sent to Athens to arrange a compromise betwen the two rival factions in GSEE. The fruits of his labor were reflected in the Citrine Agreement, which resulted in the legitimacy of the anti-communist GSEE executive, the revival of profascist trade unionists, state intervention in trade-union affairs, and the obligation of all labor organizations to abide by the agreement. Citrine's intervention in the Greek labor movement paved the way for the persecution of the socialist and communist trade unionists and the cooptation of organized labor by the right-wing elements that governed Greece during the Cold War.[2]

The KKE established the Anti-Fascist Workers Organization, ERGAS, after the Varkiza Agreement to perpetuate its influence in the labor movement. ERGAS was headed by Theos, a Communist party member, but the organization was committed to free elections as a means of allowing workers to choose their leaders. The regime opposed ERGAS's proposal because, according to a United States government report, about 70 percent of the Greek workers were leftists. When elections finally did take place in March 1946, the leftist trade-union candidates won most of the leadership positions as expected. The elections were supervised by the World Federation of Trade Unions, WFTU, a politically heterogeneous organization formed in 1945, and the British Trades Union Congress, which was a leading member of WFTU. The GSEE elections were conducted free of corruption, but the general elections brought to power the Populist party, which supported the reformist wing of the GSEE. In an apparent effort to eliminate the leftists from the GSEE, the reformist trade-union candidates immediately contested the legality of the Eighth Congress elections. The Council of State intervened in the case and declared the election results invalid.

The Populist administration announced in June 1946 that the members of the communist labor organization ERGAS were ineligible to serve on the Executive Committee of the GSEE. That was a flagrant violation of the Varkiza pact. The Tsaldaris government launched a campaign to purge the leftist leaders from the trade unions. Many leftists were arrested as part of larger plan to co-opt the labor movement and obliterate all aspects of communist and socialist influence in Greece. The High Court annulled the GSEE elections in July 1946, thereby formally confirming the legitimacy of the government-appointed GSEE Executive Committee, which was composed of Populist party members loyal to the premier. Many of the labor leaders who were appointed in the Executive Committee had served under General Metaxas and had collaborated with the Nazis during the occupation.[3]

The secretary general of the government-controlled GSEE was Fotis Makris, a notorious opportunist and a protégé of the prime minister. Makris began his ignominious career as a labor leader during the Metaxas dictatorship, but joined EEAM during the occupation. After the war, he rejoined the right-wing segment of the GSEE and was closely linked to the Populist party. He developed cordial ties with the American Federation of Labor, AFL, which was very active in the international labor movement during the Cold War, and he remained a faithful labor boss for the conservative governments throughout his career, which extended to the period of the military junta, 1967–74.[4]

Domestic and international public opinion was opposed to the blatant interference by the Tsaldaris administration in the trade-union movement. The New York *Herald Tribune* published an article on 18 April 1948 that exposed the candidates of the GSEE's Executive Committee as henchmen of the Populist party.

> The secretary-general appointed by the government in 1946 and "endorsed" by Congress in 1948, Fotis Makris, was a Populist Member of Parliament and faithful supporter of the regime; so was Theocharides, also secretary of the trade union confederation; so were Kalomiris, Antypas, and others in positions of control or influence.[5]

Free-trade unionism ended with the election of Prime Minister Tsaldaris, whose government ousted the duly elected trade-union officials and convicted them in courts-martial. The charges against the leftist labor leaders were that they "acted against national security," "against public order," and "against national peace." The government could justify such nebulous and nefarious charges quite easily because the defendants were leftists. Consequently, they were sent to prison without the right of appeal.

The duly elected secretary general of the GSEE, Dimitris Paparigas, was arrested by the police after resisting the dissolution of the Executive Committee and the confiscation of union records by the authorities. He, too, was sentenced to prison because of his leftist political affiliation. In May 1947 he was denied a visa to attend the WFTU Conference in Prague, and in July of that year he was arrested and imprisoned once again because he had testified against right-wing elements whose activities were investigated by a UN delegation. He escaped from prison in December 1947, but was arrested shortly thereafter and imprisoned for attempting to organize an independent trade-union movement. According to the authorities, Paparigas committed suicide in prison.[6]

The persecution of the leftist trade unionists and the co-optation of organized labor by the regime were absolutely essential not only for the ruling class in Greece, but also for the British and United States governments. The constituency of the KKE was in large part the working class, although the peasantry supported the left in the northern parts of the country. The consolidation of Greece as an anti-communist sphere of influence by the West necessitated the creation of an anti-communist labor movement that was docile and supported the regime's policies.

The GSEE was the principal labor central, with 1,850 local affiliates representing 200,000 members in 1947. There were, however, independent federations which constituted the opposition to the state-controlled labor confederation. The independent federations were controlled by militant leaders, but they did not constitute a real challenge to the GSEE because the latter enjoyed the backing of the state. The outbreak of the civil war enhanced the importance of the GSEE, not only to the regime, but to the United States, which was deeply entangled in Greece's internal affairs.[7]

Before the Americans were drawn into the Greek labor scene, the British TUC and the WFTU attempted to reach a compromise with Tsaldaris regarding organized labor. In the autumn of 1946 the Tsaldaris-Braine Agreement (W. H. Braine was a TUC official) provided for the release from prison of certain labor leaders. Moreover, a provisional GSEE Executive Committee was appointed until new elections were held under the supervision of international observers. That agreement was undermined by an insidious scheme of the AFL that supported Truman's Cold War foreign policy wholeheartedly and collaborated with the State Department in Europe, Latin America, Asia, and Africa to create pro-American labor organizations.

The AFL appointed Irving Brown as the European representative to undermine the solidarity of the WFTU, which included Soviet trade unions as well as Western communist and noncommunist labor organizations. Brown's task was to work with anti-communist labor leaders in Europe to divide the labor movements between pro-Soviet and pro-American. He went to Greece in February 1947 and worked closely with the Tsaldaris administration and the TUC in an effort to create a viable anti-communist GSEE. Armed with $1 million to reorganize European trade unions along anti-communist (Cold War) lines, Brown was confident that a compromise among the various labor factions in the Greek labor movement did not serve the interests of the United States. Based on Brown's recommendations, the State Department requested that the plans for unifying the disparate labor factions in Greece must be abandoned. The United States advised Tsaldaris to wait until AMAG arrived in Greece before making any decision regarding organized labor. The State Department was informed that free-trade-union elections would simply reinstate the leftist leadership in the GSEE and thus undermine the anti-communist campaign in Greece and the anti-WFTU campaign around the world. Irving Brown and the State Department agreed that the absence of a trade-union movement in Greece was preferable to a communist-dominated movement. The British disagreed with that dogmatic position since the TUC was a member of the WFTU and believed that a heterogeneous labor central was plausible.[8]

Irving Brown demanded that the GSEE withdraw its affiliation from WFTU. By May 1947 the GSEE Executive Committee had an anti-communist majority due to the efforts of the American officials and the administration in Athens. That was an inevitable turn of events because the United States had the means to accomplish its goal. As part of a European-wide effort to undermine communists in the trade unions, the AFL initiated "Operation Food." It sent 5,000 food packages to Greece, 5,000 to German trade unionists, 3,000 to Austria, and 15,000 to France, where the communists were very strong. One critic of the AFL's Cold War foreign policy has written:

> Everywhere the story was the same. Where there was a Communist-dominated union the idea was to disrupt it; where there wasn't, the idea was to immunize against it by supporting "safe" anti-Communists. Particularly shameful was Brown's endorse-

ment of Fotis Makris of Greece, and rightist adventurer who became union chief after the Communists were purged and who is now a supporter of the Papadopoulos military dictatorship.[9]

The AFL and the State Department collaborated after 1945 in a scheme designed to purge communists from trade unions in the Western Hemisphere, Africa, Asia, and Europe. The creation of anti-communist trade unions was an integral part of the containment policy. National and international anti-communist organizations created under the aegis of the AFL during the Cold War served as anti-revolutionary mechanisms that inadvertently enhanced the position of the United States in the world economy by obstructing systemic change and thus perpetuating the status quo.

On 7 June 1947, the *Wall Street Journal* exposed the State Department's scheme to infiltrate the GSEE with the intent of restructuring it, so that it would not be an obstacle to American foreign policy in Greece. The front-page article ascertained that the AMAG employed a $10,000-a-year labor expert, Clinton Golden, an official of the Steel Workers' Union, an affiliate of the Congress of Industrial Workers, CIO. Golden had served as vice president of the United States War Production Board and was a staunch anti-communist. He was placed in charge of AMAG's Labor and Manpower Division, and his task was to help Greek trade unions emulate American-style unionism.

Golden was instructed to depoliticize the Greek trade unions by removing the communists and the socialists from influential positions. Specifically, his job was to "Educate Greek laborers in the virtues of American labor unionism. This would include short courses on the ABCs of writing labor-management contracts, parliamentary procedure for electing union officers, and the structure of union constitutions." Golden operated out of the United States Embassy and AMAG headquarters in Athens. He consulted with the United States labor attaché, whose chief function was to coordinate labor policy and offer advice to the Greek Ministry of Labor and to the GSEE.[10]

The American government's policy toward all foreign trade unions was that they must remove the communist elements from positions of leadership and accept the principle of cooperation, rather than confrontation with the employers. The most important catchword of the AFL and the State Department in promoting American-style trade unionism was "free," which distinguished the ostensibly politically independent trade unions from the communist-dominated organization. Irving Brown, who was to be promoted to the position of AFL

European representative just before AMAG commenced operations, announced that he vehemently opposed free-trade unionism if it entailed the inclusion of communists in leadership positions. He denounced communism in general and the KKE in particular and argued that the "white terror" in Greece was justified on the grounds that the communists endeavored to undermine the regime. To counterpoise the widespread leftist influence in organized labor, the State Department scheduled a training program of "Greeks in the United States and elaborate Mission staff to encourage the promotion of industrial labor relations in Greece." George C. Marshall instructed Governor Griswold on 11 July 1947 that the Greek trade unions, which supported leftist factions, must be co-opted by the pro-American forces. It should be noted that the State Department, in cooperation with the AFL and the CIO, engineered similar programs to co-opt trade unions in Europe, Africa, Asia, and the Western Hemisphere.[11]

The AFL supported the Truman Doctrine and the Marshall Plan and was eager to extend its influence globally with the help of the Truman administration. The *New York Post* claimed that the ultimate goal of the United States government's collaboration with the AFL was to rid the Greek trade unions of leftists. The article continued:

> Mr. Marshall has asked the State Department to find reliable and experienced American union leaders to work with us in the Balkans. Mr. Marshall's advisers believe that US trade union leaders, having led the struggle against communism in our society, will be able to adopt an effective strategy elsewhere.[12]

The House of Representatives Appropriations Sub-Committee, which approved the Greek-Turkish Aid Bill, questioned the wisdom of the Administration's resolve to infiltrate the labor movement of a friendly sovereign nation.

Senator J. H. Overton inquired into the State Department's activities in the Greek labor movement and asked to confirm the validity of newspaper reports regarding an alleged American scheme to permeate the GSEE. The response to the senator's inquiry was that "the Labor program, which is still under discussion, has not yet been finally approved by the State Department."[13] Nothing resulted from such innocuous Congressional inquiries and criticism of the State Department's activities in Greece. President Truman's foreign policy enjoyed bipartisan support, and the domestic political climate was veering toward an increasingly conservative course.

United States Intervention in Greek Labor Affairs

As was seen in the previous chapters, conditions of the working class deteriorated rapidly after 1945 because of protracted economic dislocation. Real wages and salaries decreased by an average of about 35 percent between November 1944 and October 1947. The International Labor Organization, ILO, estimated in 1947 that prices of essential goods in Greece had risen 300 times in terms of real wages since 1939. Sweet-Escott's research corroborated the ILO's findings.

> The constant fall of the purchasing power of the drachma since liberation resulted in great hardship for the worker and salaried employees. For prices rose at least as fast as [the] external value of the drachma fell, but in the increase of wages there was the usual time lag, so that in spite of Military Liaison and UNRRA, the worker was often on the border of starvation.[14]

One of the main reasons that the Tsaldaris administration appointed its own labor leaders to the GSEE was the widespread indignation of workers amid economic dislocation. The reformists, however, were pressured by the rank-and-file to speak out against price increases and stagnant wages.

The GSEE under the reformist leadership voted on 8 October 1947 to stage a general strike from 15 to 20 October. The United States Embassy in Athens admitted in a dispatch to the State Department that the strike vote was prompted by the failure of the government and AMAG to reach an agreement on a feasible wage policy after months of deliberations. The dispatch stated:

> Wage situation three months ago critical and only at Embassy's urging have labor leaders restrained rank-and-file demands for wage increases to give AMAG time to arrive . . . organize, review entire economic situation, [and] review wage policy.[15]

The embassy's frank admission that AMAG formulated labor policy and was responsible for advising GSEE executives was a further indication of extensive American involvement in Greece's internal affairs. Such involvement resulted in a regimented labor movement that was an obstacle, rather than an impetus, to the country's socioeconomic development and democratic process.

The Greek reformist trade-union leaders displayed a sense of forbearance, while the Ministry of Labor and the American mission were trying to decide on a prudent wage policy. A general strike was imperative, however, to "take the wind from the Communist labor agitators" who allegedly capitalized on labor's discontent toward the government. The AMAG and the administration deliberated four months on a wage policy, and neither Clinton Golden nor R. S. Simpson, United States labor attaché, believed that they could prevent the impending strike unless the mission immediately approved a wage policy with substantial increases for hardship cases.[16]

The reformist leadership was overwhelmed by the relentless labor unrest, which was caused by the low standard of living as well as by the regime's repressive policies toward the opposition. A survey conducted by AMAG's Labor and Manpower Division divulged the extent of impecuniousness among the working class. The report stated that the average worker spent about 70 percent of his/her wages on food purchases alone. It continued:

> Breakfast consists of tea or coffee. Vegetables, potatoes and fish are the main dishes. Rice and macaroni are eaten seldom and meat is a luxury. . . . Families [have been] found living in caves that have been dug out of the city walls built around 1200 A.D. These caves have no windows, no floors other than the stone of the cave and no bed other than rocks.[17]

The lengthy report revealed that the majority of the dwellings were not equipped with bathroom facilities or running water. Many did not have kitchens, and it was not at all uncommon for a six-member family to reside in a single-room house. The average calorie consumption for the Greek masses was lower after the war than before. In fact, Greece's population was the most undernourished in Europe and one of the most undernourished in the world during the 1940s and early 1950s. While such vital statistics were known to American government officials in Athens, AMAG remained steadfast in its wage-control policy and refused to deviate in order to reach its deflationary targets.[18]

Governor Griswold informed his superiors in Washington on 23 October 1947 that the GSEE cancelled the general strike after the government assured a significant increase in the minimum-wage levels. Labor-union leaders of the confederation signed a collective agreement with the government on 4 November 1947, which classified wage categories for all workers and raised the wages for only 10 percent of the organized labor force. The average worker earned 65 percent of the prewar level in terms of purchasing capacity in 1947. Makris was opposed to the new collective agreement and castigated the other GSEE leaders who signed it as "stooges of the industrialists." It is quite possible, however, that he was simply showing his ostensible displeasure toward the agreement to placate the vociferous rank-and-file that mistrusted the GSEE officials.

The AMAG chief expected that the price increases, combined with wage increases, food shortages, and hoarding by the merchants, would have created new inflationary pressures on a feeble economy. Griswold was convinced that wage increases triggered an inflationary spiral that had to be controlled at some point. He recommended a wage/salary freeze after the October collective agreement to curb inflation. He did not address, however, the problem of price increases and adjustments on business and income taxes. In short, there were no proposals to alleviate the multiple causes of poverty.[19]

In anticipation of further labor unrest, Tsaldaris, who was chairman of the Cabinet Economic Policy Committee in the coalition government, conferred with United States officials on 5 December 1947. They discussed the imminent general strike by the utility and bank employees. The American advisers recommended that the existing law, affecting public employees for civilian mobilization in case of emergency, be amended to include utility employees. Moreover, the embassy and mission officials advised against any salary increases for bank employees because a precedent would be set for wage/salary increases across the board. Such a trend would have pernicious effects on the national economy and was to be avoided at all costs. Finally, the Americans recommended that remuneration for workers on strike must cease.

Tsaldaris concurred with AMAG's advice, and on 6 December 1947 he summoned a special session of the cabinet to enact the proposed anti-strike legislation. The minister of labor, Protopapadakis, was not notified that such egregious legislation was drafted. When he was informed belatedly about the entire affair, he was perplexed by the hasty steps that the cabinet adopted to pass the new law. Protopapadakis had implemented some conciliatory measures toward the GSEE and other trade unions to placate the working class and gain its confidence. After learning about the new law, he telephoned Golden and protested vigorously, charging that AMAG had been scheming to undermine his constructive policies. Golden confessed that he was ignorant of the matter and sympathized with the minister about the unjust labor law that the regime adopted. When a full cabinet meeting was held to discuss the issue, Tsaldaris maintained that he adopted the law at the mission's request.[20]

The royalist-dominated Parliament passed the anti-strike bill which became Emergency Law No. 509. It outlawed strikes, lockouts, and walkouts, and instituted the death penalty for offenders. Both the liberal and conservative parties espoused the spirit of the new law, and Prime Minister Sophoulis argued that it was a deterrent to general strikes, which had the potential of crippling the volatile national economy. American Embassy officials deliberated on the new law on 8 December and concluded that it was bound to be very unpopular. They also feared that it would invite criticism from political and labor organizations in Europe and the United States. Such considerations notwithstanding, the conferees resolved not to repudiate the law. They decided, however, that

> An effort should be made to have the Government issue a public statement interpreting the legislation as a grant of power necessary to have in time of war which it did not intend to use except when essential to the immediate security of the State.[21]

American officials met with Tsaldaris and asked him to issue a public statement clarifying the intent of Law No. 509. The vice premier's statement was modeled after the one that the mission drafted on 8 December.

The AMAG's proclamation emphasized that labor strikes had an adverse impact upon the economy and profound political reverberations amid the civil war. The new law, therefore, had been enacted for security considerations since the nation was torn by social unrest coupled with "communist aggression" against the regime. The law affected the public-health sector, national-security employees, and all workers in "essential activities." The general wording of the law was a deliberate effort to allow the government to act freely against any labor group that staged a strike. Finally, the mission's message concluded that the cabinet was compelled to adopt the drastic measures manifested in Law No. 509 for the sake of averting commercial and industrial paralysis. Tsaldaris's statement embodied all of the above points, but was placed in a partisan framework that reflected the minister's own political convictions.[22]

A wave of protests erupted after the enunciation of Law No. 509, and the GSEE demanded immediate and unconditional repeal of the anti-strike law. Griswold noted that there was widespread discontent among labor because the new law was regarded as a device to force workers to accept the November 1947 collective agreement that Makris had denounced. He informed the State Department that more strikes were inevitable given the strained relations between organized labor on the one hand and government and employers on the other.

When the news of the anti-strike law reached Western Europe, there were numerous demonstrations in support of the Greek trade unions and denunciations of the regime in Athens. The AFL and other United States labor unions also expressed grave concern about the Greek government's confrontational labor policy. Matthew Woll, one of the prominent AFL leaders involved in the organization's foreign policy, protested to the State Department and demanded full explanation for the motives behind the anti-strike law. The secretary of state replied to William Green, AFL president, that Emergency Law No. 509 was enacted hastily "at a time when the very security of Greece was in grave danger as a result of communist-inspired terror and violence, and when members of the Greek Parliament feared that outbreak of a number of strikes might bring an end to the independence of the country." He addressed a similar letter to Philip Murray, CIO president, and then released both letters to the press.[23]

State Department documents have shown beyond any reasonable doubt that the KKE was not even remotely connected with the anti-strike law because the communist influence in the labor movement had dissipated by the end of 1947. The law was directed not against communists, but against the reformists and the indignant rank-and-file. There was a strike scheduled for 8 December, two days after the law was passed, and more strikes were expected. The government and the American officials in Athens, fully cognizant of the tense labor situation, adopted Law No. 509 as a means of forcing the reluctant local labor leaders and their contentious members to accept the collective agreement. Another important consideration for the state's resoluteness to contain labor unrest was that the Ministry of Finance intended to reduce holiday (Christmas, New Year, Easter) bonuses in half, or even eliminate them. Griswold embraced that proposal in January 1948, but, according to Golden, the Ministry of Finance was behind it. In any case, the administration anticipated that there was bound to be labor unrest once the ministry's proposal was made public at a time when a wage freeze was in effect. All things considered, the coalition government prepared for a future confrontation with organized labor.

Domestic and international protests against Law No. 509 impelled the government in Athens and its American advisers to reconsider. The administration announced in January 1948 that it intended to repeal the controversial law "as soon as the democratically elected National Labor Congress, which will meet in March [1948] has chosen a responsible National Executive for the Greek labor movement." The law was repealed on 26 April 1948, for it had become a major source of embarrassment to the government and the American mission. The last thing they needed amid a civil war was to alienate their own allies in organized labor and invite undue criticism from European and American organizations.[24]

Emergency Law No. 509 exemplified the mission's overbearing role in Greek labor affairs and the extent to which the regime was subservient to the United States. If the cabinet and Parliament had opposed the labor law, the mission would probably have considered an alternative policy. The willingness of the Greek politicians to remain in power by acquiescing to American policy advice, regardless of its merits, left a legacy of political dependence that was not effaced until the collapse of the military junta in 1974.

Labor Unrest and United States Ascendancy in the GSEE

The Ninth Congress of the GSEE convened in April 1948 amid an atmosphere of antagonism between rightist and centrist factions within the organizations. The Greek government, acting on the mission's advice, had staged the GSEE congress to secure the reelection of reformist candidates. The eleven independent federations were denied participation in the congress because they had refused to collaborate with the regime and its foreign advisers. In a recent illuminating essay on the Greek labor movement, Adamantia Polis pointed out:

> By the time the Ninth Congress took place on April 10, 1948, the factions competing for control of the leadership of the trade union movement consisted essentially of opportunists, right wingers, and those who had cooperated with the Metaxas regime or the Nazis. All others had been afraid to become candidates to the Ninth Congress or even to vote.[25]

150   Intervention and Underdevelopment

A State Oversight Committee, which was composed of Ministry of Labor officials, supervised the congress's activities. Thus any freedom-of-labor organizing was eliminated by procedural preparations for which the regime was responsible. It is interesting to note that the government paid the transportation costs of delegates who came from the provinces to Athens to support the reformist candidates. Considering that only reformists participated in the event, the leadership of the GSEE was monopolized by the government-backed elements who lacked the confidence of the rank-and-file.

The GSEE congress proved that there was a growing rift within the reformist camp, despite the efforts of the Americans to unite them. The rightists denounced the centrists as "communists" and "Bulgarians." Interpersonal rivalries and local political antagonisms transcended the larger calls for anti-communist unity. Irving Brown concluded that the United States officials should have played a more direct role at the congress to mitigate the rift between the two factions. He and the other American officials in Athens sympathized with the centrists and opposed Makris's rightist faction, for it was intransigent. Tsaldaris and the royalists, however, backed Makris. The division in the political arena between conservatives and liberals was reflected in the labor movement. By October 1949, when the Tenth GSEE Congress took place, the United States had thrown its unqualified support behind the conservative politicians and, consequently, behind Makris's faction. This was an inevitable development because the rightists were more accommodating toward United States policy and interests than the vacillating centrists, who had the propensity to be more independent. Since the government in Washington sided with the conservatives in Athens, it also supported Makris, who displayed strong anti-communist convictions and collaborated with the AFL in international labor affairs.[26]

The American mission and the AFL aspired to centralize all Greek trade unions under the leadership of the GSEE so that the regime would control the labor movement. The AMAG claimed in its annual report in 1948 that it had succeeded in centralizing the functions of the Ministry of Labor and in formulating policy on its behalf. Simpson, who was responsible for the aforementioned accomplishments, was eager to use the labor movement as part of the regime's power base and to advance United States foreign policy objectives in Greece. In April 1948 he wrote that the role of the trade-union movement should have been as follows:

> 1. Remove communist saddle which has been imposed on the unions since liberation. 2. Cooperate constructively with the American aid program and 3. Eliminate the instability of the Greek labor movement as an adverse influence [to] internal political situation.[27]

The GSEE and to a lesser extent the independent federations became instruments of the State Department's Cold War policies, while the interests of the working class assumed a secondary role for the leadership of organized labor.

In assessing AMAG's achievements for 1947, Simpson wrote that Greek legislation was revised and the Greek government and trade unions were obliged to accept the principle of collective bargaining. Furthermore, the mission had made numerous efforts to centralize organized labor. Finally, it endeavored to develop a labor program "in support of the American program for aid to Greece." Simpson supported the reformist trade unionists, for they favored United States foreign-policy objectives in Greece and were receptive to the mission's advice. He concluded that while AMAG had imposed policies upon the GSEE and the Ministry of Labor, serious mistakes that had negative repercussions were made in the process. The following example illustrates his point.

> Recommendations to the Greek Government, which had the effect of decisions on matters of indirect interest to labor, were made without consulting even those leaders who were working with us. This included recommendations to dismiss 1,500 railway employees without any provisions for their subsequent subsistence.[28]

Railway workers were represented by one of the independent federations which the Americans deemed "unacceptable" because its leadership was not composed of reformists.

The GSEE sought the advice and approval of the American embassy and mission before arriving at a final decision affecting labor policy. The confederation's leaders lobbied the American offices in Athens more intensely than they lobbied the Ministries of Labor and Finance, for they realized that policy was made by American officials. Despite these conditions, which relegated the GSEE to a position subservient to that of the regime and the foreign mission, the reformist leaders deviated from the directives of the authorities on various occasions. The GSEE Executive Committee needed to prove its commitment to the interests of the membership and its ostensible independence by assuming a course of action that neither the government nor the American advisers approved.

A number of GSEE representatives conferred with United States Embassy and mission officials on 15 August 1948 to discuss labor policy as well as other matters. Ambassador Grady attempted to dissuade the Greek trade unionists from seeking wage increases. He argued that the wage freeze must remain in effect to keep inflation down. The GSEE leaders advanced the following counterarguments in support of their cause.

> 1. [The] purchasing power of Greek wages has dropped since November [1947] and is now only 40 percent of prewar, and a remedy for this situation must be found. 2. While appreciative of the difficult position of the country, not all elements of Greek population are sharing this burden; many manufacturers and merchants [are] reaping excessive profits; all labor demands is more equitable distribution of existing national income. 3. [The] task of increasing production lies with employers and government.[29]

The general index of industrial production increased six percentage points between 1947 and 1948, while real wages fell during the same period because of the American-imposed wage freeze. The argument, therefore, that wages could only rise commensurately to the rise of productivity levels could not be supported by the figures.

According to a Ministry of Labor report, the average daily wages for 294,546 workers was 15,181 drachmas per worker. In terms of purchasing power, that represented 75 percent of the prewar level. The average daily income of the entire labor force was much lower than the Ministry of Labor's figures indicated because the incomes of the organized urban workers were higher than those of the unorganized workers and peasants. One reason for the erosion in purchasing power after the collective agreement was signed in November 1947 was that the mission approved indirect tax increases and some commodity increases while freezing wages. The national income in 1939 stood at $493 million and taxes amounted to $94 million, or 19 percent of the aggregate national income. The visible national income (subterranean economy excluded) in 1948 was $354 million, and taxes amounted to

$130 million, or 37 percent of the total. The prewar direct taxes, however, accounted for 22 percent of the state's revenues, whereas in 1948 they accounted for just 17 percent, despite a rise in business taxes. If indirect taxation is taken into consideration, as it should be, when comparing the 1939 wage rates to those of 1948, the workers' purchasing power was in fact, as the GSEE claimed, 40 percent of the prewar level.[30]

Tensions between organized labor and the regime mounted in 1948 because the latter, at the mission's request, remained adamant in its wage policy. To offset any potentially rancorous action by the trade unions, the government in Athens enacted Emergency Law No. 516, which vaguely stated that anyone opposed to the regime had no right to employment. Those affected were civil servants, bank and insurance employees, and workers/employees in businesses of "common interest." At the same time, the government escalated the persecution of leftist and centrist trade unionists as part of a campaign to quell labor discontent. The entire leadership of the Greek Maritime Federation, one of the eleven independent federations, was arrested and tried on calumnious charges of complicity with the KKE.[31]

At issue was the government's and the mission's resolve to replace the Maritime Union's duly elected officials with reformist labor leaders who were loyal to the regime. European and North American trade unions regarded the Greek government's action toward the Maritime Union as a "union-busting" tactic. The National Lawyers' Guild, the CIO, and even the AFL protested to the State Department against the illegal arrests and trials of freely elected trade unionists. The American labor organizations certainly would not have protested if the Greek government had been acting purely in the name of national security by eliminating hard-core Stalinists from the federation. In any event, the American labor centrals raised serious questions about United States foreign policy toward Greece. The State Department, however, insisted that Emergency Law No. 516 was justified because of the tumescent communist threat. The National Lawyers Guild wrote to Secretary Marshall:

> The Government of Greece is sustained by the most far-reaching American aid—financial, material and military. An American representative participates in the formulation of policies carrried out by the Greek Government, and American influence is substantial in the carrying out of these policies.[32]

The State Department responded that the American Mission in cooperation with the AFL representative in Athens worked diligently to build a "free" trade-union movement—a euphemism for a right-wing, anti-communist movement.

The Greek Fur Workers Union, GFWU, which had 1,500 members in the United States and Canada, followed the example of other labor organizations in protesting the Greek regime's policy of persecution and elimination of freely elected labor officials. The GFWU demanded that the Truman administration use its influence in Athens to end the anti-labor policies of the Hellenic government. A presidential spokesman charged that the Federation of the Greek Maritime Workers was in fact illegal because its leaders were guilty of "treasonable offenses" against the regime. The administration spokesman made it clear that the offenses of the trade unionists in question were that they were communists or socialists who opposed the regime. Since the government was at war with the Democratic Army, anyone who entertained leftist political affiliation or sympathy was guilty of "treasonable offenses." Democratic principles and parliamentary practice were sacrificed in the name of the larger goal of anti-communism.[33]

Seventeen of the thirty-six defendants were acquitted, released, or given suspended sentences by the courts-martial in November 1948. Of the remaining, nine were sentenced to prison and ten were condemned to death. The government dissolved the Federation of the Maritime Workers and reorganized it under the name of Pan-Hellenic Federation of Maritime Workers. The leadership of the new federation was composed entirely of reformists who lacked the confidence of the rank-and-file but enjoyed the support of the regime. The federation held a convention in New York City on 28 October 1948. The purpose of the convention, which the State Department helped organize, was to discuss strategy for providing services to Greek seamen in American ports and methods to counter potential communist influence in the union. The task of the reformist union leaders was to meet with the Greek shipowners to arrive at an understanding on issues such as wage rates, working hours, and conditions of seamen.

The Pan-Hellenic Federation was concerned that 4,000 of its 25,000 members were unemployed, despite soaring business in the shipping industry. Moreover, there were another 2,000 seamen on the high seas working without the protection of a contract because their employers had refused to cooperate with the union during contract negotiations. The reformists advanced a number of grievances against the shipowners in an apparent gesture to win the confidence of the rank-

and-file. They realized, however, that as long as the government backed them, their union would survive. Such were the "free" trade unions that the United States helped to create in Greece during the early Cold War.[34]

The condition of the Greek workers deteriorated steadily in the last quarter of 1948 as prices rose 10 percent between October and December. The ERP Report for 1949 indicated that the mass consumer in Greece was "poverty-stricken" and added that the number of destitute people continued to rise. During the period that the wage freeze was in effect—November 1947 to November 1948—the cost-of-living index in Athens jumped from 174.6 to 247.5. Workers responded with occasional strikes, but the GSEE did not seize the opportunity to unite the labor movement and coordinate a general strike at a critical period when the regime was most vulnerable. The independent federations sanctioned sporadic strikes in the last quarter of 1948, and, according to the United States Embassy in Athens, the Ministry of Labor leaned heavily toward the unions in defiance of the administration.

In the spring of 1949, the government had to contend with widespread civil-service strikes. The public employees represented by ADEDY, the state employees' union, staged a strike on 6 April "in spite of persistent Government efforts [to] end it through persuasion, state of siege, proclamation and arrests." The state was by far the single largest employer in Greece as the size of the government bureaucracy swelled due to expansion of the patronage system and defense-related jobs. The size of the bureaucracy jumped from 85,688 in fiscal 1938–39 to 144,421 in fiscal 1948–49, representing a 68.6 percent increase for the ten-year period. Forty percent of the government employees were affiliated directly with the military and public-security sectors, while 40 percent of the remaining group were engaged indirectly in those areas. There was a correlation, therefore, between the increase in the defense budget and the burgeoning bureaucracy.

The 72,000 civil servants who went on strike on 6 April demanded higher salaries that were long overdue. The government and ADEDY had agreed in spring 1948 that the salaries of the employees would be adjusted by 1 July, but the issue remained unresolved until 25 July. At that juncture, the administration, acting on the advice of ECA/G, announced that salaries would increase by 30 percent in the form of allowances—food rations, etc. The ADEDY immediately rejected the offer and insisted on a 60 to 65 percent straight salary raise. The union argued that the cost-of-living index had reached astronomical levels since September 1947: the last time that state employees were granted a salary increase. The decline in the employees' salary level during 1947 was estimated at 37.4 percent, measured in terms of 1938 purchasing power.[35]

When the strike erupted, government services were subjected to a complete shutdown. The American chargé d' affaires wrote: "Postal, telegraph services crippled. Schools shut down. Government departments practically standstill." The government issued a statement on 9 April 1949 after consulting with United States officials.

> [The] government, having exhausted [the] last limit [of] present possibilities, decided [to] grant Government employees, over and above grants decided upon [a] total [of] three months food supplies free of charge. If employees do not resume work [on the] morning [of] April 11, they will be placed under civil mobilization.[36]

The civil servants rejected the offer because it did not make any wage concessions. In retaliation for ADEDY's position on the issue, the state enforced the civil-mobilization decree. The decree empowered all government agencies to mobilize civil servants and "also all personnel of public utility enterprises, corporate bodies, banks and transport services."

The strike was thoroughly crushed and the regime dealt a major blow to organized labor by the unsparing manner in which it applied the civil-mobilization order. In May Fotis Makris temporarily resigned as secretary general of GSEE in protest of the government's refusal to lift the wage/salary freeze. He attempted to form a coalition with the Free Trade Union Movement, headed by socialists, but the scheme failed because ultra-conservatives sabotaged the effort. Makris's venture would have failed ultimately because the regime was determined to exercise control over the labor movement. He resumed his post with GSEE after realizing that a successful independent trade union movement was impossible.[37]

The strained relations between reformist trade unionists and the government persevered throughout 1949. The Athenian gas workers went on strike in June and were followed by employees of government monopolies (salt, matches, etc.). Public-law employees and radio operators went on strike on 17 June, but the latter were forced back to their jobs by the mobilization decree. The American mission and the government in Athens had refused to negotiate a collective-bargaining agreement since November 1947. The GSEE wanted the minimum rates raised from 5,000 drachmas to 7,000 drachmas. The daily wages for unskilled male workers in 1949 ranged between $.93 and $1.73 and for females $.70 and $.87. The average daily wages for skilled laborers averaged about $2.00 a day, but the vast majority of the labor force was classified as unskilled. The demand for skilled labor increased considerably after 1947, but the state did not devote the necessary resources for technical schools and on-the-job training programs. At the same time, the underpaid skilled workers and professionals emigrated to North America, Western Europe, and Australia, thereby leaving Greece with a common problem from which Third World countries have suffered—namely "brain drain."[38]

Paul Hoffman conferred with the GSEE Executive Committee in August 1949 to discuss a number of labor issues. The trade-union representatives emphasized their continued concern about restrictions on prices of essentials and profit controls. They asked for "more direct taxation, free collective bargaining to replace the present wage controls, and greater labor participation in the planning for reconstruction." The United States officials in Athens faced a dilemma of either defending their deflationary policy or making concessions to organized labor for the sake of placating the reformist trade-union leaders whose role as anti-communist agents in the GSEE was indispensable to American foreign policy. As long as the civil war continued, the regime, the GSEE leadership, and the American Embassy deflected the workers' attention from the economic issues to the greater threat of communism. Once the Democratic Army was decimated and communism was no longer a perceptible threat to the nation, dissonance prevailed between organized labor, on the one hand, and the regime and its foreign advisers, on the other.[39]

Labor unrest erupted in October 1949 as the civil war was coming to an end. The confederation threatened a general strike unless wages were raised to keep pace with inflation. The GSEE accused the government on 6 November of failing to approve the 40 percent increase that the former proposed on 21 October 1949. The government replied that "such an increase was out of the question," leaving the GSEE no alternative but to call upon its local affiliates to prepare for a strike. At the last minute, however, Paul Porter intervened on behalf of the regime and declared that the nation's resources simply could not have sustained a general wage increase of the magnitude proposed by GSEE.

The unions responded with sporadic and uncoordinated strikes because the general strike that was scheduled for 20 November 1949 did not take place. Ambassador Grady wrote that labor unrest was a major concern for the regime as it threatened the road to recovery.

> Last fortnight brief stoppages occurred in [the] Athens-Piraeus tramway and [among] yellow bus operators; Athens-Piraeus telephone, gas, [and] monopoly workers; currant workers [in] Patras; [and] press workers of [the] *Estia* Printing Company. Also, several thousand high school teachers throughout Greece threatened [to] resign. ADEDY [government employees union] and government still bickering.[40]

Despite the intermittent strikes by local unions, organized labor failed to effect a change in government labor policy because the GSEE leadership was persuaded by the American advisers to abandon the general strike. Just before the scheduled national strike, Makris conveniently left the country to attend an international labor conference that the AFL, CIO, and TUC staged in London with the assistance of the State Department and the Central Intelligence Agency. It was at that conference that Greece came under the umbrella of the American-dominated anti-communist international labor organization.

Organized Labor Under the ICFTU

The Greek Confederation of Labor became increasingly subservient to the AFL after the Tenth Congress. In November 1949 the GSEE issued a proclamation denouncing communism as the enemy of Hellenism and of peace. The occasion for that proclamation was the founding of the International Confederation of Free Trade Unions, ICFTU, which was established as the rival to the WFTU and resolved to undermine the latter. The newly founded labor international was created for the purpose of enhancing the prestige of the AFL and to a lesser extent the CIO and TUC. Its chief aims were to combat communism throughout the world while disseminating the principles of American-style trade unionism.

The plan to form a global labor organization to rival the WFTU was masterminded by the AFL in 1947. Unlike the CIO, which became a member of WFTU when the latter was formed in 1945, the AFL had always claimed that the Soviets and their communist allies manipulated the WFTU. During the founding congress of the Inter-American Confederation of Workers, CIT, in Lima, Peru, in January 1948, the

AFL announced plans for the establishment of an anti-WFTU labor international. Serafino Romuladi, AFL's labor ambassador to Latin America—Irving Brown's counterpart in the Western hemisphere—and Liu Sun-sen, representative of the Asian Federation of Labor, formally established a secretariat at the ILO conference in July 1948, and plans were laid for the future ICFTU.

The European trade unionists resisted the proposal of a new labor international that would be under American control. There is no doubt, however, that the Marshall Plan was the catalyst to the formation of ICFTU. The TUC and CIO pressured the WFTU to endorse the Marshall Plan. When a vote was taken on the issue, the majority voted against the ERP. Consequently, the CIO and TUC, as well as other minor labor centrals, severed relations with WFTU and joined the AFL's global anti-communist movement. The United States also used its influence through the ECA to reorient the European labor centrals away from the WFTU and toward the anti-communist camp. The ECA sponsored a visit to the United States by a group of TUC leaders who met with AFL and CIO officials in March 1949 and agreed to form the ICFTU. Preparations for the founding conference were made at the ILO conference in Geneva in June 1949. A Preparatory Committee was set up that called for a new labor international. James Carey, secretary-treasurer of the CIO, delivered a strong anti-communist speech at the ILO conference, which was an indication of the ICFTU's ideological orientation. The founding conference was held in London from 28 November to 9 December 1949. There were 261 labor delegates at the ICFTU conference, representing 53 countries and about 48 million members. Three-fourths of the entire ICFTU membership, however, were Western Europeans and North Americans, representing the core sector of the world economy. Furthermore, the total donations to the ICFTU amounted to $80,000, of which the AFL contributed $25,000, the CIO $20,000, the United Mine Workers of America $1,000, the TUC £7,159, and the West German Federation of Labor £3,000. The remaining were donated by trade unions from Canada, Denmark, Sweden, Norway, and New Zealand. Considering the source of ICFTU's financing, the majority membership, and the leadership positions, the advanced countries led by the United States were destined to dominate the new labor international.[41]

The ICFTU was not free from the United States government's interference during the Cold War, for it was conceived in large part as a tool of anti-communism. The AFL and CIO collaborated with the

State Department and the CIA in founding the ICTFU and regional affiliate labor organizations in Latin America, Asia, and Africa. A major source of financing for the covert activities of these organizations was the government in Washington. A critic of the AFL has written:

> The magic weapon of this labor-CIA, apart from strigent polemic, has been and still is money—secret dollars from the US government's treasury chest. Though Brown claims he has doled out only $100,000 over two decades, a top labor figure in the Marshall Plan and AID programs who was stationed in Europe during all this period puts the figure at many millions.[42]

According to one estimate, the United States spent as much as $5 million by 1950 on international labor activities. The policy of containment was applied to the international labor movement, and the rivalry between ICFTU and WFTU exacerbated the growing rift between communist and anti-communist labor organizations throughout the world. The WFTU, which was founded as a heterogenous labor organization with the promise of coexistence between East and West, was eventually reduced to a Soviet-dominated organization. The tragedy of the Soviet-American confrontation was that both superpowers endeavored to polarize the underdeveloped nations by compelling them to choose between the two opposing camps.[43]

The Greek Confederation of Labor joined the ICFTU and denounced communism as anathema to society. The GSEE's proclamation did not address the issues of unemployment, underemployment, the rising cost of living, rampant political corruption, wage increases, and foreign interference in Greece's internal affairs. Instead the proclamation was intended to inculcate vague reformist principles to the working class. These included:

> Recognition for the right to live, for the protection of the sick and the unemployed, for justice of taxes, for equality before the law, equality in sacrifice, protection for syndicalists against persecution by employers, [and] participation in the responsibilities of rehabilitation. No Government, no class, no person, no law can refuse to satisfy these demands.[44]

In a nation of approximately 7.5 million people, with unemployment of 25 percent or higher and a refugee population of 450,000 in 1949, the

GSEE's perfunctory proclamation did not reflect the interests and aspirations of labor. Yet the conservative governments of the 1950s did not even abide by the innocuous demands of the docile confederation.

A government committee recommended on 28 November 1949 a 35 percent wage increase in the minimum rate for men and 25 percent for women. That raised women's wages to almost $1.00 and men's to $1.14. The GSEE rejected the offer and announced that there would be strikes in retaliation to the government's insensitivity to labor. The conservative elements in the country castigated the trade-union leaders as opportunists "seeking personal position, misleading the workers and playing into the hands of the Communists." The rank-and-file, however, had been pressuring the leadership to adopt more resolute steps in dealing with the employers and the regime. The confederation was compelled to approve uncoordinated strikes for the sake of preserving its own credibility and placating the indignant workers.

The ADEDY had scheduled a strike to take place on 8 December 1949, but the union's General Council, which was royalist and proAmerican, overruled the strike vote. The ADEDY's Executive Committee resigned in protest of the council's illegal measure. The government immediately appointed a new executive committee whose first resolution was to cancel the strike and demand that employees exercise restraint.

Strikes persisted despite the government's vigorous efforts to contain them by a combination of propaganda, force, or manipulation of the trade unions' leadership. Over 200,000 workers went on strike between 2 November and 9 December 1949 at various intervals. Labor unrest was so pervasive that Makris appealed to President Truman on 1 December to support the GSEE's demands. He wrote that the confederation had a number of outstanding demands that should have been fulfilled to improve the quality of life of the working class. The following were among the most serious demands that the secretary general outlined: (a) the reshaping of taxation so that the system would depend on income taxes rather than consumption taxes; (b) controls on prices and profits to curb inflation; (c) free collective bargaining and lifting of the wage freeze—protection of trade unionists from the vengeance of employers; (d) healthy housing for the poor and the reorganization of the Social Insurance Fund, IKA.[45]

President Truman was hardly the appropriate channel for the GSEE's grievances, but the fact that Makris wrote to him is indicative of the inordinate role of the United States in Greece. The condition of the Greek working class remained relatively unchanged during the 1950s, but began showing some improvement during the early 1960s as the country entered the era of "dependent" development. The cooptation of the GSEE by the right-wing conservative ruling forces prevented any significant progress in the labor movement.

After the civil war, the Greek trade unionists were resigned to the fact that American/ICFTU infiltration of the labor movement was inevitable. The GSEE leaders were more preoccupied with propaganda campaigns against communism and less concerned with the material conditions and aspirations of the Greek laborers. The confederation's new political orientation was manifested in a speech that Makris delivered over British Broadcasting Corporation radio in London after the founding of the ICFTU.

> This new international organization [ICFTU] assumes prodigious responsibilities toward the entire world, for it automatically sets itself the mission of fighting for peace in the world by removing the causes of disturbances and war. This is the body which is realizing [that] its aims will strike down communism, whose power is derived from the wretchedness of the masses.[46]

The ICFTU achieved neither peace nor prosperity for its affiliates in the Third World because its ultimate goal was to combat the spread of communism, which necessarily implied the struggle against any social revolution. Since the ICFTU and its regional affiliates often sided with American-supported reactionary regimes in the Third World, the organization served the State Department's foreign policy and was an obstacle to change, especially during the early 1950s.

The Tenth Congress of the GSEE that convened in Athens on 24 September 1950 was, as expected, organized by the ICFTU, the American mission, and the Greek government. Once again the reformist candidates who were sanctioned by the authorities easily won reelection. The workers had lost control of their unions to leaders who were accountable to the regime, the ICFTU, and American officials. The Greek labor movement underwent experiences similar to those of trade-union movements in other underdeveloped countries during the early Cold War. Labor centrals of most underdeveloped countries failed to pursue an independent course, and were manipulated from the top down by ruling parties and international organizations.[47]

The Economic Status of Organized Labor During the Early Cold War

The Greek labor movement suffered enormous political as well as economic setbacks during the Cold War due to endogenous and exogenous factors. The contributions and sacrifices of the working class to the country's economic growth were immense. But the conservative ruling class remained largely suspicious of labor and unswerving on the policy of low wages and higher productivity rates.

Four months prior to the Tenth GSEE Congress, the country was plagued by widespread strikes involving thousands of workers. Civil servants went on strike in May 1950, demanding a 50 percent salary increase. Other strikes affected the Piraeus chemical industry in August, the flour mill and macaroni factories of Piraeus, bus drivers and conductors at Athens and Piraeus, tobacco workers at Serres, bakers throughout the country, dock workers at various ports, and wool, silk, and cotton factory workers in Athens and Piraeus. Fotis Makris announced on 8 August 1950 that labor needed to fight for higher wages since it had lost 20 percent of its purchasing power during the first half of 1950. The government remained intransigent on its wage-control policy and made meager concessions due to interminable pressures from below.

Wages increased 10 percent between 1950 and 1955 although the GNP increased 25 percent between 1950 and 1953. Labor, therefore, was not compensated commensurately to the rise in productivity. The average annual income of the Greek worker in 1950 was $150 in comparison to the $260 that the Italian worker earned, the $492 that the French laborer was paid, and the $950 that the Briton made annually. Since Greece lagged far behind Western Europe in industrial development, its labor force obviously had a much lower pay scale. If the savings accrued from low wages were invested in industrial development, as was the case in the North Balkan countries, then the workers' sacrifices could have been justified. But capital flight, speculative investment, and luxury imports did not leave much capital for productive investment, as will be seen in the next chart.[48]

The average annual rise in income for the Greek worker was 2 percent between 1950 and 1955, while the average annual increase of the Western European worker was 5 to 10 percent during the same period. The following chart compares the increases in the wage and price indexes during the four years that Greece was receiving massive foreign aid.

Year	Average Wage/Salary	Wage Index	Price Index[49]
1947	10,685 drachmas	152	230.7
1948	13,160	188	325
1949	15,134	216.2	378.3
1950	18,000	257	423.7

The average wage/salary for 1947–50 represents a 40 percent decline in purchasing power in comparison to the prewar levels. According to Kyriakos Varvaressos, the income of the majority of the workers between 1939 and 1950 increased 300 to 350 times. The price of locally produced goods rose 500 times and the price of imports 400 to 450 times during the same period. Sweet-Escott arrived at the same conclusion as Varvaressos.

> Each increase in the cost of living from 1949 to 1953 has been followed by a wave of strikes, which, because they were uncoordinated, rarely succeeded in achieving any real importance in the position of the workers, and have done little more than disturb production and bring organized labor into disrepute.[50]

He went on to add that organized labor in Greece suffered a crisis in leadership because union officials owed their positions and thus their loyalty to the regime. The crisis, however, was symptomatic of American intervention in Greece, though internal factors certainly contributed to the postwar structure of trade unionism.

To place the distressed condition of the Greek labor movement during the early Cold War into perspective, the following factors must be considered. First, political repression against communist, socialist, and centrist trade unionists was rampant. The government executed 128 trade unionists between 1947 and 1950. The total number of leftists executed between July 1946 and October 1949 was 3,033—all in the name of "public security." Second, unemployment of registered workers in 1950 and 1951 was 20 percent, although production was approaching prewar levels and the economy had shown signs of a modest recovery. There were still 1,000,000 people, or one-fourth of the work force in 1953, officially classified as unemployed or underemployed with no prospects for finding work. The billions of dollars in foreign aid had created numerous positions in the defense sector as part of the ruling conservative parties' patronage network. But there were few benefits to the civilian economy.[51]

The United States Senate Foreign Relations Committee concluded in 1961 that American aid to Greece since the Truman Doctrine had not improved the condition of the lower classes. The Senate report maintained:

> While the country has registered pronounced gains, the rate of growth—owing to inordinate diversion of resources at U.S. direction to military purposes—has been exceedingly slow, and the country is plagued by unemployment (at 250,000) and underemployment (at 750,000).[52]

Fourteen years of foreign aid, combined with a massive emigration program, which accounted for the slow rate of population growth, had not resulted in the reduction of unemployment and underemployment because the country had not moved toward structural development, as was the case with Yugoslavia and most of the Eastern European countries that made considerable progress during the same period. Although the agricultural and industrial revolutions of Eastern Europe have not resulted in development comparable to that of Western Europe, partly because of the lack of natural resources, the former moved far ahead of Greece between the late 1940s and late 1960s. This growth was made possible, according to Norman J. G. Pounds, by the region's political revolution and its interdependent relationship with Russia.

> Indeed, the natural endowment of Eastern Europe is in some respects so weak that it is difficult to conceive of a thoroughgoing industrialisation—such as that which has taken place—without political support by the Soviet Union and strong ideological inspiration. In short, without the creation of socialist states, development could not have taken place on its present scale.[53]

Greece did not need a communist regime to undergo structural development, and it is not realistic to argue that the KKE would have been a panacea. It desperately needed, however, a reformist-oriented, social-democratic regime to be able to alleviate the widespread misery among the masses and keep pace with the other European nations.

The *Manchester Guardian* published an article on 13 April 1953 depicting the appalling conditions of the Greek working class at the end of the ECA/G program:

The high incidence of sickness among the working population in one of the healthiest climates in Europe can be traced to malnutrition, unsanitary housing, belated diagnosis and treatment. The 1952 Greek report to OEEC states that in the settlements of the Asia Minor refugees who came to Greece after 1922, none of the houses has a bath, 54 percent have no kitchens, and 92 percent have no lavatories. But statistics cannot fully convey the misery and degradation which prevail in some of the left-wing areas of Piraeus, where one-room shacks cluster round mud swamps infected by sewage from the town drains. Equal squalor can be found, often concealed behind the presentable facade, in the heart of Athens.[54]

The most astonishing aspect of the *Manchester Guardian* article was that it revealed how conditions for the working class had not changed since 1947, when the Labor and Manpower Divison of AMAG first conducted an investigation into this area. The benefits of the ostensibly "humanitarian" foreign aid to Greece during the Cold War did not alleviate the penurious conditions of the masses. Greece experienced modest economic growth after 1945, but there was no development until the early 1960s and then only in light industry. By 1953, when the first phase of reconstruction and economic development under ECA/G ended, the economic indicators matched the prewar levels and industrial output had moved ahead of the 1938 level. The growth in the economy, especially in manufacturing, was due to the numerous sacrifices of the working class and the peasantry. Since the private sector did not invest in new industries, the state did not initiate agrarian reform/modernization and industrial programs. Also, because American advisers were chiefly interested in strategic matters and the preservation of the free-enterprise system in Greece, none of the aforementioned can take credit for the country's economic growth.

Industrial profits between 1945 and 1950 amounted to $400 million for a handful of capitalists, while the aggregate wages for 149,843 industrial workers amounted to $300 million during the same period. Aggregate wages for workers in 1947 were 580 billion drachmas, whereas net profits were 650 billion drachmas. In 1948 wages totaled 725 billion drachmas and aggregate profits reached 1,097 billion. Such figures exemplify the disproportionate business profits at a time that the regime and the American advisers had imposed a wage freeze. If the state had had an industrial plan by which the private sector was compelled to reinvest in productive enterprises, the low wages could have been justified. But, as was noted earlier, such was not the case in the market-oriented economy.[55]

Considering that the capitalists invested a mere 10 percent annually of their resources in domestic productive enterprises, and given the infinitesimal public investment in the civilian economy during the 1940s and 1950s, the workers and peasants made inordinate sacrifices for the country's reconstruction and economic growth. The validity of this thesis was reinforced by the secretary general of the Supreme Reconstruction Council. He wrote:

> The Government therefore had good reason to maintain, as it did in its first quarterly report to the United States Economic Cooperation Administration, that the wage earners were bearing much of the burden of war and reconstruction and were consequently falling short of the necessary minimum standard of life. The decline in the purchasing power in wages which occurred during 1948 and 1949, although production increased, shows clearly enough that the improvement in the economic situation is chiefly due to the sacrifices of the working class.[56]

The Greek working class and peasantry suffered needlessly during the Cold War because sweeping social reform and state-initiated development programs would have helped alleviate socioeconomic and political problems in the countryside and the cities. If it were not for the "inordinate diversion of resources at U.S. direction to military purposes," as the Senate Foreign Relations Committee confirmed in 1961, and if the government in Washington had played a more constructive role in Greece by providing a political, rather than a military solution to the crisis in 1946, the country would have experienced a more harmonious political, economic, and social fate than it has since the Truman Doctrine. A plausible solution to the sociopolitical and economic problems would have required the formation of a center-left coalition committed to the strengthening of the state, the launching of fundamental social reforms, and the development of agriculture and industry.

Epilogue

The legacy of American intervention in Greece during the Truman presidency was that the aid recipient became dependent on the donor and was unable to undergo structural development. Moreover, the right-wing forces consolidated power after the Truman Doctrine and enjoyed virtual monopoly of the government for a generation. The rightist elements and their American supporters experienced a crisis in the political arena in the mid-1960s and disintegrated when the military junta collapsed in 1974. Finally, American intervention left a bitter legacy of deep sociopolitical divisions that have not been healed completely four decades later.

The nation's most vital institutions—the military, banks, organized labor, and civil ministries—were permeated by American missions that remained in Greece until the demise of the military junta of 1974. The first initiative to free the country from preponderate United States entanglement was made in 1981 by Prime Minister Andreas Papandreou. Although that task has proven very difficult to accomplish given Greece's inexorable economic and strategic ties to the West, his efforts at least signified the beginning of an epoch. Papandreou's initiative was inevitable with Greece's elevation into the European Economic Community and the debilitation of the United States in the world economy due to the Vietnam War and the economic challenge by Japan and Western Europe in the mid-1970s.

Some steps toward industrial development were undertaken in Greece during the early 1960s, and the country has experienced a process of dependent development. Peter Evans has argued that dependent development entails "both the accumulation of capital and some degree of industrialization of the periphery." He continues:

> Dependent development is a special instance of dependency, characterized by the association or alliance of international and local capital. The state also joins the alliance as an active partner, and the resulting triple alliance is a fundamental factor in the emergence of dependent development.[1]

Dependent development is a characteristic of semiperipheral regions in the world economy, according to Immanuel Wallerstein and "modern world-system" theorists. This phenomenon was symptomatic of ownership dependence (the expansion of transnational corporations in the Third World) and import-substitution policies (protection of the indigenous consumer-related industries by the state) that countries like Mexico, Brazil, Taiwan, South Korea, Greece, Turkey, and others adopted.[2]

The majority of the population in Greece earned its livelihood from the primary sector of production even as late as 1971. Clearly, that was an indication that the country still lagged behind Western Europe and even most of Eastern Europe. Nevertheless, there was some socioeconomic mobilization, as the following tables indicate. The first table shows that between 1940 and 1971 there was significant demographic change as the urban population increased substantially. That does not mean, however, that migration from the rural sector to the cities was due to a demand for industrial workers. The manufacturing share of the GNP was the same in 1967 as in 1950. Moreover, the percentage of the work force engaged in the secondary sector of production changes only slightly between 1951 and 1967.

Year	Urban Population	Semi-Urban	Rural[3]
1940	2,411,647	1,086,079	3,847,134
1951	2,879,994	1,130,188	3,662,619
1961	3,628,105	1,085,856	3,674,592
1971	4,667,489	1,019,421	3,081,731

Year	Work Force	Agriculture	Manufacturing	Service[4]
1928	2,745,488	53.75%	15.6%	18.6%
1951	2,839,500	48.1	18.8	33.1
1961	3,663,100	53.3	18.0	28.8
1967	3,610,000	50.1	21.2	28.7

SHARE OF THE GNP BY SECTOR[5]

Year	Agriculture	Manufacturing	Service	Total
1950	34%	25%	41%	100%
1961	31	27	42	100
1967	23.6	25.1	50.3	100

The growth in the service sector was not necessarily a positive trend since there was no corresponding increase in manufacturing. A plethora of bureaucrats who were part of a patronage system constituted a drain of public resources that could have been devoted to productive enterprises.

The population of Greece grew very slowly after 1950 partly because of the massive emigration to Europe, America, Africa, and Australia. From 1955 to 1971, 900,000 people, primarily peasants and workers, emigrated to the United States and other developed countries, while 600,000 peasants migrated to the cities in search of employment opportunities. Emigration had some positive aspects to it because of the amount of foreign capital the emigrants poured back into the Greek economy. These positive aspects were offset by the psychological torment and material hardships of the uprooted population. Moreover, the country lost many of its skilled workers and professionals, who were essential if development was to take place. For example, Greece lost more than one-fifth of its first-rate engineers between 1957 and 1961.

Rural migration was not necessarily a positive development in the absence of an expanding manufacturing sector and modernization of agriculture. The overwhelming majority of the peasants who migrated were concentrated in large cities, primarily in the capital. The Four Year Plan of the ECA/G endeavored to prevent that inevitability, but it obviously failed. The size of Athens doubled in the decade after the civil war ended, reaching 1,852,709 in 1961. The Athens metropolitan area continued to grow even after 1961, in large part due to the failure of central planning. The area provided over 50 percent of the nation's industrial employment, it received 80 percent of the aggregate imports, it paid 75 percent of the direct taxes and 65 percent of the indirect taxes, and its income was 40 percent higher than that for the rest of Greece. It was the cultural, industrial, and commercial center. Yet it was also semi-industrial, for the emphasis was on expansion of established light industry, shipping, and commerce. It has been plagued by chronic unemployment—10 percent during the 1960s—and suffers from problems similar to those of other overpopulated cities in the semiperiphery. Athens is one of the most populated cities in the world, with an archaic infrastructure that is unable to support heavy industry and high auto-traffic congestion.[6]

The rate of economic growth that the country experienced during the 1950s—an annual average of 7 percent in the GNP—was impressive. That did not translate, however, into creation of new industries or a rise in the standard of living for the masses, as might be expected. The rate of growth was attributed to phenomenal gains in shipping and banking. The shipping industry grew by 1,000 percent between 1948 and 1968, and the Greek merchant fleet accounted for 12 percent of the world's merchant marine. However, 80 percent of that industry was concentrated in the hands of twelve families who invested most of their wealth in other countries and whose ships flew foreign flags for the most part. Therefore shipping benefited the national economy to a limited degree.

Banking experienced comparable growth but, like shipping, its resources were not utilized to yield maximum benefit to Greece's systemic development. Savings increased from 835 billion drachmas in 1950 to 16,300 billion drachmas in 1960, representing a rise of 1,852 percent.[7] The banking industry was as oligopolistic as shipping, but in the case of the former the state enjoyed a controlling role. The government regulated the credit policies of all banks through the Currency Commission and controlled the National Bank of Greece. Nikos Mouzelis, a social scientist, placed the role of banking in Greece in the following perspective.

> To give an idea of the degree of concentration in banking it suffices to say that in 1962 the assets of these two concerns (the State-owned National Bank and the privately owned Commercial Bank) amounted to 96.3 percent of all Greek commercial

banks put together. . . . . Between them they handle 90 percent of the country's considerable savings, but also participate in ownership and management of an important part of the insurance and industrial sector.[8]

The state controlled the savings accounts of the public corporations, which were the principal depositors of the National Bank of Greece. Thus it controlled the largest bank. Since the state enjoyed a preponderate role in the financial network, it was within its power, assuming that the political will was there, to invest in the capital-goods sector so that the country would be less dependent on expensive manufactured goods. Such measures were carried out not only by the communist regimes of Eastern Europe, but even by Western European governments.[9]

There was a correlation between Greece's failure to invest in the capital-goods sector and its predicament of trade and financial dependence on the West. Trade deficits were quite high under UNRRA, AMAG, and ERP, but became even higher thereafter. The country's trade deficit in 1953 amounted to $102 million and reached $700 million in 1966. The total trade deficit between 1953 and 1966 was $4,642.6 million. The increase in the chronic trade imbalance was due to Greek dependence on finished goods from the United States, Canada, and Western Europe. The first table below delineates the percentage of each economic sector to the country's foreign trade.[10] The second table provides the ratio of Greek exports to imports.[11]

	Exports (%)			Imports (%)	
Year	Agr. Prod.	Minerals	Mfg. Prod.	Agr. Prod.	Mfg./Fuels
1950	80.2	3.1	17.7	27.6	72.4
1958	82.0	6.1	12.9	16.2	83.8
1962	74.8	6.4	18.8	14.0	86.0
1966	69.0	6.8	24.2	10.3	89.0

Ratio of Exports to Imports				
1950	1958	1962	1964	1965
21	41	35	32	29.5

Greece remained an exporter of agricultural products and an importer of manufactured goods and fuels. Consequently, the country experienced immense trade deficits because the terms of trade have been determined in favor of the advanced capitalist sector and at the expense of the exporters of primary products. Trade deficits also precipitated the flight of capital and thus the necessity to borrow from Western banks to finance imports, government programs, and past debts.

The indigenous capitalist class was as disinterested in the structural development of Greece as the regime during the Cold War. As Mouzelis noted:

> Greek capital, ever searching for higher profits and lower risks, preferred to orientate itself, mostly on borrowed money, towards the non-manufacturing sector, and then transfer a substantial share of its revenue whether to banks abroad or to shipping. This, not unexpectedly, resulted in Greece exhibiting the usual features of an underdeveloped economy: the tertiary sector expanded rapidly, the feeble manufacturing sector came almost to a standstill and agriculture remained badly organized.[12]

From 1952 to 1963, 62,297 million drachmas were devoted to the housing sector, 24,912 million to agriculture, and only 22,049 million to manufacturing. Thus the following asset formation resulted from the allocation of funds in three major investment sectors during the period that was ruled by right-wing governments. This chart shows the percentage of each allocation.

Housing	36%
Agriculture	15
Manufacturing	13

The greatest percentage of the GNP—3.7 to 6.2—was invested in housing, while manufacturing investment did not exceed 2.3 percent of the GNP, the lowest rate in Europe.[13]

Public investment in the economy reflected the regime's unwillingness to lessen the country's preponderate dependence on the United States and Western Europe. The average public investment in mining and manufacturing between 1948 and 1962 was 4.6 percent. The following table illustrates the direction of public investment after the enunciation of Law No. 2,687, which liberalized foreign trade and created opportune conditions for foreign investment.

Sector	1953–1957	1958–1962[14]
Transportation	19.3%	35.8%
Housing	17.1	5.3
Electrical power	28.3	20.7
Agriculture, forestry, fisheries	12.1	21.1
Mining and manufacturing	6.1	6.2
Public administration and other	17.1	10.9

Agriculture and the infrastructure continued to absorb the bulk of the public investment following the two decades after the Truman Doctrine was promulgated. If such investment in the primary sector of production and the infrastructure had resulted in resounding achievements, there would be less criticism of public investment.

The meager public and private investment in the economy by Greeks allowed foreign entrepreneurs to penetrate the domestic market, especially after Law No. 2,687 accommodated such investment. The Greek Ministry of Coordination approved 594 foreign-investment applications between 1953 and 1965, representing a total of $711.5 million of which only $281.5 was imported capital. American investors owned $229 million of the $711.5 million direct foreign investment, most of which was sunk into Greek industry and mining. France ranked second with $172.1 million, of which $167.7 million was in industry and $1.9 million in mining. While Greek capitalists had a propensity toward investments in the metropolis, American and Western European capital was sunk in Greek industry and mining. This phenomenon was characteristic of the Latin American capitalists who invested billions of dollars in the North American economy during the 1950s and 1960s, while United States-based transnational corporations dominated the Latin American oil, mining, and manufacturing sectors.[15]

Greeks living in Greece owned just 40 percent of the domestic stocks and bonds, while the remainder was in the hands of foreigners. Greek capital was also drained by foreign banks who had extended loans to Greece. The service on the public debt required 7 percent of ordinary revenues by 1964. The following chart delineates the amounts devoted to the public debt in millions of US dollars.[16]

	Before WWII	After WWII	Total
Domestic debt	$ 16.5	$357.5	$374
Foreign debt	$250	$198.5	$448.5
Debt to public corporations		$ 33.5	
Total	$266.5	$589.5	$822.5

Greece fell more deeply into debt, as was the case with Third World countries in general, during the two decades after the Truman Doctrine than in the 120 years before World War II. The excessive defense expenditure has been one of the major reasons why the country has not made more progress toward development.

American aid to Greece between 1944 and 1964 amounted to $3.984 million, most of which was absorbed by the military, as the following chart on foreign-aid allocation indicates.[17]

Allocation	Millions	%
Military expenses	$2,144	53.7%
Public investment and production	851	21.4
Budget deficit	732	18.5
US agricultural surplus	133	3.3
US mission expenses	124	3.1
Total	$3,984	100

The Senate Foreign Relations Committee pointed out in April 1961 that "Greece maintains for its size, population and resources, the greatest military establishment in the world." Greece's defense expenditure increased 180 percent from 1953 to 1961 during a period of internal sociopolitical stability and the absence of a real foreign threat. South Vietnam, whose expenditures on defense were comparable to those of Greece during the same period, was engaged in a war against North Vietnam. The Greek conservative political and military establishments were bleeding the country with a massive defense budget. The government spent 40 to 45 percent of the budget on defense between 1950 and 1956 and only 6.7 to 7.7 percent for education and 6.6 to 8.4 percent for health and welfare.[18]

The following table provides a lucid comparison of defense expenditures in relation to the gross national income of select European nations.[19]

Greece	5.4%
Turkey	2.6
Denmark	2.8
Portugal	3.1
Italy	3.2
Belgium	3.1

Greece spent 82 percent more than other NATO members for defense in terms of the gross national product, and the entire strategic network was designed to serve the interests of the United States.

The Senate Foreign Relations Committee argued that the United States was largely responsible for Greece's exorbitant defense expenditures because the State and Defense departments had placed a great deal of emphasis on the security of the Near East. The burden of the defense expenditures fell on the masses, who bore the brunt of taxation. The state's total revenues amounted to 65,989 billion, or $2.5 billion from 1950 to 1960. Indirect taxes accounted for 80 percent of government revenues and 90 percent of all revenues emanating from internal sources. The basic tax structure that existed in the 1940s remained intact as long as the conservatives enjoyed political monopoly.[20]

The absence of systemic socioeconomic change in the three decades following the Truman Doctrine was due in large part to the lack of change in the political arena. The United States was apprehensive about the consequences of political change in Greece and continued to extend its unswerving support to the conservative politicians and right-wing military establishment. The United States Senate during Kennedy's administration was concerned about the unqualified support that official Washington had extended to Greek quasi-authoritarian regimes since 1947. A Senate report noted:

> Post-1947 history makes possible a more judicious examination and reflection upon this era. The postwar tragedy may now be seen in proper focus, starting with the Metaxas quasi-fascist dictatorship in 1936. The repressive measures of that regime, which sharpened class and social conflicts, refined and abetted by the German occupation, plus the war and postwar policies of Great Britain, which were keyed to Churchill's open and avowed declaration that he had not become the King's First Minister in order to liquidate the Empire, fathered all subsequent events. There has been no political change in Greece—in

a world of change—since the last government of Venizelos the Elder (1933). Every human desire for change has been defaulted to the Communists.[21]

The report went on to point out that the State Department constantly assailed the stifling of freedom and human rights in Eastern Europe, but there was a noticeable absence of criticism of the repressive Near Eastern regimes. The Senate concluded that the United States "subsequent to 1947 has played a commanding role in the political life of the nation [Greece]." The same held true for Turkey and Iran, which were also under American strategic hegemony.

The Greek people resisted American intervention and interference in their internal affairs, despite the outpour of billions of dollars in aid and the elaborate propaganda network. The United States Embassy in Athens addressed a lengthy report to the State Department in November 1957, which ascertained that the Greeks were disgruntled with American foreign policy and were sympathetic to the nonaligned nations.

To state the matter briefly, we and our policies have become less popular with the Greeks in recent years and months and we see no evidence of the existence of any force which will reverse this trend in the immediate future, barring an immediate settlement of the Cyprus issue in a manner satisfactory to Greece or a very large increase in the amount of economic assistance.[22]

The embassy report pointed out that Greece's national interests were on a collision course with those of the United States in the Near East partly because of the perplexing Cyprus issue which compelled the government in Washington to balance its support between Ankara and Athens. Although the Cyprus question is beyond the scope of this study, it was and remains one of those areas about which Greece and the United States cannot arrive at an understanding because of their divergent geopolitical interests. American strategic hegemony in the Near East can be served best if the government in Washington continues to maintain the balance of power in the Aegean by supporting both Greece and Turkey. The Cyprus question, however, was used only as a focal point by the disgruntled Greeks of the centrist and leftist political parties against the United States. The real issue was the aspiration to achieve greater independence from the West.

According to the United States Embassy in Athens, most Greeks identified with the nonaligned nations of the world and resented the fact that their country was used politically and militarily by the United States. A public-opinion poll conducted in the mid-1950s showed that approximately half the population opposed Greece's membership in NATO. The American chargé d' affaires in Athens wrote in 1957 that the United States "has been losing ground in Greece." But since 90 percent of Greece's foreign trade was with the West, it was difficult, the chargé added, for the politicians in Athens to embark upon a course of neutrality as many people demanded. He concluded:

> The economic Ministers of the present Government are realistically aware of Greece's continuing dependence on the West as a market for her exports and as a source for capital investment, which she needs.[23]

Greece's perdurable dependence on the United States for trade, capital, and weapons, along with the conservative dominance of the government, prevented the country from embarking on a course of independent development. The demise of the military junta in 1974, which culminated in the reckless adventure to capture Cyprus that year, marked the beginning of a new era in Greek domestic and international affairs. The lower bourgeois elements, which have become the most dynamic sociopolitical sector since the mid-1960s, have opted for a reformist course that was exemplified by the Pan-Hellenic Socialist party of Andreas Papandreou during the early 1980s. His election as prime minister in 1981 and reelection in 1985 represented the first symbolic step of dismantling the complex mechanisms of Greek dependence on the United States.

In his address to Parliament on 22 November 1981, Prime Minister Papandreou stated:

> National independence, territorial integrity, popular sovereignty and democracy, *self-supporting economic and social development*, a cultural revival, the revivification of the countryside, the radical improvement of the quality of life in the towns and in the villages, social justice, and, finally, social liberation are the targets of our government. [Emphasis added.][24]

Papandreou was simply carrying out a mandate from below when he initiated the symbolic gesture toward the formation of a more just society and the redefinition of Greece's role in the world community.

Although Greece remains firmly in the Western camp, its economic, strategic, and political interests necessitated a multidimensional foreign policy and a more balanced position between East and West. This goal was to be achieved by improving relations with the communist countries for domestic as well as international considerations. Papandreou needed to placate the leftists who helped elect him, but he was also following the lead of the French socialist party and reflecting the anti-Americanism (anti-nuclear policy) among Europeans during the first Reagan administration. This position was abandoned by the mid-1980s when the economy of Greece experienced expansion and Papandreou moved to the center, resigning to the fate of Greece as a NATO and EEC member.

In the last analysis, the position of Greece in the semi-periphery of the world economy and the domestic pressures for increased democratization of society have determined its course away from the US and toward two possible alternatives—either the nonaligned, which Papandreou and some leftists and centrists seemed to favor in the early 1980s, or the more likely alternative of an independent Western category into which such diverse countries as Sweden and Portugal fit.

Notes

Chapter I

1. For extensive details concerning the origins of Greek foreign borrowing from the Great Powers, see Jon V. Kofas, *Financial Relations of Greece and the Great Powers, 1832–1862* (New York: Columbia University Press, 1981), 1–20. For more on the Greek foreign debt during the nineteenth century, see J. A. Levandis, *The Greek Foreign Debt and the Great Powers, 1821–1898* (New York: Columbia University Press, 1944). For a succinct overview regarding the impact of the Greek foreign debt on the economy, see Angelos Angellopoulos, *Oikonomika Arthra Kai Meletai, 1946–1967* (Athens, 1974), 229.

2. L. S. Stavrianos, *Greece: American Dilemma and Opportunity* (Chicago: Henry Regnery, 1952), 26. For a succinct overview of the origins of Greece's dependence on the core sector of the world economy, see Kostis Papadantonakis, "The State as Instrument of Induction to the Periphery," in Richard Rubinson, ed., *Dynamics of World Development* (Beverly Hills: Sage Publications, 1981), 43–60.

3. For more details concerning the foreign debt during the 1930s, see Jon V. Kofas, *Authoritarianism in Greece: The Metaxas Regime* (New York: Columbia University Press, 1983), 10–11; Jean Meynaud et al., *Politikes Dynameis stin Ellada* (Athens, 1974), 429.

4. Harry C. Cliadakis, "Greece, 1935–1941: The Metaxas Regime and the Diplomatic Background to World War I," (Ph.D. dissertation, New York University, 1970), 42–43.

5. For extensive details about the population that perished during World War II and the civil war, see Constantine Tsoukalas, *The Greek Tragedy* (Baltimore: Penguin Books, 1969), 91; Wray O. Candilis, *The Economy of Greece, 1944–1966* (New York: Fredrick A. Praeger, 1968), 19; Bernard Kayser, *Geographie Humaine de la Grece* (Paris: Presses Universitaires de France, 1964), 36; United Nations Relief and Rehabilitation Administration (hereafter UNRRA), *Journal* (London, 1945), 55; S. Calogeropoulos-Stratis, *La*

Grece el Les Nations Unies (New York: Manhattan Publishing, 1957), 14. For more concerning malnutrition and malaria in Greece, see George Woodbridge et al. *The History of the United Nations Relief and Rehabilitation Administration* (New York: Columbia University Press, 1950), 2:95; UNRRA, *Journal*, 55; Stavrianos, *Greece*, 192-93; Stephen Xydis, *Greece and the Great Powers, 1944-1947* (Salonica: Institute for Balkan Studies, 1963), 142; Athanasios Sbarounis, *Meletai Kai Anamniseis ek tou B' Pangosmiou Polemou* (Athens, 1950), 320-22; State Department National Archives (hereafter SDNA) 868.50/6-1946; Angellopoulos, *Oikonomika*, 1:456-59.

6. Nikos Psyroukis, *Istoria tis Synchronis Elladas, 1940-1967* (Athens, 1980), 1:238; A. D. Sismanides, "Foreign Capital Investment in Greece," *Balkan Studies* 8 (1967): 339; Candilis, *Greece*, 18-19; Angellopoulos, *Oikonimika*, 1:155; Woodbridge, *United Nations*, 2:94-96; UNRRA, *Journal*, 55; Tsoukalas, *Greece*, 91-92; Candilis, *Greece*, 18; United States Department of Commerce, *Foreign Commerce Yearbook, 1948* (Washington, D.C.: U.S. Government Printing Office, 1950), 86-87.

7. Ibid., 88; Candilis, *Greece*, 18-19; Andreas Lemos, *The Greeks and the Sea* (London: Cassell, 1976), 179; Department of Commerce, *Foreign Commerce Yearbook, 1948*, 89. For more extensive details on the destruction of the Greek merchant marine, see SDNA, 868.5151/7-247, No. 5163, and Psyroukis, *Istoria*, 1:238-39. Sismanides, "Foreign Capital," 339; Public Records Office, Foreign Office (hereafter F.O.), 371, R 24/52/19, No. 97; Frank Smothers et al., *Report on the Greeks* (New York: Twentieth Century Fund, 1948), 72; Psyroukis, *Istoria*, 1:239.

8. Woodbridge, *United Nations*, 2:96

9. Department of State, *Foreign Relations of the United States, 1945* (hereafter FRUS) (Washington, D.C.: U.S. Government Printing Office, 1969), 8:221.

10. For a biographical sketch of Ambassador MacVeagh, see John O. Iatrides, ed., *Ambassador MacVeagh Reports: Greece, 1933-1947* (Princeton: Princeton University Press, 1980), 4-7; *New York Times*, 7 December 1947.

11. FRUS, 1945, 8:221.

12. Candilis, *Greece*, 28.

13. FRUS, 1945, 8:221. There are a number of useful books that deal with the Athens Revolt. The most judicious study from a liberal perspective is by John O. Iatrides, *Revolt in Athens* (Princeton: Princeton University Press, 1972). For a leftist interpretation, see F. N. Gregoriades, *Istoria tou Emphiliou Polemou, 1945-1949* (Athens, 1963-65). The cost of the Athens Revolt has been estimated at $250 million. See L. S. Stavrianos, *The Balkans since 1453* (New York: Holt, Rinehart and Winston, 1958), 827-28. For more details on the reconstruction cost estimates, see Angellopoulos, *Oikonomika*, 1:157-61.

14. For extensive analysis regarding UNRRA's origins, see Woodbridge, *United Nations* 1:3-12. For more on the role of the United States in UNRRA, see Herbert Feis, *From Trust to Terror* (New York: W. W. Norton, 1970), 227; Thomas G. Patterson, *Soviet-American Confrontation* (Baltimore: The Johns Hopkins University Press, 1973), 20-21, 76-86; D. F. Fleming, *The Cold War and Its Origins* (London: George Allen and Unwin, 1961), 1:430; David Horowitz, *The Free World Colossus* (New York: Hill and Wang, 1965), 69-70. Sbarounis, *Meletai*, 279-87. For extensive details regarding the ML, see F.O. 371/R2381/52/19, No. 26; F.O. 371/R2381/52/19, No. 28. Also, see William H. McNeill, *The Greek Dilemma* (New York: J. B. Lippincott, 1947), 169. For more about George Papandreou's defense of his government-in-exile, see Konstantinos Komnenos, *Georgios Papandreou* (Athens, 1965), 451-77; George Papandreou, *The Third War* (Athens, 1948), 16. For a succinct appraisal of Papandreou's government-in-exile, see Andreas Papandreou, *E Demokratia sto Apospasma* (Athens, 1974), 76-84, and Dominique Eudes,

The Kapetanios, translated from the French by John Howe (New York: Monthly Review Press, 1972), 127–60. The single authoritative account on ELAS is by Stefanos Sarafes, *O ELAS* (Athens, 1964). Also see Panos Lagdas, *Aris Velouhiotis* (Athens, 1965).

15. For more on Great Britain's state of the economy during the immediate postwar years and the impact it had on Anglo-Greek relations, see Psyroukis, *Istoria,* 1:243–46. For details on England's financial bankruptcy after Lend-Lease, see Joseph Marion Jones, *The Fifteen Weeks* (New York: Brace and World, 1964), 6–9, 78–80; F. S. Northedge, *Descent from Power* (London: George Allen and Unwin, 1974), 38–40; Keith Hutchison, *The Decline of British Capitalism* (Hamden, Conn.: Archon Books, 1966), 271–88.

16. McNeill, *Dilemma,* 134–35. EAM was formed in September 1941 and was organized as a coalition of six socialist parties and the KKE. For the official record of EAM, see Greek Communist party, *Episima Keimena, 1940–1945* (Athens, 1973), 5:387–537. For a revisionist analysis of EAM, see Pavlos Nepheloudis, *Stis Piges tes Kakodaimonias, Ta Vathytera Aitia tis Diaspasis tou KKE, 1918–1968* (Athens, 1974), 142–54. For conservative critiques of EAM, see D. G. Kousoulas, *Revolution and Defeat* (London: Oxford University Press, 1965), 147–87; Edgar O'Ballance, *The Greek Civil War* (New York: Frederick A. Praeger, 1966), 49–86.

17. SDNA, 868.51/4–547.

18. For more details on British interference in Greece's financial affairs during the nineteenth century, see Kofas, *Financial Relations.* For more on British interference in Greece's political affairs see T. S. Couloumbis et al., *Foreign Interference in Greek Politics* (New York: Pella Publications, 1976). For more regarding the subservience of the Service Governments to the British government, see Meynaud, *Politikes Dynameis,* 402–6, and Stephen Rousseas, *Death of a Democracy* (New York: Grove Press, 1967), 81. For a critique of British policy in Greece, see Stavrianos, *Greece,* 146. For more on United States policy toward the Near East during the demise of the British empire, see Richard J. Barnet, *Intervention and Revolution* (New York: World, 1968), 106. For more on the Churchill-Stalin informal agreement regarding the spheres-of-influence issue, see Winston Churchill, *Triumph and Tragedy* (Cambridge, Mass.: Houghton Mifflin, 1953), 226–28. The thesis that Stalin remained aloof of Greek affairs during the early Cold War had been advanced by a number of scholars. See Stavrianos, *Greece,* 184; William McCagg, *Stalin Embattled, 1943–1948* (Detroit: Wayne State University Press, 1978), 67–8; Geoffrey Chandler, *The Divided Land: An Anglo-Greek Tragedy* (London, 1959); James E. Nathan and James K. Oliver, *United States Foreign Policy and World Order* (Boston: Little, Brown, 1976), 44–50.

19. Bickham Sweet-Escott, "Greece in the Spring of 1949," *International Affairs* 25 (October 1949):452.

20. Department of Commerce, *Foreign Investments of the United States* (Washington, D.C.: U.S. Government Printing Office, 1950), 48.

21. The United Kingdom looked to the United States for financial assistance after Lend-Lease ended. See Howard K. Smith, *The State of Europe* (New York: Alfred A. Knopf, 1950), 27–29; Richard J. Gardner, *Sterling-Dollar Diplomacy in Current Perspective* (New York: Columbia University Press, 1980), 178–84; Psyroukis, *Istoria,* 1:270. For a historical perspective on the sterling-dollar competition, see James McMillan and Bernard Harris, *The American Take-Over of Britain* (New York, 1968), 114–25. For analysis regarding the supremacy of the dollar in the international economy, see Henry Aubrey, *The Dollar in World Affairs* (New York: Frederick A. Praeger, 1964), 109. The thesis that New York became the center of the world economy has been advanced by many scholars, including Immanuel Wallerstein, *The Capitalist World-Economy* (New York:

Cambridge University Press, 1979), 31–32; Harry Magdoff, *The Age of Imperialism* (New York: Monthly Review, 1967), 81–84.

22. F.O. 371/R2420/52/19, No. 97; FRUS, 1945, 8:193–95. For the text of the Anglo-Greek Agreement on distribution of supplies, see Woodbridge, *United Nations*, 3:224–28. Nikolaos Plastiras was a Venizelist officer in the interwar period. He succeeded Papandreou in January 1945. The ultra-royalists drove him out of office on 17 April 1945. For more details, see Georgis Katsoulis, *Istoria tou Kommounistikou Kommatos Elladas* (Athens, 1977), 6:17–23; J. C. P. Carey and A. G. Carey, *The Web of Modern Greek Politics* (New York: Columbia University Press, 1968), 137–38; Spyros K. Theodoropoulos, *Ap' To Dogma Truman sto Dogma Junta* (Athens, 1976), 22–23. Woodbridge, *United Nations*, 2:101; Bickham Sweet-Escott, *Greece: A Political and Economic Survey, 1939–1953* (London: Royal Institute of International Affairs, 1954), 97; FRUS, 1945, 8:202–3.

23. FRUS, 1945, 8:205–6. Stavrianos, *Balkans*, 820–26; C. M. Woodhouse, *Apple of Discord* (London: Hutchinson, 1948), 98–100, 228; Katsoulis, *Istoria*, 6:18–23. For President Roosevelt's response to Churchill's proposal, see FRUS, 1945, 8:207–8. For more on UNRRA's structure and the text of the UNRRA Agreement with Greece, see LeRoy Bennett, *International Organizations* (Englewood Cliffs, N.J.: Prentice-Hall, 1977), 214; Sweet-Escott, *Greece*, 97; Woodbridge, *United Nations*, 3:289–95, and F.O. 371/R7717/52/19, No. 246; F.O. 371/R9684/52/19, No. 67.

24. FRUS, 1945, 8:122. Woodhouse, *Apple of Discord*, 232–33, 237; and Stavrianos, *Greece*, 142, 151. Iatrides, *Revolt*, 241; Rousseas, *Democracy*, 79; O'Ballance, *Civil War*, 90, 101, 103; Psyroukis, *Istoria*, 1:266; A. Papandreou, *Democracy*, 85; G. M. Alexander, *The Prelude to the Truman Doctrine* (New York: Oxford University Press, 1982), 109–11.

25. FRUS, 1945, 8:213.

26. Ibid., 8:232–33; Candilis, *Greece*, 28–29; Alexander, *Truman Doctrine*, 124.

27. SDNA, 868.5151/6–2145, No. 1,203.

28. Cited in FRUS, 1945, 8:233; Sweet-Escott, *Greece*, 26.

29. FRUS, 1945, 8:222, 234–35; Psyroukis, *Istoria*, 1:282–83.

30. Sbarounis, *Meletai*, 286; Woodbridge, *United Nations*, 2:262–65; Diomides D. Psilos, "Postwar Economic Problems in Greece," in *Economic Development Issues: Greece, Israel, Taiwan, Thailand* (New York: Committee for Economic Development, 1963), 34.

31. FRUS, 1945, 8:273.

32. Stavrianos, *Greece*, 158–59; Psyroukis, *Istoria*, I:284.

33. SDNA, 868.50/6–1946, No. 2810.

34. Candilis, *Greece*, 30; Psyroukis, *Istoria*, 1:284; Woodhouse, *Apple of Discord*, 237–40; Stavrianos, *Greece*, 159.

35. Cited in Katsoulis, *Istoria*, 6:15; see F.O. 371/R1758/7/19, No. 20.

36. Cited in Smothers, *Greeks*, 75.

37. A. W. Sheppard, *Britain in Greece* (London, 1947), 20; Smothers, *Greeks*, 74.

38. Alexander, *Truman Doctrine*, 123.

39. Chrysos Evelpides, *Oikonomiki and Koinoniki Istoria Ellados* (Athens, 1950), 112.

40. Smothers, *Greeks*, 75.

41. Sweet-Escott, *Greece*, 127.

42. SDNA, 868.5151/6–2145, No. 1,203; Candilis, *Greece*, 38; Woodhouse, *Apple of Discord*, 237–38.

43. Sweet-Escott, *Greece*, 127; F.O. 371 R 1591, No. 285.

44. Meynaud, *Politikes Dynameis*, 377; Stavrianos, *Greece*, 157; Woodhouse, *Apple of Discord*, 238; C. M. Woodhouse, "Summer 1943: The Critical Months," in Phyllis Auty

and Richard Clogg, eds., *British Policy Towards Wartime Resistance in Yugoslavia and Greece* (London: Macmillan Press, 1975), 117–33; and Richard Clogg, "Pearls from Swine: The Foreign Office Papers, S.O.E. and the Greek Resistance," in ibid., 195, 200. For extensive details concerning UNRRA's difficulties in distributing supplies, see Woodbridge, *United Nations*, 2:104–23. For more about the Greeks who profited from UNRRA, see Smothers, *Greeks*, 75; Katsoulis, *Istoria*, 6:25; Psyroukis, *Istoria*, 1:285. For more about the use of UNRRA as a political weapon against the communists, see Theodoropoulos, *Dogma Truman*, 24–25; Chandler, *Divided Land*, 184; Sheppard, *Greece*, 30; and Lyall Wilkes, "British Missions and Greek Quislings," *New Statesman and Nation* 33 (1947):88–89. For MacVeagh's defense of the profiteers, see FRUS, 1945, 8:269.

45. Smith, *Europe*, 227–28.

46. Katsoulis, *Istoria*, 6:168; Psyroukis, *Istoria*, 1:283–85.

47. F.O. 371/GR1101/2, No. 10; *New York Times*, 15 December 1947; ibid., 18 December 1947; Department of Commerce, *Foreign Relations Yearbook, 1949* (Washington, D.C.: U.S. Government Printing Office, 1951), 93–94.

48. Angellopoulos, *Oikonomika*, 1:108.

49. SDNA, 868.51/10-245, No. 1,264; Angellopoulos, *Oikonomika*, 1:107, 109–110.

50. Candilis, *Greece*, 29; *New York Times*, 11 September 1945; Stavrianos, *Greece*, 159; Candilis, *Greece*, 30–31; SDNA, 868.51/10-245, No. 1,264.

51. FRUS, 1945, 8:224–28, 238–39, 242–43; C. M. Woodhouse, *The Struggle for Greece, 1941–1949* (New York: Beekman/Esanu Publishers, 1976), 148; Stavrianos, *Greece*, 160–62; Hutchison, *British Capitalism*, 300–301; Feis, *From Trust to Terror*, 229. For more on the debate regarding the merits of UNRRA, see Arthur Vandenberg, Jr., *The Private Papers of Senator Arthur Vandenberg* (Boston: Houghton Mifflin, 1952), 66–64; Horowitz, *Free World*, 70–71; SDNA, 868.50/6-1946, No. 2,810.

52. FRUS, 1945, 8:241–42, 246–47; Smith, *Europe*, 94; Robert H. Ferrell, *George C. Marshall* (New York: Cooper Square Publishers, 1966), 107–8; Walter Millis, ed., *The Forrestal Diaries* (New York: Viking Press, 1951), 210, 234.

53. *New York Times*, 10 September 1945, 11 September 1945; FRUS, 1945, 8:152–53, 250–51, 262–63; F. J. Dobney, *Selected Papers of Will Clayton* (Baltimore: The Johns Hopkins University Press, 1971), 185–89.

54. Eudes, *Kapetanios*, 252–54; Stavrianos, *Greece*, 162; Woodhouse, *Apple of Discord*, 252–53; Alexander, *Truman Doctrine*, 144–48; F.O. 371/R1588/17001/19, No. 286; Meynaud, *Politikes Dynameis*, 81. FRUS, 1945, 8:263; Theodoropoulos, *Dogma Truman*, 17; Nikolaos Stavrou, *Allied Politics and Military Intervention* (Athens, 1976), 61.

55. FRUS, 1945, 8:252.

56. Ibid., 8:253–54, 263–67; Xydis, *Greece*, 175–80; Heinz Richter, "The Varkiza Agreement and the Origins of the Civil War," in John O. Iatrides, ed., *Greece in the 1940s* (London: University Press of New England, 1981), 166–80.

57. Cited in Stavrianos *Greece*, 160. Bevin informed Atlee on 15 November 1945 that the English economy was in crisis due to shortages in materials, industrial power, and equipment. See Francis Williams, *Twilight of Empire* (New York: A. S. Barnes, 1960), 125–27. For more details concerning the domino theory, see Vandenberg, *Private Papers*, 338–39; Stephen Ambrose, *Rise to Globalism* (New York: Penguin Books, 1978), 146–47; Richard J. Walton, *Henry Wallace, Harry Truman and the Cold War* (New York: Viking Press, 1976), 143–44.

58. Komnenos, *Papandreou*, 496. Woodhouse, *Apple of Discord*, 253; FRUS, 1945, 8:178–79, 297–98; Alexander, *Truman Doctrine*, 14–51; Theodoropoulos, *Dogma Truman*, 33–34; Stavrianos, *Greece*, 161.

59. FRUS, 1945, 8:285.
60. SDNA, 868.50/4–446, No. 2,481; Candilis, *Greece*, 36.
61. *New York Times*, 23 December 1945. Katsoulis, *Istoria*, 6:78. Regarding the status of banks, see Candilis, *Greece*, 71.
62. FRUS, 1945, 8:286.
63. For the text of the Varkiza Agreement, see EAM *White Book, May 1944–March 1945* (Athens, [n.d.]), 97–113. For more details about the KKE's position after the Varkiza Agreement, see *Episima Keimena, 1940–1945*, 5:358–61; Antonio Solaro, *Istoria tou Kommounistikou Kommatos Elladas* (Athens, 1975), 170; Nepheloudis, *KKE*, 251–52; Sarafes, *ELAS*, 362–63; Lagdas, *Velouhiotis*, 481–501; Eudes, *Kapetanios*, 243–63. For more details on the "white terror" and the position of the British as well as the Greek authorities in Athens toward the right-wing elements, see Smothers, *Greeks*, 34–35; Smith, *Europe*, 223; Tsoukalas, *Tragedy*, 95.
64. For more Grivas, see Komnenos Pyromaglou, *O Kartales kai e Epohe tou* (Athens, 1965), 555–58; Eudes, *Kapetanios*, 156. For more about the "Xists," see Tsoukalas, *Tragedy*, 93–94; Maurice Edelman, "Greece: A Reply to Mr. Bevin," *New Statesman and Nation* 31 (1946); Stavrou, *Allied Politics*, 42–44; Smothers, *Greeks*, 34; Pyromaglou, *Kartales*, 237, 311–15; Stavrianos, *Greece*, 88–89; Tsoukalas, *Tragedy*, 93; Wilkes, "British Missions," 88.
65. Smith, *Europe*, 238.
66. Nikos C. Alivizatos, "The Emergency Regime and Civil Liberties, 1946–1949," in Iatrides, *Greece*, 220–22; Central Committee of the KKE, *Voethema Yia tin Istoria tou KKE* (Athens, 1975), 233; Psyroukis, *Istoria*, 1:267; Katsoulis, *Istoria*, 6:16; Tsoukalas, *Tragedy*, 94.
67. Cited in Chandler, *Divided Land*, 142–43.
68. Stavrianos, *Greece*, 153–54, 160; Eudes, *Kapetanios*, 244; Wilkes, "British Missions," 88; Sheppard, *Greece*, 12–15. A. Papandreou, *Democracy*, 113.
69. For more details concerning Kanellopoulos and EON, see Kofas, *Authoritarianism*, 88–94.
70. FRUS, 1945, 8:298; Katsoulis, *Istoria*, 6:76–78.
71. SDNA, 868.5151/1–1046, No. 3,644.
72. FRUS, 1945, 8:275, 282.
73. Xydis, *Greece*, 141; Angellopoulos, *Oikonomika*, 1:123, 139–45; Feis, *From Trust to Terror*, 215–17; Paterson, *Confrontation*, 241–43; Vandenberg, *Private Papers*, 278–85; C. J. Bartlett, *The Rise and Fall of Pax Americana* (New York: St. Martin's Press, 1974), 104–6; SDNA, 868.50/446, No. 2,481; SDNA, 868.50/6–1946, No. 2,810; *New York Times*, 19 January 1946; Alexander, *Truman Doctrine*, 167. For the complete text of the Agreement, see FRUS, 1946, 8:100–104.
74. Candilis, *Greece*, 33; Angellopoulos, *Oikonomika*, 1:234.
75. FRUS, 1946, 7:103.
76. Angellopoulos, *Oikonomika*, 1:234–35; *New York Times*, 27 January 1946. Kommounistiko Komma Elladas, *Saranta Chronia tou KKE, 1918–1958* (Athens, 1958), 548.
77. SDNA, 868.5151/2–546, No. 2,036; FRUS, 1946, 7:89–90, 95–96, 103; Angellopoulos, *Oikonomika*, 1:236. *New York Times*, 19 January 1946, 27 January 1946; Xydis, *Greece*, 152–53.
78. Candilis, *Greece*, 34. For similar views, see L. S. Wittner, *American Intervention in Greece, 1943–1949* (New York: Columbia University Press, 1982), 171; Psyroukis, *Istoria*, 1:286.
79. SDNA, 868.5151/6–2446, No. 2,833; Alexander, *Truman Doctrine*, 194–95.

80. SDNA, 868.51/3-1047.
81. Eudes, *Kapetanios,* 299.
82. For more details concerning the controversial March 1946 elections, see Meynaud, *Politikes Dynameis,* 78-85; Theodoropoulos, *Dogma Truman,* 39-41; Gregoris Daphnis, *Ta Ellinika Politika Kommata, 1821-1961* (Athens, 1961). For more details about the Greek loan from the United States Federal Reserve Bank, see FRUS, 1946, 7:260.
83. SDNA, 868.5151/11-746, No. 6,106.

Chapter II

1. Alexander, *Truman Doctrine,* 164.
2. For the text of Lend-Lease, see Walter C. Langsam, ed., *Documents and Readings in the History of Europe since 1918* (New York: J. B. Lippincott, 1951), 914-18. For analysis regarding the origin of Lend-Lease, see Ambrose, *Globalism,* 43-45; Gardner, *Diplomacy,* 40-42; McMillan and Harris, *Britain,* 24-25. Total Lend-Lease aid amounted to $50 billion. See Aubrey, *World Affairs,* 6-7. For more details about the termination of Lend-Lease, see Fleming, *Cold War,* 1:269-70; Ambrose, *Globalism,* 120-21; George F. Kennan, *Memoirs, 1925-1950* (Boston: Little, Brown, 1967), 266-69. For more on the British reaction to the termination of Lend-Lease, see Williams, *Empire,* 132-34; Northedge, *Descent from Power,* 44; Feis, *From Trust to Terror,* 230-31; Gardner, *Diplomacy,* 188-207; Paterson, *Confrontation,* 162-64. For analysis regarding the Ottawa Conference, see Walter L. Arnstein, *Britain Yesterday and Today* (Lexington, Mass.: D. C. Heath, 1971), 57-58; Hutchison, *British Capitalism,* 255-57; and Gardner, *Diplomacy,* 154-58.
3. Northedge, *Descent from Power,* 41-42.
4. Williams, *Empire,* 134; Gaddis Smith, *Dean Acheson* (New York: Cooper Square Publishers, 1972), 32-33; Psyroukis, *Istoria,* 1:286. For a critique of the American loan to England, see McMillan and Harris, *Britain,* 28-32; Walter LeFeber, ed. *The Origins of the Cold War, 1941-1947* (New York: John Wiley and Sons, 1971), 81-84. For more details about England's financial predicament between June 1946 and June 1948, see Ferrell, *Marshall,* 100-101; Northedge, *Descent from Power,* 45. Smith, *Europe,* 78; Paul Baran and Paul Sweezy, *Monopoly Capital* (New York, Monthly Review Press, 1966), 159-60, 175-76, 212. The United States financial network dominated the international economy after 1945. See Magdoff, *Imperialism,* 67-100; Aubrey, *World Affairs,* 171-205; Nikos Svoronos, *Episkopisi tis Neoellinikes Istorias* (Athens, 1976), 145.
5. FRUS, 1946, 7:176.
6. Smothers, *Greeks,* 71; Candilis, *Greece,* 69; *Foreign Commerce Yearbook, 1948,* 93. For extensive details on the Populist government, see Stavrianos, *Greece,* 163-71; Tsoukalas, *Tragedy,* 96-97; Solaro, *Istoria,* 183-84; Katsoulis, *Istoria,* 6:75-93.
7. *New York Times,* 2 July 1946.
8. Ibid.; Stavrou, *Allied Politics,* 59, 63-64.
9. FRUS, 1946, 7:182, 184, 187-88, 190; *New York Times,* 2 July 1946; Alexander, *Truman Doctrine,* 203-4.
10. Gregoris Daphnis, *Sophocles Eleftheriou Venizelos* (Athens, 1970), 280-82; SDNA, 868.516/12-1545, No. 2,003; SDNA, 868.516/1-946, No. 113.
11. For a favorable biography of Karamanles, see Maurice Genevoix, *The Greece of Karamanles* (London: Doric Publications, 1973). Karamanles moved to the forefront of the political arena in 1956 with the backing of the United States. See A. Papandreou,

Democracy, 140–44; Meynaud, *Politikes Dynameis*, 234–75; For more details on the mission's initial contacts, see FRUS, 1946, 7:190–91. For more details concerning the role of Henry Wallace during the early Cold War, see Ronald Radosh and L. P. Liggio, "Henry A. Wallace and the Open Door," in Thomas G. Paterson, ed., *Cold War Critics* (Chicago: Quadrangle Books, 1971), 76–107. For more about the mission's deals with American officials, see Daphnis, *Venizelos*, 287–89.

12. SDNA, 868.51/8-2346, Office Memo. T. C. Kariotis, "American Economic Penetration of Greece in the Late Nineteen Forties," *Journal of the Hellenic Diaspora* 4 (1979): 87.

13. SDNA 868.5151/7-247, No. 5,163; Daphnis, *Venizelos*, 284–86; Lemos, *Greeks*, 180, 183, 185, 186; Katsoulis, *Istoria*, 6:157, Psyroukis, *Istoria*, 1:241, 290. The Greek shipowners had in 1945 "27 million pounds sterling on deposit in London as a result of insurance collected on ships lost during the war." SDNA, 868.51/10-245, No. 1,624. Eudes, *Kapetanios*, 299; Meynaud, *Politikes Dynameis*, 376; Queen Fredericka of the Hellenes, *A Measure of Understanding* (London: Macmillan, 1971), 154–55; Smothers, *Greeks*, 176; SDNA, 5151/7-247, No. 5,163.

14. Xydis, *Greece*, 233; Lemos, *Greeks*, 199; Meynaud, *Politikes Dynameis*, 380.

15. Cited in Eudes, *Kapetanios*, 300.

16. FRUS, 1946, 7:201; Daphnis, *Venizelos*, 287–89, 386–87.

17. For more details concerning the deteriorating relations between Washington and Moscow during Truman's first year in office, see Smith, *Acheson*, 33–35; Paterson, *Confrontation*, 25–26; Xydis, *Greece*, 355–59; Fleming, *Cold War*, 1: Ch. 13. For more about the Soviet Union's objections to the British military presence in Greece, see Evangelos Averoff-Tosizza, *By Fire and Axe* (New York: Caratzas Brothers, 1978), 158–60; D. G. Kousoulas, *The Price of Freedom* (Syracuse, N.Y., 1953), 156–59; H. N. Howard, "United States Policy Towards Greece in the United Nations," *Balkan Studies*, 8 (1966): 265; Van Coufoudakis, "The United States, the United Nations, and the Greek Question, 1946–1952," in Iatrides, *Greece*, 279–81; Katsoulis, *Istoria*, 6:137. For more details on the Ukrainian representatives' objections concerning Greece, see Kousoulas, *Freedom*, 159–60; Daphnis, *Venizelos*, 400. The most comprehensive account concerning the Greek question before the United Nations in 1946 is Xydis, *Greece*, 236–354. Greece acquired the Dodecanese islands after World War II, but did not realize its territorial ambitions in the north. See Kousoulas, *Freedom*, 142–45. For more on the plebiscite, see Carey and Carey, *Greece*, 140–41; Theodoropoulos, *Dogma Truman*, 44–49; George Papandreou, *Politika Keimena* (Athens, 1950), 2:150–61; Chandler, *Divided Land*, 167–70; Stavrianos, *Greece*, 174–75. In March 1946 Atlee hinted that his government would withdraw its troops from Greece and the entire Near East to concentrate on Africa. See Xydis, *Greece*, 184.

18. Xydis, *Greece*, 228. SDNA, 868.50/6-1946, No. 281.

19. For the Communist party's perspective on the "white terror," see *Verite Sur la Grece* (Belgrade, 1945), 164–77, 193–229; Katsoulis, *Istoria*, 6:142.

20. Barnet, *Intervention*, 98. The United States granted $10 million in surplus property credit to Greece in August 1946. See Xydis, *Greece*, 476.

21. Ibid., 400–401.

22. FRUS, 1946, 6:235–37.

23. Ibid., 7:240–44.

24. Horowitz, *Free World*, 54–64; John Bagguley, "The World War and the Cold," in David Horowitz, ed., *Containment and Revolution* (Boston: Beacon Press, 1967), 112–14. The United States rejected Stalin's loan request in 1946, while extending loans to West-

ern European and Latin American countries. Stalin concluded that the West was building an anti-communist bloc under America's leadership. See Feis, *From Trust to Terror*, 70–74; Thomas G. Paterson, "The Dessent of Senator Claude Pepper," in Paterson, *Cold War*, 120–24.

25. Cited in Horowitz, *Containment*, 11.

26. Robert Engler, *The Politics of Oil* (New York: Macmillan Press, 1961), 202; Woodhouse, *Apple of Discord*, 275. On the issue of the United States search for minerals and the Cold War, see Alfred E. Eckes, Jr., *The United States and the Global Struggle for Minerals* (Austin: University of Texas Press, 1979), 135–45. Magdoff argued that America's Cold War policy furthered capitalist interests that were on an outward-oriented course. Magdoff, *Imperialism*, 200. A number of revisionist historians argue along similar lines. See Gabriel Kolko, *Main Currents in American History* (New York: Pantheon Books, 1984), 348–60. The most important domestic dimension of the Cold War policy of containment was that it served as an impetus for McCarthyism. One of the best historical studies on this subject is by Athan Theoharis, *Seeds of Repression: Harry S. Truman and the Origins of McCarthyism* (Chicago: Quadrangle Books, 1971).

27. Cited in Stavrianos, *Greece*, 178.

28. FRUS, 1946, 7:282.

29. Ibid., 7:286; Daphnis, *Venizelos*, 403; Xydis, *Greece*, 433–36; Stavrianos, *Greece*, 178–80; Katsoulis, *Istoria*, 6:149–50, 156–57.

30. Cited in FRUS, 1947, 5:6–7.

31. Xydis, *Greece*, 378, 438; SDNA, 868.516/5-747, No. 3,990; FRUS, 1946, 7:252; ibid., 7:253–54; Candilis, *Greece*, 40.

32. FRUS, 1946, 7:250.

33. Sheppard, *Britain*, 19.

34. Smith, *Europe*, 226–27; Eudes, *Kapetanios*, 275–76.

35. For extensive details on the Porter mission's preliminary work, see Xydis, *Greece*, 462–65; Jones, *Fifteen Weeks*, 75–76. For more details on the resignation of Tsaldaris and the composition and appointment of the cabinet, see Papandreou, *Politika Keimena*, 2:197–99; Stavrianos, *Greece*, 179–80; Daphnis, *Venizelos*, 403–4; FRUS, 1947, 5:3–5; Woodhouse, *Apple of Discord*, 276; Theodoropoulos, *Dogma Truman*, 54–55; SDNA, 868.50/2-1747, AMAG; A. Papandreou, *Democracy*, 103.

36. SDNA, 868.50/2-1747, AMAG.

37. Cited in Katsoulis, *Istoria*, 6:26.

38. FRUS, 1946, 7:226–27; ibid., 1947, 5:22–27; Barnet, *Intervention*, 106; Ferrell, *Marshall*, 78–79; Jones, *Fifteen Weeks*, 78–83; Kuniholm, *Cold War*, 406–7; Arnstein, *Britain*, 303–6; Hutchison, *British Capitalism*, 293–300; Harry S. Truman, *Memoirs* (Garden City, N.Y.: Doubleday, 1956), 2:99; Daphnis, *Venizelos*, 412; Feis, *From Trust to Terror*, 188.

39. FRUS, 1947, 5:28. MacVeagh charged that the KKE was Soviet-controlled and the government in Moscow intended to extend its power over the Aegean. See FRUS, 1946, 7:226–27.

40. O'Ballance, *Civil War*, 121; Averoff-Tosizza, *Fire and Axe*, 171; Woodhouse, *Apple of Discord*, 181–82; Howard F. Gosnell, *Truman's Crises* (Westport, Conn.: Greenwood Press, 1980), 345. For more on Stalin's policy toward the West, see McCagg, *Stalin*, 31–35. The KKE committed a grave error by allowing two years to pass before making a definite decision to stage a revolution. This was later recognized and admitted by the new leadership after the civil war. See *Saranta Chronia*, 646; Todd Gittlin, "Counter-Insurgency: Myth and Reality in Greece" in Horowitz, *Containment*, 163–64; Daphnis, *Venizelos*, 413.

41. Stavrianos, *Greece*, 174; Katsoulis, *Istoria*, 6:112-18.
42. FRUS, 1947, 5:40. For excerpts from the secretary's speech, see Jones, *Fifteen Weeks*, 103, 107-9. Kennan, *Memoirs*, 354-67. For a critique of "containment," see Henry H. Berger, "A Conservative Critique of Containment: Senator Taft on the Early Cold War Program," in Horowitz, *Containment*, 125-37; R. J. Donovan, *Conflict and Crisis* (New York: W. W. Norton, 1977), 279, 72. FRUS, 1947, 5:42.
43. FRUS, 1947, 5:42.
44. Ibid., 42-44; Jones, *Fifteen Weeks*, 81-82; Stavrianos, *Greece*, 180.
45. FRUS, 1947, 5:49; Xydis, *Greece*, 479-80. Marshall wrote to the president on 26 February that the United States must take over Britain's role in the Near East, considering the geopolitical importance of the area. See Kariotis, "Greece," 87.
46. FRUS, 1947, 5:54.
47. Truman, *Memoirs*, 2:100-101.
48. Ibid., 231.
49. The seeds of American imperialism were planted by the bourgeois leaders of the War of Independence. By 1800 the United States set out to become an empire emulating the mother country. This thesis has been developed by a number of historians, including Richard Van Alstyne, *The Rising American Empire* (Chicago: Quadrangle Books, 1960), ch. 4; and William Appleman Williams, *Empire as a Way of Life* (New York: Oxford University Press, 1980). The thesis that underdevelopment is the direct result of imperialist exploitation is reflected in many recent Third World studies based on the dependency model. See Richard Harris, ed., *The Political Economy of Africa* (New York: Shenkman Publishing, 1975); Ronald H. Chilcote and Joel C. Edelstein, eds., *Latin America: The Struggle with Dependency and Beyond* (New York: John Wiley and Sons, 1974).
50. FRUS, 1947, 5:46-47; Walter Millis, ed., *The Forrestal Diaries* (New York: Viking Press, 1951), 248-49.
51. Cited in Gardner, *Diplomacy*, 300. For Acheson's views, see Jones, *Fifteen Weeks*, 141.
52. Vandenberg, *Private Papers*, 340.
53. Kennan, *Memoirs*, 316-17.
54. Jones, *Fifteen Weeks*, 151-52; FRUS, 1947, 5:63-64; Truman, *Memoirs*, 2:103-4; Smith, *Acheson*, 46; Vandenberg, *Private Papers*, 338-39.
55. FRUS, 1947, 5:69-71, 73-75; Jones, *Fifteen Weeks*, 153; SDNA, 868.51/3-347, Office Memo.
56. F.O. 371/R341/141/11; F.O. 371/R342/141/11; FRUS, 1947, 5:79-89, 90, 102; Millis, *Forrestal*, 251; Jones, *Fifteen Weeks*, 164-65.
57. FRUS, 1947, 5:108.
58. Truman, *Memoirs*, 2:104; Feis, *From Trust to Terror*, 192; Jones, *Fifteen Weeks*, 167-68; Millis, *Forrestal*, 251-52. Keenan, *Memoirs*, 320; Ambrose, *Globalism*, 148-49; Charles Bohlen, *Witness to History* (New York: W. W. Norton, 1973), 261; Truman, *Memoirs*, 2:105; Jones, *Fifteen Weeks*, 155-6.
59. For the complete text of the Truman Doctrine, see *Public Papers of the the Presidents, Harry S. Truman, 1947* (Washington, D.C.: U.S. Government Printing Office, 1963), 176-80. For the president's afterthoughts, see Truman, *Memoirs*, 2:105-8. For a critical appraisal of the Doctrine, see Fleming, *Cold War*, 1:441-42; Horowitz, *Free World*, 73-74; Kuniholm, *Cold War*, 247-48; and Susan Hartman, *Truman and the 80th Congress* (Columbia: University of Missouri Press, 1971), 53-55.
60. Berger, "Containment," 125-26.
61. Kolko, *History*, 364.

62. Cited in Katsoulis, *Istoria*, 6:158-59.
63. Gittlin, "Counter-Insurgency," 169; Hartman, *Truman*, 60-63; Jones, *Fifteen Weeks*, 171-73; Ferrell, *Marshall*, 84-85. For more details concerning the contemporary critics of the Truman Doctrine, see Berger, "Containment," 128-30; Paterson, "Claude Pepper," 128-31; Wittner, *Intervention*, 80-84, 86-90; William C. Pratt, "Senator Glen C. Taylor: Questioning American Unilateralism" in Paterson, *Cold War*, 146-49; and Horowitz, *Free World*, 71. For details about the UN Commission's composition, goals, and findings, see Harry N. Howard, *The United Nations and the Problem of Greece* (Washington, D.C.: U.S. Government Printing Office, 1947). For an analysis from a revisionist perspective, see Eudes, *Kapetanios*, 281-88; Rousseas, *Democracy*, 85-87. For Truman's policy toward the UN, see George T. Mazuman, "America's U.N. Commitment, 1945-1953," *The Historian*, 60 (1978): 323. For commentary on the commission's report by a key member, see Howard, "United Nations," 267-72. For extensive analysis, see Woodhouse, *Struggle*, 197-98; Eudes, *Kapetanios*, 188-90; Katsoulis, *Istoria*, 6:138-41; Kenneth Matthews, *Memoirs of a Mountain War: Greece, 1944-1949* (London, 1972), 136-54.
64. Fleming, *Cold War*, 1:450-53; Xydis, *Greece*, 496; Rousseas, *Democracy*, 84; Berger, "Containment," 127; Ambrose, *Globalism*, 151. For extensive details concerning Wallace as a critic of the Truman administration's foreign policy, see Edward L. and Frederick H. Schapsmeir, *Prophet in Politics: Henry A. Wallace and the War Years, 1945-1965* (Ames: University of Iowa Press, 1970), ch. 10; see also Walton, *Wallace*, 72-137.
65. Barnet, *Intervention*, 97.
66. Gittlin, "Counter-Insurgency," 141.

Chapter III

1. For more details concerning the reception of the Truman Doctrine in Greek political circles, see Smothers, *Greeks*, 197-98; Rousseas, *Democracy*, 87-88; Psyroukis, *Istoria*, 1:195-96; and *Public Papers of the Presidents, Truman*, 180. For the Porter mission recommendations, see F.O. 371/GR2609, No. OF 48/10/6; F.O. R1841, No. 342; FRUS, 1947, 5:131-34; Theodoropoulos, *Dogma Truman*, 63-64; Economic Cooperation Administration, *Greece Country Report* (Washington, D.C.: U.S. Government Printing Office, 1949), 2-3; Hugh Seton-Watson, *The East European Revolution* (New York: Frederick A. Praeger, 1950), 332; FRUS, 1947, 5:136-37; Barnet, *Intervention*, 123.
2. Hartman, *Truman*, 60-63; Jones, *Fifteen Weeks*, 182-85; Feis, *From Trust to Terror*, 204; Ferrell, *Marshall*, 95; FRUS, 1947, 5:99; *Public Papers of the Presidents, Truman*, 254-55; Fleming, *Cold War*, 1:450; Schapsmeir, *Wallace*, 174; Walter Lippman, *The Cold War* (New York: Harper Torchbooks, 1972), 43-47; Barton J. Bernstein, "Walter Lippman and the Early Cold War," in Paterson, *Cold War*, 39-41. For the complete text of the agreement, see FRUS, 1947, 5:185-86. For commentary, see Tsoukalas, *Tragedy*, 106; Angellopoulos, *Oikonomika*, 1:128-33; Kariotis, "Greece," 87-88, 94.
3. FRUS, 1947, 5:186.
4. William H. McNeill, *Greece: American Aid in Action, 1947-1956* (New York: Twentieth Century Fund, 1957), 35.
5. Democratic Organization of Greece, *Third Blue Book* (Athens, 1950), 19.
6. FRUS, 1947, 5:177-78; Stavrianos, *Greece*, 193.
7. FRUS, 1947, 5:204; Sheppard, *Britain*, 9; S. Agapitides, "Wage Policy in Greece," *International Labor Review* 61 (1950): 243-44; FRUS, 1947, 5:204-05. For more details about the expenses of the Royal House, see SDNA, 868.51/7-847, Office Memo.
8. Department of State, *Second Report to Congress on the United States Relief Program*

192 Notes

(Washington, D.C.: U.S. Government Printing Office, 1947), 21; Department of State, *Third Report to Congress on the United States Relief Program* (Washington, D.C.: U.S. Government Printing Office, 1948), 37.

9. For extensive details on the government troops vs. those of the Democratic Army, see Katsoulis, *Istoria*, 6:176-77; Nepheloudis, *Istoria*, 283-84; Barnet, *Intervention*, 125; Psyroukis, *Istoria*, 1:350; Eudes, *Kapetanios*, 294.

10. Sheppard, *Britain*, 14-15.

11. William H. McNeill, *The Metamorphosis of Greece since World War II* (Chicago: University of Chicago Press, 1978), 87; Solaro, *Istoria*, 187; Eudes, *Kapetanios*, 294; SDNA, 868.50/1-748, No. 4,383; F.O. 371/RG1011/1, No. 7; F.O. 371/RG1101/1, No. 5; Stavrianos, *Greece*, 193; Katsoulis, *Istoria*, 6:195.

12. FRUS, 1947, 5:202, 215-16; Wittner, *Intervention*, 101-2; Theodoropoulos, *Dogma Truman*, 67.

13. FRUS, 1947, 5:219-20.

14. McCagg, *Stalin*, 241-43.

15. Ibid., 271-72, 386; Eudes, *Kapetanios*, 296; Katsoulis, *Istoria*, 6:173-75; Nikos Svoronos, "Greek History, 1940-1950," in Iatrides, *Greece*, 13.

16. Cited in FRUS, 1947, 5:231.

17. Gittlin, "Counter-Insurgency," 164; McNeill, *American Aid*, 37; FRUS, 1947, 5:222-24.

18. F.O. 371/R340/14/19; FRUS, 1947, 5:76-77.

19. C. A. Munkman, *American Aid to Greece* (New York: Frederick A. Praeger, 1958), 63-64.

20. FRUS, 1947, 5:191-92.

21. FRUS, 1947, 5:291; Eudes, *Kapetanios*, 299; Candilis, *Greece*, 71; Sweet-Escott, *Greece*, 192; SDNA, 868.516/5-747, No. 3,990; Smothers, *Greece*, 72-74.

22. *Foreign Commerce Yearbook, 1949*, 91-92; FRUS, 1947, 5:341-42, 420-21; Candilis, *Greece*, 49; FRUS, 1947, 5:413-14. For extensive details concerning Griswold's role in the Greek political arena, see G. Papandreou, *Politika Keimena*, 274-77; Katsoulis, *Istoria*, 6:181; Rousseas, *Democracy*, 90; Stavrianos, *Greece*, 187-89; Eudes, *Kapetanios*, 301; Woodhouse, *Apple of Discord*, 279.

23. SDNA, 868.5151/1-1648, No. 4.

24. *Second Report to Congress*, 18.

25. SDNA, 868.50/4-2348, No. 481, Enclosures 2-6; SDNA, 868.18/12-1947; Eudes, *Kapetanios*, 299.

26. SDNA, 868.00/12-1147; SDNA, 868.5017/11-147, No. 180.

27. Cited in SDNA, 868.5151/10-3147.

28. SDNA, 868.5017/11-147, No. 180; FRUS, 1947, 5:421; SDNA, 868.50/12-1147. Also see *New York Times*, 12 October 1947. Professor Kariotis's research, which was based on archival material, confirmed the *New York Times* report that Griswold's powers were extensive and superseded the Greek government's authority. See Kariotis, "Greece," 91; FRUS, 1947, 5:378-88.

29. Ibid., 5:398.

Chapter IV

1. For the complete text of General Marshall's speech, see Department of State, *Bulletin* 16 (15 June 1947): 1159-60. For more details concerning the inception of the

Marshall Plan, see Smith, *Acheson*, 49-51; Truman, *Memoirs*, 2:113; Kennan, *Memoirs*, 325-29; Jones, *Fifteen Weeks*, 199-203; Department of Commerce, *Foreign Trade, 1939-1949* (Washington, D.C.: U.S. Government Printing Office, 1950), 42; Ferrell, *Marshall*, 105-6. For more details about the postwar economic factors that played an important part in the Truman Administration's foreign policy, see Paterson, *Confrontation*, 16-18. For more on Europe's economic predicament, see Bartlett, *Pax Americana*, 107; Ferrell, *Marshall*, 100-103; Gardner, *Diplomacy*, 302-3; and Raymond Mikesell, *Foreign Exchange in the Postwar World* (New York: Twentieth Century Fund, 1954), 100-102. President Truman asked Congress on 19 December 1947 to appropriate $17 billion for the ERP. When the program terminated on 31 December 1951, Congress had actually allocated $13.015 billion. See Economic Cooperation Administration, *Report to the Committee on Foreign Relations* (Washington, D.C.: U.S. Government Printing Office, 1948), 3; Also see Jacob Rubin, *Your Hundred Billion Dollars* (New York: Chiton Books, 1964), 49.

2. Nathan and Oliver, *World Order*, 103-5; Horowitz, *Free World*, 75-82; Kennan, *Memoirs*, 330-45.

3. Eckes, *Minerals*, 157.

4. Ibid., 158; Donald Dozer, *Are We Good Neighbors?* (Gainsville: University of Florida Press, 1959), 236. On the issue of Latin American dependence on the Untied States, there are many useful studies based on the dependency model and class analysis. For an overview perspective, see Alonso Aguilar, *Pan-Americanism: From Monroe to the Present*, trans. Asa Zatz (New York: Monthly Review Press, 1968); also see James Cockcroft et al., eds., *Dependence and Underdevelopment: Latin America's Political Economy* (Garden City, N.Y.: Doubleday/Anchor, 1972). For a succinct essay on the specific issue of United States militarization of Latin America, see M. T. Klare and Cynthia Arnson, "Exporting Repression: U.S. Support for Authoritarianism in Latin America," in Richard Fagen, ed., *Capitalism and the State in U.S.-Latin American Relations* (Stanford: Stanford University Press, 1979), 138-68. For more details about the ECA's functions, see Rubin, *Billion Dollars*, 41-49. For more about Europe's reciprocal obligations toward the United States under the ERP, see Eckes, *Minerals*, 159; Baran and Sweezy, *Capital*, 190-91.

5. FRUS, 1949, 6:453.

6. United Nations, General Assembly, *Official Records* (Lake Placid, N.Y.: United Nations, 1947), 86-88.

7. McNeill, *American Aid*, 47; Katsoulis, *Istoria*, 6:237; *Foreign Commerce Yearbook, 1951*, 395, 380, 413, 517; Sweet-Escott, *Greece*, 194; Katsoulis, *Istoria*, 6:237-39.

8. SDNA, 868.516/11-1848, No. 1,121; A. A. Fatouros, "Building Formal Structures of Penetration: The U.S. in Greece, 1947-48," in Iatrides, *Greece*, 251; Candilis, *Greece*, 46.

9. SDNA, 868.516/11-1848, No. 1,121.

10. Munkman, *Aid*, 72; McNeill, *American Aid*, 229; Candilis, *Greece*, 46.

11. Mouzelis, *Underdevelopment*, 119; Candilis, *Greece*, 48.

12. SDNA, 868.51/8-3048, AMAG-1,521; SDNA, 868.51/8-648, No. 239.

13. Cited in SDNA, 868.51/8-618, No. 239.

14. SDNA, 868.51/10-848, No. 1,015.

15. SDNA, 868.50/5-148, No. 69; SDNA, 868.51/12-1249, No. 864. Direct taxes in fiscal 1948-49 accounted for 17.3 percent of the revenues, or 501 billion drachmas. Indirect taxes were 82.7 percent of the revenues, or 2,391 billion drachmas. See SDNA, 868.5042/12-149, No. 6,991.

16. OEEC, *Progress and Problems of the European Economy* (Fifth Annual Report of the OEEC) (Paris, 1954), 124; Sweet-Escott, *Greece*, 192; Munkman, *Aid*, 71-72.

17. OEEC, *Europe the Way Ahead* (Fourth Annual Report to the OEEC) (Paris, 1952), 274.
18. Angellopoulos, *Oikonomika*, 1:301.
19. Munkman, *Aid*, 71–72.
20. Ibid., 72. Nicholas A. Michas, "Economic Development, Social Mobilization and the Growth of Public Expenditures in Greece," *American Journal of Economics and Sociology*, 39 (1980): 39. Yiannes Roubatis, "The United States and the Occupational Responsibilities of the Greek Armed Forces, 1947–1987," *Journal of the Hellenic Diaspora* 6 (1979): 39–57. For Papandreou's defense and foreign-policy objectives see *Greek Government Programme Presented by the Prime Minister Andreas G. Papandreou* (Athens, 1981), 8–16.
21. FRUS, 1949, 6:454–55.
22. SDNA, 868.50/11–2748, No. 1,148. For more about Stefanopoulos, see Meynaud, *Politikes Dynameis*, 89. For the entire text of the speech, see SDNA, 868.50/11–2748, No. 1,148.
23. Sweet-Escott, *Greece*, 108–9.
24. For the specifics of the Four Year Plan, see ERP, *Greece*, 29, 30–34; SDNA, 868.50/11–2748, No. 1,148. F.O. 371/R35/1102/19, No. 378; F.O. 371/R11166/1102/19, No. 224; F.O. 371/R8032/1102/19, No. 143E.
25. Sweet-Escott, *Greece*, 108; ERP, *Greece*, 29–30, 42–43; F.O. 371/R8032/1102/19, No. 143E; FRUS, 1949, 6:229.
26. SDNA, 868.50/9–2349, A–615. For more details about Hoffman and his functions, see Hadley Arkes, *Bureaucracy and the Marshall Plan* (Princeton, N.J.: Princeton University Press, 1972), 100–102. For more about the reconstruction program, see ERP, *Greece*, 111–12; also see F.O. 371/RG1102/2, No. 78E.
27. Munkman, *Aid*, 57; SDNA, 868.50/6–2749, A–406; SDNA, 868.50/9–1649, Office Memo.
28. Stavrianos, *Greece*, 214–15.
29. SDNA, 868.50/7–2649, A–471.
30. F.O. 371/WG1101/3, No. 32E; F.O. 371/RG1102/18, No. 195E; F.O. 371/RG1102/15, No. 190E; F.O. 371/RG1101/1, No. 5; Candilis, *Greece*, 57, 65; Psilos, "Economic Problems," 38; Sweet-Escott, *Greece*, 194.
31. Angellopoulos, *Oikonomika*, 1:297.
32. Candilis, *Greece*, 146. The OEEC report of 1954 provided the following observation about the decline of investment in Greece's productive sector: "Gross investment measured at 1951 prices fell by 1,700 billion (27 percent) from 1951 to 1952, being no more than 12.7 percent of available resources as against an average of 17.5 percent from 1949 to 1951." OEEC, *European Economy*, 125.
33. Andreas G. Papandreou, *A Strategy for Economic Development* (Athens, 1962), 18–19.
34. Sweet-Escott, *Greece*, 107, 193; Candilis, *Greece*, 79; Sweet-Escott, *Greece*, 112–13. For more on how United States foreign policy affects the structural underdevelopment of the Third World, see the useful anthology in Fann and Hodges, *Imperialism*. Also see Andre Gunder Frank, *Latin America: Underdevelopment or Revolution* (New York: Monthly Review Press, 1969).
35. SDNA, 868.50/7–2649, A–471; SDNA, 868.50/9–1649, Office Memo. For more about the Bretton Woods system, see A. L. K. Acheson et al., eds., *Bretton Woods Revisited* (Toronto: University of Toronto Press, 1972); Edward S. Mason and Robert E. Asher, *The World Bank since Bretton Woods* (Washington, D.C.: The Brookings Institution, 1973). For a critical appraisal of the Bretton Woods system from a Marxian perspec-

tive, see Magdoff, *Imperialism*, 144–49; Eduardo Galeano, "Latin America and the Theory of Imperialism," in Fann and Hodges, *Imperialism*, 216–17; and Cheryl Payer, *The Debt Trap: The IMF and the Third World* (New York: Monthly Review Press, 1974), 22–26.

36. OEEC, *Europe the Way Ahead*, 271.
37. Angellopoulos, *Oikonomika*, 306–7.
38. SDNA, 611.81/11–457, No. 308. For a recent study on United States foreign economic policy and commerical relations with Eastern Europe, see Stephen A. Garrett, "The Economics of American Trade with Eastern Europe: The Carrot or the Stick?" *East European Quarterly* 15 (1981): 485–508.
39. *Third Blue Book*, 22.
40. Candilis, *Greece*, 52–53.
41. SDNA, 868.5042/12–149, No. 6,991; Katsoulis, *Istoria*, 6:303; Psyroukis, *Istoria*, 1:400; Tsoukalas, *Tragedy*, 114; *Third Blue Book*, 124–25; F.O. 371/RG1102/9, No. 818; F.O. 371/RG1101/1, No. 5.
42. ERP, *Greece*, 28.
43. Agapitides, "Wage Policy," 243.
44. A. Papandreou, *Economic Development*, 23–25; A. Pepelasis and P. A. Yotopoulos, *Labor Surplus in Greek Agriculture, 1950–1960* (Athens, 1962), 57–66; Angellopoulos, *Oikonomika*, 1:295; OEEC, *Europe the Way Ahead*, 271–73.
45. Seton-Watson, *Revolution*, 335.
46. John R. Lampe and Marvin R. Jackson, *Balkan Economic History, 1550–1950* (Bloomington: Indiana University Press, 1982), 561.
47. Seton-Watson, *East European*, 254.
48. For more regarding the economic progress of the Balkans, see Lampe and Jackson, *Economic History*, 576–99; Norman J. G. Pounds, *Eastern Europe* (Chicago: Aldine, 1969), 145–85; Fred Singleton and Bernard Carter, *The Economy of Yugoslavia* (New York and London: St. Martin's/Croom Helm, 1982), 128–32; John Michael Montias, *Economic Development in Communist Rumania* (Cambridge, Mass.: M.I.T. Press, 1967), 23–53; Bogoslav Dobrin, *Bulgarian Economic Development since World War II* (New York: Praeger Publishers, 1973), 143–68.
49. *Third Blue Book*, 22–23; Sweet-Escott, *Greece*, 115; Tsoukalas, *Tragedy*, 129; SDNA, 611.81/10–560, No. 325. For more details about the role of the United States and the Colombian steel mill, see F.O. 371/81492, AL 1101/1, No. 1; F.O. 371/81492, AL 1300/1300/11, No. 8; Jon V. Kofas, *Dependence and Underdevelopment in Colombia* (Tempe: Center for Latin American Studies), 1986.
50. Cited in Tsoukalas, *Tragedy*, 129.
51. For more details about dumping in Greece, see *Third Blue Book*, 25. For a general study on the issue of dumping by the advanced countries, see Hamza Alavi and Amir Khurso, "Pakistan: The Burden of Aid," in R. I. Rhodes, ed., *Imperialism and Underdevelopment* (New York: Monthly Review Press, 1970), 62–77; SDNA, 868.506–2749, A–406; FRUS, 1949, VI, 232; Chandler, *Divided Land*, 197–99; F.O. 371/RG1011/1, No. 7.
52. Cited in the *Third Blue Book*, 117.
53. Sweet-Escott, *Greece*, 155; Candilis, *Greece*, 61. SDNA, 868.50/12–149, No. 6,991. For more on the taxation issue, see Angellopoulos, *Oikonomika*, 1:298–99.
54. Candilis, *Greece*, 75.
55. For complete details about Greece's induction into NATO, see Theodore A. Couloumbis, *Greek Political Reaction to American and NATO Influences* (New Haven: Yale University Press, 1966), 33–50. For analysis of the mission's policy directives to the

Greek government, see McNeill, *American Aid*, 229; Candilis, *Greece*, 53; Sweet-Escott, *Greece*, 113–14; OEEC, *European Economy*, 127; Sweet-Escott, *Greece*, 113; F.O. 371/WG1011/1, No. 13; F.O. 371/RG1101/10, No. 1,095.

56. Cited in *Third Blue Book*, 17, 21.

57. For more concerning Papagos, see A. Papandreou, *Democracy*, 126–34; Meynaud, *Politikes Dynameis*, 93–96; Carey and Carey, *Greece*, 149–57. For more about the devaluation of the drachma and Markezines's revelations, see Sweet-Escott, *Greece*, 154; Psyroukis, *Istoria*, 2:83–84; F.O. 371/WG1101/5, No. 65E.

58. Kariotis, "Greece," 91–92. It should be noted that in January 1952 the ECA was formally abolished and replaced by the Mutual Security Agency, MSA, whose purpose was solely strategic. See Rubin, *Billion Dollars*, 57–58; Robert A. Packanham, *Liberal America and the Third World* (Princeton: Princeton University Press, 1973), 49–50; Felix Gilbert, *The End of the European Era, 1890 to the Present* (New York: W. W. Norton, 1984), 432. The Foreign Office has recently declassified documents which revealed that the British government was convinced that American advisers in Athens were in control of the country. See F.O. 371/RG1011/1, No. 7; F.O. 371/RG1102/3, No. 79; F.O. 371/WG1011/1, No. 13; Meynaud, *Politikes Dynameis*, 430–31; F.O. 371/WG1101/11, No. 161E.

59. Cited in Sismanides, "Foreign Capital," 342.

60. Ibid., 342–43. A recent study dealing with direct foreign investment in Greece is by A. Gregorogiannes, *To Xeno Kefalaio stin Ellada* (Athens, 1980). This is not a scholarly work and it primarily covers the decade of the 1970s. Nevertheless, it has some useful information on the issue of decapitalization of Greece. For a broader look at the issue of capital flight from the Third World to the metropolis, see Magdoff, *Imperialism*, 155–56; Galeano, "Imperialism," 217; L. S. Stavrianos, *Global Rift: The Third World Comes of Age* (New York, 1981), 440–56.

Chapter V

1. For extensive details on the rise of the Greek working-class movement, see Giannes Kordatos, *Istoria tou Ellinikou Ergatikou Kinimatos* (Athens, 1972), 21–56; Giannes Zevgos, *Syntome Metete tis Ellinikes Istorias* (Athens, [n.d.]), 2:112–14; D. K. Nikoles, *Istorike Poreia tou Ellinikou Ethnous, 1863–1941*. For more about the condition of the working class under the Metaxas regime, see Chrystos Jecchines, *Trade Unionism in Greece* (Chicago: Roosevelt University Press, 1967), 20; and Kofas, *Authoritarianism in Greece*, 65–67. For more about EEAM, see Wittner, *Intervention*, 193; Adamantia Polis, "U.S. Intervention in Greek Trade Unions, 1947–1950," in Iatrides, *Greece*, 263–64; Woodhouse, *Apple of Discord*, 33; Stavrianos, *Greece*, 69–70, 73–74.

2. For more analysis on the condition of labor after the Varkiza Agreement, see Jecchines, *Unionism*, 104; Sweet-Escott, *Greece*, 139; Polis, "U.S. Intervention," 267–68; Richter, "Civil War," 170–71.

3. F.O. 371/R11178/130/19, No. 205; F.O. 371/R9908/130/19, No. 1,051; F.O. 371/R10225/130/19, No. 1,512. Also see Sheppard, *Britain*, 21; *Third Blue Book*, 70; Jecchines, *Unionism*, 96; Wittner, *Intervention*, 194; Meynaud, *Politikes Dynameis*, 182; Sweet-Escott, *Greece*, 140; Ronald Radosh, *American Labor and United States Foreign Policy* (New York: Random House, 1969), 338–39. For the origins of the WFTU, see Louis Saillant, *The World Federation of Trade Unions in the Service of all Workers of all Countries* (Paris, 1960). For a critical appraisal of the WFTU, see Lewis L. Lorwin, *The International Labor Move-*

ment (New York: Harper Brothers, 1953), 201–5; and John Windmuller, *American Labor and the International Labor Movement, 1940–1953* (Ithaca, N.Y.: Cornell University Press, 1954), 16–66. SDNA, 868.51/6–1347; SDNA, 868–5043/11–348; Richter, "Civil War," 171; F.O. 371/R15703/20/19; F.O. 371/R15722/20/19; F.O. 371/R15840/30/19; F.O. 371/R16158/20/19, No. A/7/13/47.

4. Polis, "U.S. Intervention," 266; Radosh, *American Labor*, 338–40.
5. Cited in the *Third Blue Book*, 70.
6. SDNA, 868.5043/11–348; F.O. 371/R11365/130/19, No. 1,717; F.O. 371/R11325/130/19, No. 1, 707; *Third Blue Book*, 72.
7. SDNA, 868.51/6–1347; Jecchines, *Unionism*, 111, 120–21.
8. Wittner, *Intervention*, 195–201; Jecchines, *Unionism*, 86–95; Sheppard, *Britain*, 22–24. For extensive details about the recognition of Makris's rightist faction by the British authorities, see F.O. 371/R11394/130/19, No. 16. For details regarding the establishment of the GSEE provisional executive, see F.O. 371/R11440/130/19, No. 1,732. For more on the Tsaldaris-Braine Agreement, see F.O. 371/R17177/130/130, No. 114. For more concerning Tsaldaris's decision to break the Tsaldaris-Braine Agreement, see F.O. 371/R18456/130/19, No. 2,704. For more on Brown's functions in Europe, see Radosh, *American Labor*, 309; Lorwin, *Labor Movement*, 236; Windmuller, *Labor Movement*, 76–77; Roy Godson, *American Labor and European Politics* (New York: Crane, Russak, 1976), 106–7; Philip Taft, *Defending Freedom: American Labor and Foreign Affairs* (Los Angeles: Nash, 1973), 163–75.
9. Sydney Lens, "Labor Lieutenants and the Cold War," in Burton Hall, ed., *Autocracy and Insurgency in Organized Labor* (New Brunswick, N.J.: Transaction Books, 1972), 317.
10. SDNA, 868.51/6–1347; Jecchines, *Unionism*, 112.
11. Ibid.; FRUS, 1947, 5:222–24, 246.
12. Cited in Eudes, *Kapetanios*, 280.
13. SDNA, 868.51/6–1247; Agapitides, "Wage Policy," 258–59.
14. Sweet-Escott, *Greece*, 102.
15. SDNA, 868.5045/10–1047.
16. Ibid. The Minister of Labor had proposed a wage increase, but the Currency Committee opposed it. See F.O. 371/R1428/7/19, No. 253.
17. For the complete report, see SDNA, 868.5042/12–149, No. 6,991.
18. For complete details concerning the condition of the working class, see Agapitides, "Wage Policy," 247; Meynaud, *Politikes Dynameis*, 22; Wittner, *Intervention*, 206; Angellopoulos, *Oikonomika*, 1:305.
19. SDNA, 868.5045/10–2349, AMAG–382; Jecchines, *Unionism*, 113–14; Sweet-Escott, *Greece*, 134; Wittner, *Intervention*, 206–08; SDNA, 868.51/12–1949, AMAG–694.
20. SDNA, 868.5045/12–1047, No. 65.
21. F.O. 371/R579/102/19, No. 17/4/48; F.O. 371/R596/102/19, No. 17/3/48; Psyroukis, *Istoria*, 1:379–80; SDNA, 868.5045/12–1047, No. 65; *Third Blue Book*, 71.
22. For the proclamation of AMAG as well as Tsaldaris's announcement, see SDNA, 868.5045/1–2948, Office Memo; F.O. 371/R146/102/19, No. 9.
23. SDNA, 868.51/12–1947, AMAG–694; SDNA, 868.5045/1–2948, Office Memo, Enclosures #1 and #2.
24. SDNA, 868.5045/12–1047, No. 65; SDNA, 868.5045/1–2948; Jecchines, *Unionism*, 114; Psyroukis, *Istoria*, 1:380; *Third Blue Book*, 71.
25. Polis, "U.S. Intervention," 272.
26. Jecchines, *Unionism*, 115, 118, 120–21; Wittner, *Intervention*, 209–14.

27. SDNA, 868.50/4–2348, No. 481, Enclosure #2.
28. Ibid.
29. SDNA, 868.5045/8–2748, No. 1,683.
30. Candilis, *Greece*, 49; Agapitides, "Wage Policy," 250; SDNA, 868.5043/12–149, No. 6,991.
31. SDNA, 868.5043/11–348; Psyroukis, *Istoria*, 1:382–83.
32. SDNA, 868.5043/11–348.
33. SDNA, 868.5043/11–1248; F.O. 371/R13919/102/19; F.O. 371/R13971/102/19; F.O. 371/R14513/102/19.
34. SDNA, 868.5043/11–1248; SDNA, 868.5043/10–3149; F.O. 371/R16158/20/19, No. A/7/13/47; F.O. 371/R16404/20/19; SDNA, 868.5043/10–3149.
35. SDNA, 868.5045/12–1148, No. 2,529; ERP, *Greece*, 15, 27; Candilis, *Greece*, 69; Sweet-Escott, *Greece*, 194; F.O. 371/R255/10119/19, No. 51/2/49; SDNA, 868.5045/4–1349, No. 733; Psyroukis, *Istoria*, I, 393; SDNA, 868.50/72649, No. A–471; Agapitides, "Wage Policy," 250.
36. SDNA, 868.5045/4–1349, No. 753.
37. Ibid.; Seton-Watson, *Revolution*, 334; Jecchines, *Unionism*, 135. For more details on the ADEDY strike, see F.O. 371/R4789/10119/19, No. 20; F.O. 371/R6579/10119/19, No. 22; F.O. 371/R767/10119/19, No. 23.
38. SDNA, 868.50/6–22749, No. A–406; SDNA, 868.5042/12–149, No. 6,991. For more details about Greek emigration, see McNeill, *Metamorphosis*, 209–17; Psyroukis, *Istoria*, 2:38–40. For more on the "brain drain," see Walter Adams, *The Brain Drain* (New York: Macmillan, 1968).
39. SDNA, 868.50/9–2349, No. A–615. The American officials in Greece obliged the host government to declare the celebration of Labor Day in September, as is the American tradition, rather than in May, as is the case in most countries of the world. Jecchines, *Unionism*, 129.
40. SDNA, 868.5045/11–1649, No. 2,299.
41. Serafino Romualdi, *Presidents and Peons* (New York: Funk and Wagnals, 1967), 78–79; Lorwin, *Labor Movement*, 262–66, 274; Windmuller, *Labor Movement*, 151–53, 156–59.
42. Lens, "Cold War," 319.
43. For extensive details on the ICFTU's programs and activities, see International Confederation of Free Trade Unions, *The First Ten Years* (Brussels, 1959); Taft, *Defending Freedom*, 147–62. For critical views of the ICFTU and the role of the AFL and the United States government in the organization, see Philip Agee, *Inside the Company: CIA Diary* (New York: Bentham Books, 1978), 68–69; Winslow Peck, "The AFL-CIA," in Howard Frazier, ed., *Uncloaking the CIA* (New York: Free Press, 1978), 158–61, 230–38. For a critical appraisal of the WFTU, see Blair A. Ruble, *Soviet Trade Unions* (Cambridge: Cambridge University Press, 1981), 124–37. For more on the impact of the WFTU and ICFTU in Africa, see Ioan Davies, *African Trade Unions* (Baltimore: Penguin Books, 1966), 188–216.
44. SDNA, 868.5042/12–149, No. 6,991.
45. Ibid.; SDNA, 868.5041/11–3049, No. 2,395; F.O. 371/RG1101/1, No. 5; SDNA, 868.5045/12–849, No. 2,445; SDNA, 868.5042/12–149, No. 6,991; *Third Blue Book*, 72; IKA was controlled by an American official who ran the agency dictatorially and earned the contempt of the Greek officials.
46. Cited in Jecchines, *Unionism*, 129.
47. Ibid., 143; *Third Blue Book*, 74–75; Sweet-Escott, *Greece*, 141; F.O. 371/RG1101/2,

No. 10; F.O. 371/RG1101/10, No. 1,095; F.O. 371/RG1011/1, No. 7. For more on United States labor policy toward the Third World, see Hobart A. Spalding, Jr., "US and Latin American Labor: The Dynamics of Imperialist Control," in June Nash et al., *Ideology and Social Change in Latin America* (New York: Gordon and Breach, 1977), 55–83.

48. F.O. 371/RG1101/8, No. 875; *Third Blue Book*, 74; Psyroukis, *Istoria*, 2:87, 110.
49. Angellopoulos, *Oikonomika*, 1:303; *Third Blue Book*, 130.
50. Sweet-Escott, *Greece*, 142.
51. Ibid., 141–42; Angellopoulos, *Oikonomika*, 1:295; Tsoukalas, *Tragedy*, 95; *Third Blue Book*, 68, 72; Katsoulis, *Istoria*, 6:302–3; P. Pavlopoulos, *A Statistical Model for the Greek Economy, 1949–1959* (Amsterdam: North-Holland, 1966), 3–4.
52. SDNA, 611.81/4–1261.
53. Pounds, *Eastern Europe*, 143.
54. Cited in Sweet-Escott, *Greece*, 132.
55. *Third Blue Book*, 119, 131. Industrial income for 1948 amounted to 1.9 billion drachmas, according to the government in Athens. Wages accounted for 870 million drachmas, taxes for 70 million, and profits for 960 million. See SDNA, 868.5042/12–149, No. 6,991.
56. Agapitides, "Wage Policy," 245.

Epilogue

1. Peter Evans, *Dependent Development: The Alliance of Multinational, State, and Local Capital in Brazil* (Princeton, N.J.: Princeton University Press, 1979), 32.
2. Wallerstein, *World-Economy*, 20–22; Richard Rubinson, ed., *Dynamics of World Development* (Beverly Hills: Sage Publications, 1981), 69–118.
3. Kostas Vergopoulos, *To Agrotiko Zitima stin Ellada* (Athens, 1975), 211.
4. Psyroukis, *Istoria*, 2:24; Lampe and Jackson, *Economic History*, 597; D. S. Stathis, *The Record of Greece* (Athens, 1962), 42.
5. Ibid., 43; Psyroukis, *Istoria*, 2:29; Lampe and Jackson, *Economic History*, 597.
6. Labor shortages were manifested in the mid-1960s as 25.9 percent of the work force had emigrated from 1951 to 1970. See McNeill, *Metamorphosis*, 117. The rate of the population growth was less than 1 percent between 1950 and 1971. See Michas, "Economic Development," 45. For more on the brain drain affecting Greece, see George Coutsoumaris, "Greece," in Adams, *Brain Drain*, 166–82; Kayser, *Greece*, 132. McNeill maintained that the population of Athens was 1,378.5 million in 1951 and 2,540.2 million in 1971. Fifty-six percent of all Athenians in 1960 were immigrants. McNeill, *Metamorphosis*, 4, 105. For more details about the problems of overurbanization, see Tsoukalas, *Tragedy*, 127; Angellopoulos, *Oikonomika*, 1:328.
7. Tsoukalas, *Tragedy*, 134; Pavlopoulos, *Greek Economy*, 24–25; Psyroukis maintained that the GNP grew 4 percent annually between 1950 and 1963, while the average annual expenditure for the same period was 7.6 percent higher than the GNP. Psyroukis, *Istoria*, 2:57, 117, 123.
8. Mouzelis, *Underdevelopment*, 119.
9. Ibid., 118; Candilis, *Greece*, 126.
10. Psyroukis, *Istoria*, 2:36–37.
11. Ibid., 37.
12. Mouzelis, *Underdevelopment*, 121.
13. Tsoukalas, *Tragedy*, 132.

14. Candilis, *Greece*, 146; Pavlopoulos, *Greek Economy*, 11–12.
15. Sismanidis, "Foreign Capital," 346–47; Angellopoulos, *Oikonomika*, 1:230.
16. Meynaud, *Politikes Dynameis*, 460–61.
17. Ibid., 420–21; Psyroukis, *Istoria*, 2:69–70.
18. SDNA, 611.81/1261; Psyroukis, *Istoria*, 2:70, 85.
19. Angellopoulos, *Oikonomika*, 1:214.
20. SDNA, 611.81/1261; Psyroukis, *Istoria*, 2:84–85.
21. SDNA, 611.81/1261.
22. SDNA, 611.81/11–457. No. 308.
23. Ibid.
24. *Greek Government Programme*, 5.

Bibliography

I. Archives

A. Great Britain Public Records Office, Foreign Office. Selected files on Greece.
B. United States Freedom of Information Act. Department of State. Selected files on Greek-American Relations.
C. United States National Archives, Department of State. Selected files on Greek finances, labor, and commerce.

II. Published Documents

Economic Cooperation Administration. *Report to the Committee on Foreign Relations* (Washington, D.C.: U.S. Government Printing Office, 1949).
———. *Economic Recovery Program: Greece, Country Report* (Washington, D.C.: U.S. Government Printing Office, 1949).
Ethniko Apeleftheriko Metopo, EAM. *Lefki Vivlos, Mais 1944–Martis 1945* (National Liberation Front. White Book, May 1944–March 1945) (Trikala, 1945).
Greek Government Programme Presented by the Prime Minister Andreas Papandreou (Athens: General Secretariat for Press and Information, 1981).
Kommounistiko Komma Elladas. *Episima Keimena, 1940–1945* (Greek Communist Party, Official Documents, 1940–1945) (Athens, 1973).
———. *Saranta Chronia tou Kommounistikou Kommatos Elladas, 1918–1959* (Greek Communist Party, Forty Years of the Greek Communist Party, 1918–1958) (Athens, 1958).

———. *Voithima Gia tin Istoria tou KKE* (Greek Communist Party, A Guide for the History of the Greek Communist Party) (Athens, 1975).
Langsam, Walter C. *Documents and Readings in the History of Europe Since 1918* (Philadelphia: J. B. Lippincott, 1951).
Organization for European Economic Cooperation. *Europe the Way Ahead* (Fourth Annual Report of the OEEC) (Paris, 1952).
———. *Progress and Problems of the European Economy* (Fifth Annual Report of the OEEC) (Paris, 1954).
Public Papers of the Presidents. Harry S. Truman, 1947 (Washington, D.C.: U.S. Government Printing Office, 1963).
United Nations General Assembly. *Official Records* (Lake Placid, N.Y.: United Nations, 1947).
United States Department of Commerce. *Foreign Commerce Yearbook, 1948* (Washington, D.C.: U.S. Government Printing Office, 1950).
———. *Foreign Commerce Yearbook, 1949* (Washington, D.C.: U.S. Government Printing Office, 1951).
———. *Foreign Commerce Yearbook, 1951* (Washington, D.C.: U.S. Government Printing Office, 1953).
Department of State. *Bulletin* 16 (15 June 1947): 1159–60.
———. *Foreign Relations of the United States, 1945*, Vol. 8 (Washington, D.C.: U.S. Government Printing Office, 1969).
———. *Foreign Relations of the United States, 1946*, Vol. 7 (Washington, D.C.: U.S. Government Printing Office, 1969).
———. *Foreign Relations of the United States, 1947*, Vol. 5 (Washington, D.C.: U.S. Government Printing Office, 1971).
———. *Foreign Relations of the United States, 1948*, Vol. 4 (Washington, D.C.: U.S. Government Printing Office, 1974).
———. *Foreign Relations of the United States, 1949*, Vol. 6 (Washington, D.C.: U.S. Government Printing Office, 1977).
———. *Second Report to Congress on the United States Relief Program* (Washington, D.C.: U.S. Government Printing Office, 1947).
———. *Third Report to Congress on the United States Relief Program* (Washington, D.C.: U.S. Government Printing Office, 1948).

III. Biographies, Diaries, and Memoirs

Bolhen, Charles. *Witness to History*. New York: W. W. Norton, 1973.
Bullock, Alan. *Ernest Bevin*. New York: W. W. Norton, 1983.
Churchill, Winston S. *Triumph and Tragedy*. Boston: Houghton Mifflin, 1953.
Daphnis, Gregoris. *Sophocles Venizelos, 1894–1964*. Athens, 1970.
Dobney, F. J., ed. *Selected Papers of Will Clayton*. Baltimore: Johns Hopkins University Press, 1971.
Ferrell, Robert H. *George C. Marshall*. New York: Cooper Square Publishers, 1966.
Fredericka, Queen of the Hellenes. *A Measure of Understanding*. London: Macmillan, 1971.
Genevoix, Maurice. *The Greece of Karamanles*. London: Doric Publications, 1973.
Iatrides, John O., ed. *Ambassador MacVeagh Reports: Greece, 1933–1947*. Princeton: Princeton University Press, 1980.

Jones, Joseph Marion. *The Fifteen Weeks*. New York: Harcourt, Brace and World, 1964.
Kennan, George F. *Memoirs, 1925-1950*. Boston: Little, Brown, 1967.
Komnenos, Konstantinos. *Georgios Papandreou*. Athens, 1965.
Lagdas, Panos. *Aris Velouhiotis*. 2 vols. Athens, 1965.
Matthews, Kenneth. *Memoirs of a Mountain War: Greece, 1944-1949*. London, 1972
Millis, Walter, ed. *The Forrestal Diaries*. New York: Viking Press, 1951.
Papandreou, Andreas. *E Demokratia sto Apospasma* (Democracy at Gunpoint). Athens, 1974.
Papandreou, George. *Politika Keimena* (Political Documents). Athens, 1950.
Pyromaglou, Komnenos. *O Georgios Kartalis kai e Epoche tou, 1934-57* (George Kartalis and His Times, 1934-57). Athens, 1964.
Sarafis, Stefanos. *O ELAS*. Athens, 1964.
Sbarounis, Athanasios I. *Meletai kai Anamniseis tou B' Pangosmiou Polemou* (Studies and Recollections of the Second World War). Athens, 1950.
Smith, Gaddis. *Dean Acheson*. New York: Cooper Square Publishers, 1972.
Truman, Harry S. *Memoirs*. 2 vols. Garden City, N.Y.: Doubleday, 1956.
Vandenberg, Arthur. *The Private Papers of Senator Vandenberg*. Boston: Houghton Mifflin, 1952.

IV. Articles

Agapitidis, S. "Wage Policy in Greece," *International Labour Review* 51 (January-June 1950): 242-73.
Alavi, Hamza, and Amir Khusro. "Pakistan: The Burden of U.S. Aid," in R. I. Rhodes, ed., *Imperialism and Underdevelopment*. New York: Monthly Review Press, 1970.
Alivizatos, Nikos C. "The Emergency Regime and Civil Liberties, 1946-1949," in John O. Iatrides, ed., *Greece in the 1940s*. London: University Press of New England, 1981.
Baggulley, John. "The World War and the Cold War," in David Horowitz, ed., *Containment and Revolution*. Boston: Beacon Press, 1967.
Berger, Henry. "A Conservative Critique of Containment: Senator Taft on the Early Cold War Program," in David Horowitz, ed., *Containment and Revolution*. Boston: Beacon Press, 1967.
Bernstein, Barton J. "Walter Lippman and the Early Cold War," in Thomas G. Paterson, ed., *Cold War Critics*. Chicago: Quadrangle, 1971.
Clogg, Richard. "Pearls from Swine: The Foreign Office Papers, S.O.E. and the Greek Resistance," in Phyllis Auty and Richard Clogg, eds., *British Policy Towards Wartime Resistance in Yugoslavia and Greece*. London: Macmillan Press, 1975.
Coufoudakis, Van. "The United States, the United Nations and the Greek Question, 1946-1952," in John O. Iatrides, ed., *Greece in the 1940s*. London: University Press of New England, 1981.
Coutsoumaris, George. "Greece," in Walter Adams, ed. *The Brain Drain*. New York: The Macmillan Company, 1968.
Edelman, Maurice. "Greece: A Reply to Mr. Bevin," *New Statesman and Nation* 31 (March 1946).
Fatouros, A. A. "Building Formal Structures of Penetration: The United States in Greece, 1947-1948," in John O. Iatrides, ed., *Greece in the 1940s*. London: University Press of New England, 1981.

Galeano, Eduardo. "Latin America and the Theory of Imperialism," in K. T. Fann and D. C. Hodges, eds., *Readings in U.S. Imperialism*. Boston: An Extending Horizons Book, 1971.
Garrett, Stephen A. "The Economics of American Trade with Eastern Europe: The Carrot or the Stick?" *East European Quarterly* 15 (Winter 1981): 485–510.
Gittlin, Todd. "Counter-Insurgency: Myth and Reality in Greece," in David Horowitz, ed., *Containment and Revolution*. Boston: Beacon Press, 1967.
Howard, Harry N. "United States Policy Towards Greece in the United Nations, 1946–1950," *Balkan Studies* 8 (Summer 1967): 263–96.
Jonas, (Bodenheimer) Susanne. "Dependency and Imperialism: The Roots of Underdevelopment," in K. T. Fann and D. C. Hodges, eds., *Readings in U.S. Imperialism*. Boston: An Extending Horizons Book, 1971.
Kariotis, Theodore C. "American Economic Penetration of Greece in the Late Nineteen Forties," *Journal of the Hellenic Diaspora* 6 (Winter 1979): 86–94.
Klare, M. T., and Cynthia Arnson. "Exporting Repression: U.S. Support for Authoritarianism in Latin America," in Richard Fagen, ed., *Capitalism and the State in U.S.–Latin American Relations*. Stanford: Stanford University Press, 1979.
Lens, Sydney. "Labor Lieutenants and the Cold War," in Burton Hall, ed., *Autocracy and Insurgency in Organized Labor*. New Brunswick, N.J.: Transaction Books, 1972.
Mazuman, George T. "America's UN Commitment, 1945–1953," *The Historian* 60 (February 1978): 309–30.
Michas, Nicholas A. "Economic Development, Social Mobilization and the Growth of Public Expenditures in Greece," *American Journal of Economics and Sociology* 39 (1980): 31–48.
Papadantonakis, Kostis. "The State as Instrument of Induction to the Periphery," in Richard Rubinson, ed., *Dynamics of World Development*. Beverly Hills: Sage Publications, 1981.
Peck, Winslow. "The AFL-CIA," in Howard Frazier, ed., *Uncloaking the CIA*. New York: The Free Press, 1969.
Polis, Adamantia. "U.S. Intervention in Greek Trade Unions, 1947–1950," in John O. Iatrides, ed., *Greece in the 1940s*. London: University Press of New England, 1981.
Pratt, William C. "Senator Glen C. Taylor: Questioning American Unilateralism," in Thomas G. Paterson, ed., *Cold War Critics*. Chicago: Quadrangle Books, 1971.
Psilos, Diomedes D. "Postwar Economic Problems in Greece," in *Economic Development Issues: Greece, Israel, Taiwan and Thailand*. New York: Committee for Economic Development, 1968.
Richter, Heinz. "The Varkiza Agreement and the Origins of the Civil War," in John O. Iatrides, ed., *Greece in the 1940s*. London: University Press of New England, 1981.
Roubatis, Yiannes P. "The United States and the Occupational Responsibilities of the Greek Armed Forces, 1947–1987," *Journal of the Hellenic Diaspora* 6 (Spring 1979): 39–57.
Sismanides, S. D. "Foreign Capital Investment in Greece," *Balkan Studies* 8 (Summer 1967): 339–52.
Spalding, Jr., Hobart A. "U.S. and Latin American Labor: The Dynamics of Imperialist Control," in June Nash et al., *Ideology and Social Change in Latin America*. New York: Gordon and Breach, 1977.
Svoronos, Nicolas. "Greek History, 1940–1950: The Main Problems," in John O. Iatrides, ed., *Greece in the 1940s*. London: University Press of New England, 1981.
Sweet-Escott, Bickham. "Greece in the Spring of 1949," *International Affairs* 25 (1949): 442–52.

United Nations Relief and Rehabilitation Administration *Journal* (Third Session of Council), No. 6, 1945.
Wilkes, Lyal. "British Missions and Greek Quislings," *New Statesman and Nation* 33 (1947): 88-90.
Woodhouse, C. M. "Summer 1943: The Critical Months," in Phyllis Auty and Richard Clogg, eds., *British Policy Towards Wartime Resistance in Yugoslavia and Greece*. London: Macmillan Press, 1975.

V. Monographs, Dissertations, and General Accounts

Acheson, A. L. K., et al., eds., *Bretton Woods Revisited*. Toronto: University of Toronto Press, 1972.
Adams, Walter, ed. *The Brain Drain*. New York: Macmillan Press, 1968.
Agee, Philip. *Inside the Company: CIA Diary*. New York: Bantam Books, 1978.
Aguilar, Alonso. *Pan-Americanism: From Monroe to the Present*. Translated from the Spanish by Asa Zatz. New York: Monthly Review Press, 1968.
Alexander, G. M. *The Prelude to the Truman Doctrine*. New York: Oxford University Press, 1982.
Alstyne, Richard Van W. *The Rising American Empire*. Chicago: Quadrangle Books, 1960.
Ambrose, Stephen E. *Rise to Globalism*. New York: Penguin Books, 1978.
Angellopoulos, Angelos. *Oikonomika Arthra kai Meletai, 1946-1967* (Economics Articles and Studies, 1946-1967). 2 vols. Athens, 1974.
Arkes, Hadley. *Bureaucracy and the Marshall Plan*. Princeton: Princeton University Press, 1972.
Arnstein, Walter. *Britain Yesterday and Today*. Lexington, Mass.: D. C. Heath, 1971.
Aubrey, Henry G. *The Dollar in World Affairs*. New York: Frederick A. Praeger, 1964.
Auty, Phyllis, and Richard Clogg, eds. *British Policy Towards Wartime Resistance in Yugoslavia and Greece*. London: Macmillan Press, 1975.
Averoff-Tosizza, Evangelos. *By Fire and Axe*. Translated from the Greek by Sarah Arnold Rigos. New York: Caratzas Bros., 1978.
Baldwin, David A. *Foreign Aid and American Foreign Policy*. New York: Frederick A. Praeger, 1966.
Baran, Paul, and Paul Sweezy. *Monopoly Capital*. New York: Monthly Review Press, 1966.
Barker, Elizabeth. *The British Between the Superpowers, 1945-50*. Toronto: University of Toronto Press, 1983.
Barnet, Richard J. *Intervention and Revolution*. New York: World, 1968.
Bartlett, C. J. *The Rise and Fall of Pax Americana*. New York: St. Martin's Press, 1974.
Bennett, A. LeRoy. *International Organizations*. Englewood Cliffs, N.J.: Prentice-Hall, 1977.
Calogeropoulos-Stratis, S., et al. *La Grece et les Nations Unies*. New York: Manhattan Publishing, 1957.
Candilis, Wray O. *The Economy of Greece, 1946-1966*. New York: Frederick A. Praeger, 1968.
Carey, J. P. C., and A. G. Carey. *The Web of Modern Greek Politics*. New York: Columbia University Press, 1968.
Chandler, Geoffrey. *The Divided Land: An Anglo-Greek Tragedy*. London, 1959.
Chilcote, Ronald H., and Joel C. Edelstein, eds. *Latin America: The Struggle with Dependency and Beyond*. New York: John Wiley and Sons, 1974.

Bibliography

Cliadakis, Harry C. "Greece, 1935–1941: The Metaxas Regime and the Diplomatic Background to World War II" (Ph.D. dissertation, New York University, 1970).
Cockcroft, James, et al., eds. *Dependence and Underdevelopment: Latin America's Political Economy*. Garden City, N.Y.: Doubleday/Anchor, 1972.
Couloumbis, Theodore A. *A Greek Political Reaction to American and NATO Influences*. New Haven: Yale University Press, 1966.
——— et al. *Foreign Interference in Greek Politics*. New York: Pella, 1976.
Daphnis, Gregoris. *Ta Ellinika Politika Kommata, 1821–1961* (The Greek Political Parties, 1821–1961). Athens, 1961.
Davies, Ioan. *African Trade Unions*. Baltimore: Penguin Books, 1966.
Democratic Organization of Greece. *Third Blue Book*. (somewhere in the North Balkans, n.d.).
Dobrin, Bogoslav. *Bulgarian Economic Development Since World War II*. New York: Praeger, 1973.
Donovan, R. J. *Conflict and Crisis*. New York: W. W. Norton, 1977.
Dozer, Donald M. *Are We Good Neighbors? Three Decades of Inter-American Relations, 1930–1960*. Gainesville: University of Florida Press, 1959.
Eckes, Jr., Alfred E. *The United States and the Global Struggle for Minerals*. Austin: University of Texas Press, 1979.
Engler, Robert. *The Politics of Oil*. New York: Macmillan Press, 1961.
Eudes, Dominiques. *The Kapetanios*. Translated from the French by John Howe. New York: Monthly Review Press, 1972.
Evans, Peter. *Dependent Development: The Alliance of Multinational, State and Local Capital in Brazil*. Princeton: Princeton University Press, 1979.
Fagen, Richard, ed. *Capitalism and the State in U.S.–Latin American Relations*. Stanford: Stanford University Press, 1979.
Fann, K. T., and D. C. Hodges, eds. *Readings in U.S. Imperialism*. Boston: An Extending Horizons Book, 1971.
Feis, Hert. *From Trust to Terror*. New York: W. W. Norton, 1970.
Fleming, D. F. *The Cold War and its Origins, 1917–1960*. 2 vols. London: George Allen and Unwin, 1961.
Frank, Andre Gunder. *Latin America: Underdevelopment or Revolution*. New York: Monthly Review Press, 1969.
Frazier, Howard, ed. *Uncloaking the CIA*. New York: The Free Press, 1978.
Freeland, Richard M. *The Truman Doctrine and the Origins of McCarthyism*. New York: Alfred A. Knopf, 1972.
Gardner, Richard N. *Sterling-Dollar Diplomacy in Current Perspective*. New York: Columbia University Press, 1980.
Gilbert, Felix. *The End of the European Era, 1890 to the Present*. New York: W. W. Norton, 1984.
Godson, Roy. *American Labor and European Politics*. New York: Crane, Russak, 1976.
Gosnell, Harold F. *Truman's Crises*. Westport, Conn.: Greenwood Press, 1980.
Gregoriades, F. N. *Istoria tou Emphiliou Polemou, 1945–1949* (History of the Greek Civil War, 1945–1949). Athens, 1963–65.
Hall, Burton, ed. *Autocracy and Insurgency in Organized Labor*. New Brunswick, N.J.: Transaction Books, 1972.
Harris, Richard, ed. *The Political Economy of Africa*. New York: Shenkman, 1975.
Hartman, Susan. *Truman and the 80th Congress*. Columbia: University of Missouri Press, 1971.

Howard, Harry N. *The United Nations and the Problem of Greece.* Washington, D.C.: U.S. Government Printing Office, 1947.
Horowitz, David, ed. *Containment and Revolution.* Boston: Beacon Press, 1967.
———. *The Free World Colossus.* New York: Hill and Wang, 1965.
Hutchison, Keith. *The Decline and Fall of British Capitalism.* Hamden, Conn.: Archon Books, 1966.
Iatrides, John O., ed. *Greece in the 1940s.* London: University Press of New England, 1981.
———. *Revolt in Athens.* Princeton: Princeton University Press, 1972.
International Confederation of Free Trade Unions. *The First Ten Years.* Brussels, 1959.
Jecchines, Chrystos. *Trade Unionism in Greece.* Chicago: Roosevelt University Press, 1967.
Katsoulis, Georgis D. *Istoria tou Kommounistikou Kommatos Elladas* (History of the Greek Communist Party). 6 vols. Athens, 1980.
Kayser, Bernard. *Geographie Humaine de la Grèce.* Paris: Presses Universitaires de France, 1964.
Kofas, Jon V. *Authoritarianism in Greece: The Metaxas Regime.* New York: East European Monographs/Distributed by Columbia University Press, 1983.
———. *Financial Relations of Greece and the Great Powers, 1832–1862.* New York: East European Monographs/Distributed by Columbia University Press, 1981.
———. *International and Domestic Politics in Greece During the Crimean War.* New York: East European Monographs/Distributed by Columbia University Press, 1980.
Kolko, Gabriel. *Main Currents in Modern American History.* New York: Pantheon Books, 1984.
Kordatos, Yiannes. *Istoria tou Ellinikou Ergatikou Kinimatos* (History of the Greek Working-Class Movement). Athens, 1972.
———. *Istoria tis Neoteris Elladas* (History of Modern Greece). 5 vols. Athens, 1957–58.
Kousoulas, D. G. *Revolution and Defeat.* Oxford: Oxford University Press, 1964.
———. *The Price of Freedom.* Syracuse, N.Y.: Syracuse University Press, 1953.
Kuniholm, B. R. *The Origins of the Cold War in the Near East.* Princeton: Princeton University Press, 1980.
Lampe, John R., and Marvin R. Jackson. *Balkan Economic History, 1550–1950.* Bloomington: Indiana University Press, 1982.
LeFeber, Walter, ed. *The Origins of the Cold War, 1941–1947.* New York: John Wiley and Sons, 1971.
Lemos, Andreas. *The Greeks and the Sea.* London: Cassell, 1976.
Levandis, J. A. *The Greek Foreign Debt and the Great Powers, 1821–1898.* New York: Columbia University Press, 1944.
Lippman, Walter. *The Cold War.* New York: Harper Torchbooks, 1972.
Lorwin, Lewis L. *The International Labor Movement.* New York: Harper Brothers, 1953.
McCagg, William. *Stalin Embattled.* Detroit: Wayne State University Press, 1978.
McMillan, James, and Bernard Harris, *The American Take-Over of Britain.* New York, 1968.
McNeill, William H. *Greece: American Aid in Action, 1947–1956.* New York: Twentieth Century Fund, 1957.
———. *The Greek Dilemma: War and Aftermath.* Philadelphia: J. B. Lippincott, 1947.
———. *The Metamorphosis of Greece Since World War II.* Chicago: University of Chicago Press, 1978.

208 Bibliography

Magdoff, Harry. *The Age of Imperialism*. New York: Monthly Review Press, 1969.
Mason, Edward S., and Robert E. Asher. *The World Bank since Bretton Woods*. Washington, D.C.: The Brookings Institution, 1973.
Meynaud, Jean, et al. *Politikes Dynameis stin Ellada* (Political Forces in Greece). Athens, 1974.
Mikesell, Raymond F. *Foreign Exchange in the Postwar World*. New York: Twentieth Century Fund, 1954.
Minter, William. *Imperial Network and External Dependency: The Case of Angola*. Beverly Hills: Sage Publications, 1972.
Montias, John Michael. *Economic Development in Communist Rumania*. Cambridge, Mass.: The M.I.T. Press, 1967.
Mouzelis, Nikos P. *Modern Greece: Facets of Underdevelopment*. New York: Holmes-Meier, 1978.
Munkman, C. A. *American Aid to Greece*. New York: Frederick A. Praeger, 1958.
Nash, June, et al. *Ideology and Social Change in Latin America*. New York: Gordon and Breach, 1977.
Nathan, James A., and James K. Oliver. *United States Foreign Policy and World Order*. Boston: Little, Brown, 1976.
Nepheloudis, Pavlos. *Stis Piges tis Kakodaimonias: Ta Vathytera Aitia tis Diaspasis tou KKE* (To the Source of Misfortune: The Deeper Causes of the Split of the Greek Communist Party). Athens, 1974.
Nikoles, Dimitris K. *Istorike Poreia tou Ellinikou Ethnous, 1863–1941* (Historical Course of the Greek Nation, 1863–1941). Athens, 1978.
Nirumand, Bachman. *Iran: The New Imperialism in Action*. New York: Monthly Review Press, 1964.
Northedge, F. S. *Descent from Power*. London: George Allen and Unwin, 1974.
O'Ballance, Edgar. *The Greek Civil War*. New York: Frederick A. Praeger, 1966.
Packanham, Robert A. *Liberal America and the Third World*. Princeton: Princeton University Press, 1973.
Papandreou, Andreas. *A Strategy for Greek Economic Development*. Athens, 1963.
Papandreou, George. *The Third War*. Athens, 1948.
Pepelasis, A., and P. A. Yotopoulos. *Labor Surplus in Greek Agriculture*. Athens, 1962.
Paterson, Thomas G., ed. *Cold War Critics*. Chicago: Quadrangle Books, 1971.
———. *On Every Front*. New York: W. W. Norton, 1979.
———. *Soviet-American Confrontation*. Baltimore: Johns Hopkins University Press, 1973.
Pavlopoulos, P. *A Statistical Model for the Greek Economy, 1949–1959*. Amsterdam: North-Holland, 1966.
Payer, Cheryl. *The Debt Trap: The International Monetary Fund and the Third World*. New York: Monthly Review Press, 1974.
Pounds, Norman J. G. *Eastern Europe*. Chicago: Aldine, 1969.
Psyroukis, Nikos. *Istoria Synchronis Elladas* (History of Contemporary Greece). 3 vols. Athens, 1976.
Radosh, Ronald. *American Labor and United States Foreign Policy*. New York: Random House, 1969.
Rhodes, R. I., ed. *Imperialism and Underdevelopment*. New York: Monthly Review Press, 1970.
Romualdi, Serafino. *Presidents and Peons*. New York: Funk and Wagnals, 1967.
Rousseas, Stephen. *The Death of a Democracy*. New York: Grove Press, 1967.
Rubin, Jacob A. *Your Hundred Billion Dollars*. New York: Chiton Books, 1967.

Bibliography 209

Rubinson, Richard, ed. *Dynamics of World Development*. Beverly Hills: Sage Publications, 1981.
Ruble, Blair A. *Soviet Trade Unions*. Cambridge: Cambridge University Press, 1981.
Saillant, Louis. *The World Federation of Trade Unions in the Service of all Workers in all Countries*. Paris, 1960.
Sanders, Jerry. *Peddlers of Crisis: The Committee on the Present Danger*. Boston: South End Press, 1982.
Schapsmeir, Edward L., and F. H. Schapsmeir. *Prophet in Politics: Henry A. Wallace and the War Years, 1945–1965*. Ames: Iowa University Press, 1970.
Seton-Watson, Hugh. *The East European Revolution*. New York: Frederick A. Praeger, 1950.
Sheppard, A. W. *Britain in Greece*. London, 1947.
Singleton, Fred, and Bernard Carter. *The Economy of Yugoslavia*. New York/London: St. Martin's Press/Croom Helm, 1982.
Smith, Howard K. *The State of Europe*. New York: Alfred A. Knopf, 1950.
Smothers, Frank, et al. *Report on the Greeks*. New York: Twentieth Century Fund, 1948.
Solaro, Antonio. *Istoria tou Kommounistikou Kommatos Elladas*. (History of the Greek Communist Party). Athens, 1975.
Stathis, D. S. *The Record of Greece*. Athens, 1962.
Stavrianos, L. S. *Global Rift: The Third World Comes of Age*. New York: William Morrow, 1981.
———. *Greece: American Dilemma and Opportunity*. Chicago: Henry Regnery, 1952.
———. *The Balkans Since 1453*. New York: Holt, Rinehart and Winston, 1958.
Stavrou, A. *Allied Politics and Military Interventions*. Athens, 1976.
Svoronos, Nikos G. *Episkopise tis Neoellinikes Istorias* (A Survey of Modern Greek History). Athens, 1976.
Sweet-Escott, Bickham. *Greece: A Political and Economic Survey, 1939–1953*. London: Royal Institute of International Affairs, 1954.
Taft, Philip. *Defending Freedom: American Labor and Foreign Affairs*. Los Angeles: Nash, 1973.
Theodoropoulos, Spyros. *Ap' to Dogma Truman sto Dogma Junta* (From the Truman Doctrine to the Junta Doctrine). Athens, 1976.
Theoharis, Athan. *Seeds of Repression: Harry S. Truman and the Origins of McCarthyism*. Chicago: Quadrangle Books, 1971.
Tsoukalas, Constantine. *The Tragedy of Greece*. Baltimore: Penguin Books, 1969.
Venezis, Elias. *Chroniko tis Trapezes Ellados: Istoria mias Eikosipentaetias, 1928–1952* (Chronicle of the Bank of Greece: History of a Twenty-five-Year Period). Athens, 1955.
Vergopoulos, Kostis. *To Agrotiko Zetema stin Ellada* (The Agrarian Question in Greece). Athens, 1975.
Vérité sur la Grèce. Belgrade, 1945.
Wallerstein, Immanuel. *The Capitalist World-Economy*. New York: Cambridge University Press, 1979.
Walton, Richard J. *Henry A. Wallace, Harry S. Truman and the Cold War*. New York: The Viking Press, 1976.
Weisner Duran, Eduardo. *Paz del Rio*. Bogotá: Universidad de los Andes, 1963.
Williams, Francis. *Twilight of Empire*. New York: A. S. Barnes, 1960.
Williams, William Appleman. *Empire as a Way of Life*. New York: Oxford University Press, 1980.

Windmuller, John P. *American Labor and the International Labor Movement, 1940–1953.* Ithaca, N.Y.: Cornell University Press, 1954.
Wittner, Lawrence S. *American Intervention in Greece, 1943–1949.* New York: Columbia University Press, 1982.
Woodbridge, George, et al. *The History of the United Nations Relief and Rehabilitation Administration.* 3 vols. New York: Columbia University Press, 1950.
Woodhouse, C. M. *Apple of Discord.* London: Hutchinson, 1948.
———. *The Struggle for Greece, 1941–1949.* New York: Beekman/Esanu, 1976.
Xydis, Stephen G. *Greece and the Great Powers, 1944–1947.* Thessalonike: Institute for Balkan Studies, 1963.
Zevgos, Yiannes. *Syntome Melete tis Neoellinikes Istorias* (A Brief Survey of Modern Greek History). Athens, (n.d.).

Index

Acheson, Dean, 37, 46, 48, 49, 56, 64, 76, 80, 81, 82, 83
ADEDY, 155–56, 158, 161
Africa, 14, 66, 109, 141, 142, 143, 160, 171
Agapitides, S., 127
Anti-Fascist Workers' Organization, ERGAS, 138–39
Agreement of Greek Aid, 90–92
Albania, 74, 75, 128, 129
American Federation of Labor, AFL, 139, 140–43, 148, 150, 153, 158
American Mission for Aid to Greece, AMAG, 42, Ch. 3, 141–48, 173
Anglo-Greek Trade Organization, 47
Arbenz, Jacobo, 66
Asia, 17, 66, 83, 108, 109, 141, 142, 143, 160
Asian Federation of Labor, 159
Athens Revolt, 2, 7, 10, 12, 16, 17, 20, 39, 63, 93, 137
Atlee, Clement, 28, 45, 53, 54, 55, 63, 69, 73, 77, 93
Austin, Warren, 85
Axis Powers, 1
   occupation of Greece, 8, 10, 36

Bevin, Ernest, 32, 40, 53, 68, 77
Bosch, Juan, 66
Bretton Woods System, 31, 52, 124
British Economic Mission, 24
Brown, Irving, 141–42, 150
Bulgaria, 6, 74, 75, 128
Byrnes, James, 32, 36, 47, 55

Carey, James, 159
Central Intelligence Agency, CIA, 66, 117, 158, 160
Central Loan Committee, 98, 121–22
China, 1, 13, 65, 66, 95–96
Churchill, Winston, 14, 16, 18, 19, 32, 36, 62, 177
Civil War (see Greece, Third Round)
Citrine Agreement, 138
Citrine, Walter, 138
Clark General John, 45
Clayton, William G., 19, 57, 59, 60, 80
Clifford, Clark, 79, 83
Collado, Emilio, 60
Colombia, 130, 135
Committee on the Present Danger, 86
Communist Party of Greece, 1–2, 16, 35,

37, 39–40, 42, 62, 65, 69, 74–79, 84, 96–98, 138
Communists, 18, 40, 42, 55, 62, 64, 74–79, 94, 141–42, 150, 161, 178
Congress of Industrial Organizations, CIO, 143, 148, 153, 158
Coombs, Charles, 111
Counterpart Account, 98, 123
Crimean War, 7
Currency Committee, 45, 46, 47, 48, 71, 89, 98, 99, 111–13, 172
Cyprus, 116, 178, 179

Damaskinos, Archbishop, 19, 35, 36, 61
Democratic Army, 16, 72, 74, 91, 92, 94–96, 102, 154, 157
Dimitrov, Georgi, 1
Domino Theory, 36, 83, 84, 87

EAM (see National Liberation Front)
Eccles, Marriner, 60
Economic Consultative Committee, 45
Economic Cooperation Administration, ECA, 109–10
Economou-Gouras, Paul, 77
EDES (see National Republican Greek League)
ELAS (see National Liberation Army)
Emergency Law No. 509, 147–49
Emergency Law No. 516, 153–54
EON (see National Youth Organization)
European Recovery Program, ERP, (see Marshall Plan)
Export-Import Bank, 19–23, 56, 57, 68, 70, 81, 90

Fleet, General James Van, vii, 109–10, 116–17
Foreign Trade Administration, 89, 98, 124
Forrestal, James, 79, 95
Four Year Plan, 108–20, 171–72
France, 5, 78, 108, 109, 116, 125, 141, 163

General Agreement on Tariffs and Trade, GATT, 104
General Confederation of Labor, GSEE, 137–47, 148–53, 155–58, 160–63
George II, King of the Hellenes, 2, 14, 62, 63, 64

Germany, 8, 10, 11, 14, 43, 69, 78, 124, 125, 129
Golden, Clinton, 142, 145, 146–47, 148
Gonatas, Stylianos, 72
Grady, Henry F., 110, 113–14, 130, 152, 158
Great Britain,
 dependence on the United States, 17
 financial relations with Greece, 5–7, 15
 investments in Greece, 16–17
 loans from the United States, 51–53
 loans to Greece, 43–50, 93
 Military Liaison, 14, 17, 18, 32, 144
 military occupation of Greece, 39, 42, 61–62, 73, 81–82
 revolt of 1944, 2, 10, 16
 struggle for hegemony over Greece, 31–36, 52–55
Great Depression, 5, 20
Greece,
 and Great Powers, 5–6
 destruction during World War II, 8–12
 emigration, 171
 financial dependence on England, 5–7
 foreign-capital investment, 103–4, 133–35, 171–76
 foreign debt, 5–6, 15, 175–76
 government-in-exile, 13–14
 merchant marines, 9–10, 55, 57–60, 153–55, 172
 reconstruction plan, 118–32
 "Third Round," 16, 35, 62–64, 68–69, 97–98, 162
 War of Independence, 5, 7, 25
 World War II destruction, 8–13
Greek-American Economic Cooperation Agreement, 110
Greek Fur Workers' Union, GFWU, 154
Greek-Italian Agreement, 119
Greek Maritime Federation, 153–54
Greek-Turkish Aid Bill, 90, 99, 143
Griswold, Dwight, 95, 97, 101, 102, 103, 104–5, 110, 113, 143, 145, 146, 148
Grivas, Colonel G., 40
Guatemala, viii, 66

Harriman, Averell, 60
Havlik, Hubert F., 79

Index   213

Henderson, Loy, 36, 76, 90, 97, 101
Hoffman, Paul, 120, 127, 157

IKA, Social Insurance Fund, 161
India, 14
Inter-American Confederation of Workers, CIT, 158–59
International Bank for Reconstruction and Development, (IBRD), 48, 55, 60, 70, 130
International Confederation of Free Trade Unions, ICFTU, 158–60, 162
International Labor Organization, ILO, 144, 159
International Monetary Fund, IMF, 70, 124
Invarchapel, Lord, 76, 77
Iran, 3, 61, 66, 109, 117, 132, 178
Italy, 8, 36, 108, 109, 116, 125, 163

Jackson, R.G.A. 33, 34
Joint Policy Committee, 18–19, 32
Jones, Joseph Marion, 83

Kanellopoulos, Alexander, 42
Kanellopoulos, Panayiotis, 34, 37, 69
Karamanlis, Constantine, 56, 130–31
Kassimatis, George, 34–35, 36
Kennan, George F., 65–66, 76, 80, 108
KKE (see Communist Party of Greece)

Labor, 24, 33, 113
   and economic status, 163–67
   and international organizations, 138, 140, 141, 158–60, 162
   and Varkiza Agreement, 138–39
Labor and Manpower Division of AMAG, 142, 145, 166
Labor strikes, 38, 144–48, 155–61, 163
Latin America, 66, 71, 83, 97, 104, 109, 118, 141, 159, 160, 175
Lend-Lease, 38, 51, 85
"Liberty" ships, sale of, 58–60
Lippman, Walter, 90
London Agreement, 43–50, 62
Lyons, Sir Edmund, vii, viii

Maben, Buel, 32
MacMillan, Harold, 19

MacNeill, Hector, 36–37, 44
MacVeagh, Lincoln, 11, 17, 19, 23, 28, 32, 33, 36, 37, 38, 39, 42, 43, 56, 63, 64, 68, 72, 74, 81, 93, 97, 110
Makris, Fotis, 139, 142, 148, 150, 156, 161–62
Mao Tse-tung, 1
Maoist revolution, 96, 107
Markezines, Spyros, 103, 134
Marshall, George, C., 73, 76, 81, 105, 143, 153
Marshall Plan, (ERP) 53, 76, 78, 95–96, 107–11, 122, 124, 143, 159, 160, 173
Maximos, Demetrios, 56, 71–72, 73, 89, 90, 94
Metaxas, General John, 1–2, 6–7, 8, 42, 137, 139, 177
Molotov, V. M., 96
Morgan, William D., 35, 36
Mossadeq, Mohammad, 66
Munkman, C. A., 99, 112, 116, 120, 123

National Liberation Army, (ELAS), 14, 40
National Liberation Front (EAM), 2, 15, 39, 84
National Republican Greek League, (EDES), 28
National Security Council (NSC #68), 86
National Youth Organization, (EON), 42
Nazis, 9, 40, 139
   and Greek collaborators, 8, 24, 41, 94
Near East, 3, 7, 16, 56, 63, 64, 77, 81, 83, 177, 178
North Atlantic Treaty Organization, NATO, 107, 115, 132, 135, 177, 179, 180
Northern Tier, 3, 61, 64, 117

Organization for European Economic Co-operation, OEEC, 115, 117, 124, 126, 127, 130, 166, 180

Pan-Hellenic Federation of Maritime Workers, 154–55
Pan-Hellenic Socialist Party, 179
Papagos, Alexandros, 116, 133–34
Papandreou, Andreas, ix, 116, 123, 169, 179–80

Index

Papandreou, George, 14, 55, 69
Paparigas, Dimitris, 140
Paris Conference on Reparations, 8, 44
Paris Peace Conference, 60
Partsalidis, Dimitris, 74
Paterson, Gardner, 48
Pepper, Claude, 84–85
Plastiras, Nikolaos, 17, 19, 97
Populist party, 37
Porter, Paul, 59, 67, 72, 73, 74, 76, 89–90, 129, 133, 157
Porter Mission, 60, 67, 71, 89, 129

Reagan Doctrine, vii
Refugees, 95, 101–2, 105, 130–31
Romuladi, Serafino, 159
Roosevelt, Franklin, 18, 60
Rural migration, 170–72
Rumania, 6, 128
Russia, vii, 5

Sbarounis, A., 14
Schultz, George, vii
Scobie, Ronald, 17
Security Battalions, 40, 72
Sideris, George, 17
Simpson, R. S., 145, 151
Sofianopoulos, John, 73
Sophoulis, Themistocles, 37, 38, 43, 45, 46–47, 48, 69, 97, 101, 103, 147
Soviet bloc, 3, 80, 85, 108
Soviet Union, 13, 16, 36, 37, 57, 61–62, 63, 65–66, 75, 78, 86, 96–97, 107, 125, 141, 158, 165
Stalin, Josef, 39, 42, 65–66, 74, 75, 96, 98
Stefanopoulos, Stefanos, 117–18
Stettinius, Edward, 17
Strasbourg Congress, 96

Taft, Robert A., 84–85
Taylor, Glen, 84–85
Taylor, Wayne C., 19
Third Round (see Greece, Third Round)
Third World, viii, ix, 3, 12, 20, 30, 36, 53, 55, 66, 67, 70, 72, 79, 83, 86–7, 109, 110, 118, 121, 130, 132, 134, 135, 162, 170, 176
Trades Union Congress, TUC, 138, 140, 141, 158, 159

Truman, Harry S., vii–viii, 51, 63, 65, 67, 78–79, 82–83, 143, 161
  policy toward Greece, 2–3, 13, 20, 33
  reaction to London Agreement, 46–49
  Venizelos Mission, 56–61
Truman Doctrine, vii–viii, 3, 6, 13, 35, 54, 59, 64, 66, 74–87, 89, 96, 100, 103, 107, 115, 143, 165, 167, 169, 177
Tsaldaris, Constantine, 48, 49, 54–56, 57, 58, 62–64, 67, 68, 71, 100, 103, 139, 141, 146–47, 150
Tsaldaris-Braine Agreement, 140–41
Tsouderos, Emanuel, 43, 45, 47, 97
Turkey, 3, 36, 61, 65, 76, 77, 78, 79, 81, 82, 109, 116, 117, 125, 170, 177, 178

Unemployment, 127, 164, 165
United Mine Workers of America, 159
United Nations, 36, 61, 64, 75, 83–85, 90, 108, 140
United Nations, Food and Agricultural Administration, 25, 63
United Nations Relief and Rehabilitation Administration, UNRRA, 10, 13–24, 26, 28, 29, 31–35, 38, 44–45, 54, 55, 68, 70, 71, 73, 93, 144, 173
United States,
  aid to Greece, 5, 23
  counterinsurgency operations, 80–98
  investments in Greece, 16
  and labor policy in Greece, ch. 5
  policy toward Tsaldaris regime, 62–66
  preeminent role in the world economy, 13
USSR (see Soviet Union)

Vandenberg, Arthur, 80
Varkiza Agreement, 12–13, 15, 39, 40, 41, 55, 62, 137–39
Varvaressos, Kyriakos, 19–31, 48, 49, 164
Venizelos, Sophocles, 56–60, 69
Vietnam, 65, 66, 86, 108, 170, 176
Vishinsky, Andrej, 61, 110
Voulgaris, Admiral, 19, 23, 25, 27, 32

Wallace, Henry A., 57, 60, 85
West German Federation of Labor, 159
White Terror, 40–43, 72, 75, 94

Winant, John, 37, 46
Woll, Matthew, 148
Woodbridge, George, 10
World Federation of Trade Unions, 138, 140, 141, 158–59, 160
World War II, 2, 5, 7, 11, 26, 64, 107
Workers' National Liberation Front, EEAM, 137, 139

"X" organization, 40

Yugoslavia, 6, 7, 39, 74, 75, 96, 100, 109–10, 128, 165

Zachariadis, Nikos, 39, 75
Zhdanov, Andrej, 96
Zervas, Napoleon, 27–28, 72

www.ingramcontent.com/pod-product-compliance
Lightning Source LLC
Chambersburg PA
CBHW031550300426
44111CB00006BA/244